W9-BEW-388

JOKES
JOKES
JOKES

VERBAL ABUSE EDITION

Steve Ochs

Published by National Lampoon Press

National Lampoon, Inc. • 8228 Sunset Boulevard • Los Angeles • CA 90046 • USA

AMEX:NLN

NATIONAL LAMPOON, NATIONAL LAMPOON PRESS and colophon are trademarks of National Lampoon

National lampoon, jokes jokes jokes, verbal abuse edition / by Steve Ochs -- 1st ed.

p. cm.

ISBN-10: 0978832388
ISBN-13: 978-0978832384 - $11.95 U.S. - $14.95 Canada

Book Design and Production by
JK NAUGHTON

Cover by
Sam McCay

COPYRIGHT © 2007 by NATIONAL LAMPOON

ALL RIGHTS RESERVED

PRINTED IN THE UNITED STATES OF AMERICA

1   3   5   7   9   10   8   6   4   2

JULY 2007

WWW.NATIONALLAMPOON.COM

NATIONAL LAMPOON ®

Contents

The Tragic Tale of Johnny Bunghole

Okay, there is no Johnnie Bunghole. This is just the foreword, but I knew that you would be unable to prevent yourself from reading any piece with the word, 'bunghole' in the title.

Welcome to National Lampoon's Jokes, Jokes, Jokes, II: Verbal Abuse Edition. That's right; our first joke book was so popular we couldn't wait to put out another one that would insult the very people who bought the first one! That would be *you*, d*@khead.

Sorry.

I'm kind of a "method" writer, so to bring reality to the material; I try to embody the POV of the piece. In this case that meant becoming completely sexist and racist. And I thought I was doing a good job of keeping it suppressed, but not according to my big-mouthed Polack wife!

Sorry.

This book is my thesis; my introduction to the hate-based community. With this book I can prove that I am as biased and closed-minded as any hater out there. Granted, there are few polarizing hypocrites, like Ted Haggard or Newt Gingrich, who give hate professionals a bad name, but by and large hate is still reliable.

I would never purport to be a KKK-level hater. They have been answering America's hate needs since 1866. They're the only hate group with greatest hits. What would a KKK appearance be like without the big cross-burning closer?

And, being remotely Jewish (more on that inside), I will never be able to hate anybody the way everybody hates the Jews! There are Jew haters out there that make the KKK look quaint. You've never seen a guy in a ghost costume (or whatever the f#@k that is the KKK wears) stand next to a Jew and blow himself up, have you? *That's* some hate we could all learn from.

Almost as many people hate black people. I am using the term 'black people' not 'African American' for two reasons: one, that's just what they'd want me to do, and two, because I don't *mean* African Americans, I mean black people from all over the world you nationalistic, segregationist twat.

Sorry.

The only thing Jews have over blacks in the most hated race-race is that, while black people are blamed for all kinds of things, Jews are blamed for actually using their mighty powers to direct the lives of others and deprive them of the things they want and need. Now, *that* is a hate hook!

Mexican hate doesn't even come close. Even the people who would rather see them in their own country rotting next to a mud puddle, actually kind of like them. Mexican hatred is pure economics, while black and Jew hate are passionate. But my new hater comrades will find that I've skewered them appropriately.

Everyone else is left to stew in a potpourri of incidental *hateables*. The Irish are drunks, the Italians are dangerous, the Asians – who knows what their story is! Etc.etc.

The only group almost completely left out of the book is the middle easterners. This is very important because leaving them out illustrates my final pitch for official hater membership. You see, most groups will hear your insults and just think you're a jerk, but some of our olive-skinned brothers of the desert will put out what you call your *Fatwa*.

This means they call on all Muslims to kill you. Now, I'm not egomaniacal enough to think that any Muslim or Islamic Extremist would bother to kill me even if I was to kneel down and face off with him from the other side of his prayer rug… five times a day. But, and here's where I get the big points, like all the other pro-level haters, deep down inside, I'm a cowardly pussy. Hate isn't something you get out in front of; it's something you hide behind.

So, for all you kike, WOP, frog, beaner, beast, fag/dyke, mick, geriatric, gimp, gook, a-holes, I hope this book helps keep you all in your places.

Sorry,

Steve Ochs

Part I

Demographics

Whores

I have never been with a whore. This is not to suggest that I've never paid for it; oh, I've paid for it alright. But I have never had sex by way of commerce. I do, however, have friends who swear by it. I can certainly see the logic to it; no date, no pretense, no awkward good byes. And to those who say that the missing element of deep love, trust and understanding ruins sex, I say, really? When was the last time you were feeling "fond" at the threshold of a crazy nut?

I've met a couple of hookers and, seriously, I think they were into me.

I can't imagine how negotiations with a person of the evening isn't the most insulting conversation you could have. "Yes, I understand that you have put a great many miles on your ass and assessed its value as accurately as you can, but I am looking at the ass in question and I think your best value is going to be using it as a trade in."

There should be a Kelly's Blue Book for hooker ass. I'd like to see someone restore some of the classics.

Head – More than what lives above her neck; head is the name of her primary service! However, the commonly used term "give head" is inaccurate – a hooker "gives" nothing. Should be "rents head."

Somehow good tits are immune to skankafication. Even Courtney Love's tits are welcome guests, regardless of their arguably skanky escort. Tits also bear the distinction of being the only widely accepted erogenous zone that does not transfer disease. Therefore, it should actually cost more to fuck them.

Nose – Drug introduction portal. Sucks up the dollars faster than she can... suck up the dollars.

Tongue – More muscular than Superman's dick (trust me, I saw the video). Inspires postage stamps to cry, "Don't put that thing on me!"

What the pre-ops really envy. Science can build a better vagina, but only God hands out the hips, bitch. Needed for placing hands upon while skeptically suggesting that, No, someone, Di-int.

Money Maker – The "Money Maker" is often shaken, always stirred.

A good hooker supports herself with her knees. Male hookers sometimes have ironic name of Neil.

Those streets won't walk themselves. Heels plus heroin equals *America's Funniest Ho Videos*.

Common Indicators That You Are A

WHORE

After a lengthy tour of sea duty, an old sailor finally gets some shore leave. Fortunately, a nearby brothel had been recommended to him by some of his younger shipmates.

The old sailor walked over to the brothel, where he chose his girl and began. "How am I doing?" he asked her.

"Three knots," she replied.

"Three knots? What does that mean?" asked the sailor.

The girl answered, "You're not hard. You're not in. And, you're not getting your money back."

* * *

George Washington and his men had just finished a big battle and were tired and wounded. They were walking for miles looking for a place to stay when they came upon this very small broken-down shack.

Washington asked the man who answered the door if he had room to help some of his men as they were tired and sick. The man said, "As you can see I only have room for one man."

So Washington picked out his most wounded man, Private Cox, to stay there. Then he left with the rest of his men looking for another place.

After walking for several miles more, they finally saw this big beautiful mansion on a hill and proceeded to the mansion. Washington rang the bell and a beautiful woman came to the door, and asked him what he wanted. Washington explained that he had just fought a terrible battle and that some of his men were wounded and that they were all tired and needed some shelter and a place to rest.

The Madam explained that the place was actually a bordello, but that they would be happy to take in him and his men. In fact, she was excited about it. She asked, "How many men do you have?"

Washington answered, "About 99 men without Cox."

The madam replied, "You've got to be kidding me!"

* * *

Last Halloween, all eyes turned to stare as a gorgeous hooker walked into the costume party stark naked. The alarmed host rushed to intercept her. "Where's your costume?" he hissed through clenched teeth.

"This is it," the beautiful woman calmly explained. "I came as Adam."

"Adam?" her host exploded! "You don't even have a dick!"

"I just got here," the hooker replied. "Give me a few minutes."

* * *

A young blond woman, named Anna Bowie, called the local police department and reported that she had recently been sexually assaulted.

The sheriff's department officer who answered the phone, asked, "When did this happen, Miss Bowie?"

Anna replied, "Sir, it happened last week."

The sheriff then asked, "Why did you wait until now to report it?"

"Well," Miss Bowie replied. "I didn't know that I was assaulted until the check bounced."

* * *

One afternoon, the old drunk stumbled into a podiatrist's office, mistaking it for a whorehouse. The nurse asked him his name, then told him to go behind the screen and stick it out.

So, naturally, the old drunk weaved over the screen, dropped his pants, and stuck his thing through the screen.

The nurse walked over, shrieked, and dropped her tray of instruments. "That's not a foot!" she screamed.

The old drunk replied, "Sshorry, lady! I didn't know there was a minimum."

* * *

A hooker in a hurry to get home leaves her john's room wearing nothing, but a loose coat. As she crosses the street, a drunk driver skids around the corner and hits her sending her flying into the air, and landing unconscious on her back with her charms exposed to the world.

As a crowd gathers, a gentleman places his hat upon the hooker's crotch in order to minimize her exposure. In the meantime, the drunk driver hardly aware he just hit someone, staggers over to see what all the fuss is about.

Noticing the near-naked woman lying exposed on the street, he points to the strategically placed hat and slurs in a loud voice, "Well, the first thing we gotta do is get that guy outta there!"

* * *

A woman wanted a pet to keep her company at home while her husband, Harry, was off at work and the children were in school. After some research, she decided a parrot would fit her needs nicely. It wouldn't be as much work as a dog or a cat, and it would be very interesting to hear it speak, but unfortunately they were quite expensive.

One day on a shopping trip she spotted a large, beautifully colored parrot and asked the owner of the store for the price of the bird. The owner said he would let it go for $50. Delighted that such a rare and beautiful bird wasn't more expensive, she agreed to buy it.

Before accepting her money, the owner said, "I should tell you first that this bird used to live in a whorehouse. Sometimes it says some pretty... well... embarrassing stuff."

The woman was so attracted to the bird and the excellent price that she decided to buy it anyway.

When she got home she placed the bird's cage in her living room and waited patiently for it to say something.

The bird studied his new surroundings, and his new owner, and finally said, "New house, new madam." The woman was a little taken at the implication of what she had just heard, but after a few minutes decided that it wasn't really all that bad. When her two teenage daughters came in from school, the bird looked them over and said, "New house, new madam, new whores!" After their initial surprise was over, the girls joined their mother in laughter.

Shortly after 5 o'clock, the woman's husband came home from work. The bird looked at him, the mother, and the girls and said, "New house, new madam, new whores, same old faces. Hi Harry!"

* * *

Mr. Brown, the old history teacher, had a dirty mouth. He was always saying something off-color or suggestive. One day after class, Sally approaches his desk with a flock of girls in tow.

"Mr. Brown," she said, "We are tired of your filthy remarks and we aren't going to put up with them anymore. The next time you say something nasty in class, we are all going to complain to the principal."

Mr. Brown was silent and the girls stormed off thinking they had cowed him. The next day as everyone arrived in class, Mr. Brown read the newspaper. The bell rang, but he continued to read.

Finally, he looked up and said, "Oh girls, you should find this interesting. The government is recruiting whores to go to Afghanistan and screw the servicemen over there for $100 a day."

All at once the girls get up and head for the door.

"Wait a minute!" shouted Mr. Brown. "The boat doesn't leave 'till Thursday!"

* * *

A man came down with the flu and was forced to stay home. He was glad for the interlude because it taught him how much his wife loved him. She was so thrilled to have him around that when a delivery man or the mailman arrived, she ran out and yelled, "My husband's home! My husband's home!"

* * *

"So let me get this straight," the prosecutor says to the defendant. "Every day when you came home from work early you found your wife in bed with some strange man."

"That's correct," says the defendant.

"And finally," continues the prosecutor, "you took out a pistol and shot your wife, killing her."

"That's correct," says the defendant.

"Then my question to you is, why did you shoot your wife and not her lover?" asked the prosecutor.

"It seemed easier," replied the defendant, "than shooting a different man every day!"

* * *

John and Jill, a lady of the evening, were about to go into John's apartment. But before he could open his door, Jill said, "Wait a minute, I can tell how a man makes love by how he unlocks his door."

John says, "Well, give me some examples."

Jill proceeds to tell him, "Well, the first way is, if a guy shoves his key into the lock, and opens the door hard, then that means he is a rough lover and that isn't for me."

"The second way is if a man fumbles around and can't seem to find the hole, then that means he is inexperienced and that isn't for me either."

Then Jill said, "Honey, how do you unlock your door?"

John proceeds to say, "Well, first, before I do anything else, I lick the lock."

* * *

One day, three friends went to this gentlemen's club. One of the friends wanted to impress the other two, so he pulls out a $10 bill. The dancer came over to them, and the one friend licked the $10 bill and put it on her butt.

Not to be outdone the other friend pulls out a $50 bill. He calls the girl back over, licks the $50, and puts it on her other cheek.

Now the attention is focused on the third guy. He got out his wallet, thought for a minute, then swiped his ATM card down her crack, and grabbed the 60 bucks.

* * *

A guy walks in and sits down at a bar. The side of his face is bruised and bleeding so the bartender asks, "What in the world happened to you, buddy?"

The guy says, "Oh I got in a fight with my girlfriend and I called her a two-bit whore."

"Yeah?" asks the bartender. "What did she do?"

"She hit me with her bag of quarters!"

* * *

There was a man who wanted a pure wife. So he started to attend church to find such a woman. He met a gal who seemed nice so he took her home.

When they got there, he whipped out his manhood and asked "What's this?"

She replied, "A cock."

He thought to himself that she is not pure enough.

A couple of weeks later he met another gal and soon took her home. Again, he pulled out his manhood and asked the question.

She replied, "A cock."

He was angry because she seemed more pure than the first but, oh well.

A couple of weeks later he met a gal who seemed real pure. She wouldn't go home with him for a long time but eventually he got her to his house.

He whipped it out and asked, "What is this?"

She giggled and said, "A pee-pee."

He has finally found his woman.

They get married but after several months every time she sees his member she giggles and says, "That's your pee-pee."

He finally breaks down and says, "Look this is not a pee-pee, it is a cock."

She laughs and says, "No it's not, a cock is ten inches long and black."

* * *

A teacher asked the students in her class, "What do you want out of life?"

A young girl in the front row raised her hand and said, "All I want out of life is four animals."

"Really?" asked the teacher. "What four animals would that be?"

"A mink on my back, a jaguar in my garage, a tiger in my bed and a jackass to pay for it all," the girl replied.

* * *

Two Irishmen were digging a ditch directly across from a brothel. Suddenly, they saw a rabbi walk up to the front door, glance around and duck inside.

"Ah, will you look at that?" one ditch digger said. "What's our world comin' to when men of th' cloth are visitin' such places?"

A short time later, a Protestant minister walked up to the door and quietly slipped inside.

"Do you believe that?" The workman exclaimed. "Why, 'tis no wonder th' young people today are so confused, what with the example clergymen set for them."

After an hour went by, the men watched as a Catholic priest quickly entered the whore house.

"Ah, what a pity," the digger said, leaning on his shovel. "One of th' poor lasses must be ill."

* * *

A very shy guy goes into a bar and sees a beautiful woman sitting at the bar. After an hour of gathering up his courage he finally goes over to her and asks, tentatively, "Um, would you mind if I chatted with you for a while?"

She responds by yelling, at the top of her lungs, "No, I won't sleep with you tonight!" Everyone in the bar is now staring at them.

Naturally, the guy is hopelessly and completely embarrassed and he slinks back to his table.

After a few minutes, the woman walks over to him and apologizes. She smiles at him and says, "I'm sorry if I embarrassed you. You see, I'm a graduate student in psychology and I'm studying how people respond to embarrassing situations."

To which he responds, at the top of his lungs, "What do you mean, $200?"

* * *

A man met a beautiful lady and he decided he wanted to marry her right away. She said, "But we don't know anything about each other."

He said, "That's all right, we'll learn about each other as we go along." So she consented, and they were married, and went on a honeymoon to a very nice resort.

So one morning they were lying by the pool, when he got up off of his towel, climbed up to the ten-meter board and did a two and a half-tuck gainer, this was followed by a three rotations in jackknife position, where he straightened out and cut the water like a knife. After a few more demonstrations, he came back and lay down on his towel.

She said, "That was incredible!"

He said, "I used to be an Olympic diving champion. You see, I told you we'd learn more about each other as we went along."

So she got up, jumped in the pool, and started doing laps. After about thirty laps she climbed back out and lay down on her towel hardly out of breath.

He said, "That was incredible! Were you an Olympic endurance swimmer?"

"No," she said. "I was a hooker in Venice and I worked both sides of the Grand Canal."

* * *

A young man and his date were parked on a back road some distance from town. They were about to have sex when the girl stopped.

"I really should have mentioned this earlier, but I'm actually a hooker and I charge $20 for sex." The man reluctantly paid her, and they did their thing.

After a cigarette, the man just sat in the driver's seat looking out the window. "Why aren't we going anywhere?" asked the girl.

"Well, I should have mentioned this before, but I'm actually a taxi driver, and the fare back to town is $25."

* * *

A hooker goes to the drug store to buy her pimp some toiletries. A clerk comes up to help her and asks if she needs assistance.

"I'm looking for some deodorant for my new husband John, but I don't know what type he uses."

The clerk says, "Is it the ball type?"

"No," says Judi, it's for his underarms."

A man goes to a whore house. The madam is out of women, but since the man is Polish she thinks she can get away with a blow up doll and he will never know the difference.

The man comes out after being in the room for five minutes. "How was it?" asks the madam.

"Not good at all," says the man. "I bit her nipple, she let out this huge fart and then flew out the window!"

* * *

A man was seated next to a stiff-looking Baptist minister on a flight to Wichita. After the plane was airborne, the flight attendant came around for drink orders. The man asked for a whiskey and soda, which he got. The attendant then asked the minister if he would also like a drink.

The minister replied in disgust, "I'd rather be savagely raped by a brazen whore than let liquor touch these lips."

The man then handed his drink back to the attendant and said, "I didn't know there was a choice."

* * *

While on a train ride, three nuns were getting to know each other and decided to confess to one another what their greatest sins were.

"My greatest sin is sex," says the first nun. "One week each year I go out and work as a prostitute. Of course, I put all the money I earn into the poor box."

"My greatest sin is drinking," admits the second nun. "Each year I take the money from the poor box and go out drinking for a whole week."

As they are both waiting for the third nun to tell her greatest sin, she just sits there without saying a word.

Finally, the first nun says to her, "Come on Sister, we've told you our greatest sins, now you must tell us yours."

"Okay," says the third nun, "my greatest sin is that I gossip and I cannot wait to get off this train."

* * *

A fellow is ordered by his doctor to lose a minimum of 75 pounds because of the serious health risks involved with being so overweight. Baffled as to how on earth he was ever going to be able to accomplish this, he runs across an ad in the newspaper for a "Guaranteed Weight Loss Program."

Skeptical, but desperate, he calls them and subscribes to the 3-day/10-pound weight loss program.

The next day there's a knock on his door and when he answers it, standing before him is an athletic, beautiful, 20-year-old hooker dressed in nothing but a pair of Nike running shoes, and a sign around her neck.

She introduces herself as a representative of the weight loss company. The sign around her neck reads, "If you can catch me, you can have me!" Without giving it a second thought, he takes off after her. A few miles later, huffing and puffing, he finally catches her and has his way with her.

After they finish, she leaves and he thinks to himself, "I really like the way this company does business!" For the next two days, the same girl shows up and the same thing happens. On the fourth day, he weighs himself and is thrilled to find he has lost 10 pounds as promised.

So, he calls the company and subscribes to their 5-day/20-pound program. As expected, the following day there's a knock on his door and there stands the most gorgeous, sexy woman he has ever seen in his life, wearing nothing but Reebok running shoes and a sign around her neck that reads, "If you catch me, you can have me!" He's out the door after her in a flash.

This gal is in excellent shape and it takes him a while to catch her, but when he does, it's worth every cramp and wheeze. She is, by far, the best he has ever had. For the next four days, the same routine happens and, much to his delight, on the fifth day he weighs himself and finds he's lost another 20 pounds as promised!!

Deciding to go for broke, he calls the company and subscribes to their 7-day/50-pound program! "Are you sure, sir?" the company representative asks. "This is our most rigorous program!"

"I'm positive," he replies. "I haven't felt this good in years!"

The next day there's a knock on his door and when he answers it, standing before him is Richard Simmons wearing nothing but a pair of pink racing spikes, and a sign around his neck that reads, "If I catch you, I can have you!"

* * *

Q & A Roundup
Whores

Q What's the difference between a prostitute, a nymphomaniac, and a blond?

A The prostitute says, "Aren't you done yet?"
The nympho says, "Are you done already?"
The blond says, "Beige... I think I'll paint the ceiling beige."

Q What do you call a prostitute with no legs?

A Cash and Carry.

Q What do you call kids born in a whore house?

A Brothel sprouts.

Q What do you get when you cross a computer with a whore?

A A fucking know it all.

Q How are a lawyer and a prostitute different?

A The prostitute stops fucking you after you're dead.

God and the Godly

Look, I don't want to get into it with you, but I don't know or care if there's a God. I actually list my religion as "Apathist." It would seem the arbitrary nature of Godly acts upon the Earth and universe are so disparate that it really doesn't matter what I think. I get hit by a car and die, God took me. I live, God spared me, and I should thank God I'm alive. If I'm disabled, I will ask for God's help in my recuperation... where was he when that car was headed my way? Meanwhile the guy who hit me gets forgiven by God and probably thanks God that he wasn't hurt. Really, what changes?

Instead, I brave a world unprotected by holy verse. And I believe there should be more people who think the way I do. I hope to God this book sells.

Halo – One important way to look Godly is good lighting. So, in His infinite wisdom, God invented the halo; a portable, self-directing light source. It also presents an appearance of angelic innocence. We can see how helpful that is in classic mannerist paintings. When you're hanging out in a garden with chicks barely wearing a yard or two of flowing fabric, you don't want anyone to know what you're really thinking.

God sees all. Ev-er-y-thing. Think about that the next time you're spanking it to an ad in Maxim.

God sees all but speaks to very few. Here in the good ol' US of A, he prefers the company of slicked back preachers, beady eyed polit-icos and Grammy winners.

Nipples – You think yours are superfluous?

Hands – Big. Can palm a thunderclap. Many people have claimed to have been touched by the hand of God, but in most cases the church settled out of court.

Balls – I don't know where to go with this. I mean there's the Earth Mother theory out there and Sun Gods and what have you. If all things come from God then God would have to be, um, kind of endowed with all... things. That could suggest "cycles." That would explain the war, poverty and famine. God's PMSing.

Common Indicators That You Are

GOD

Four nuns were standing in line at the gates of Heaven. Peter asks the first if she has ever sinned.

"Well, once I looked at a man's penis," she said.

"Put some of this holy water on your eyes and you may enter heaven," Peter told her. Peter then asked the second nun if she had ever sinned.

"Well, once I held a man's penis," she replied.

"Put your hand in this holy water and you may enter heaven," he said. Just then the fourth nun pushed ahead of the third nun. Peter asked her, "Why did you push ahead in line?"

She said, "Because I want to gargle before she sits in it!"

* * *

Two nuns cycling down a cobbled street. The first one says "I've never come this way before."

The second one replies, "Must be the cobbles."

* * *

A sailor and a priest were playing golf. The sailor took his first shot missed and said, "Fuck, I missed."

Surprised, the priest replied, "Don't use that kind of language or God will punish you."

The sailor took aim and hit his second shot. Again he missed and under his breath he said, "I fucking missed again."

The priest overheard and replied, "My son, please don't use that language or God will punish you."

The sailor took his third shot and once again he couldn't help mutter, "Oh fuck…"

The priest said, "That's it! God will certainly punish you." Suddenly a bolt of lightning came down and killed the priest.

In the distance a deep voice said, "FUCK, I Missed!"

* * *

In heaven, the angels asked God where he would spend his next holiday.

God said, "Not on Earth. Last time I went there, I left a girl pregnant and those people haven't stopped talking about it since!

* * *

God said to Adam, "I've got some good news and some bad news. First the good news. I have given you a brain and a penis. The bad news... I've only given you enough blood to work one of them at a time!"

* * *

One Friday, there were three nuns riding on a mountain road. They were coming around a turn when a semi rammed into them head on, killing them instantly. When they arrived at the pearly gates, they noticed a sign that said 'Closed for Remodeling.' One nun knocked on the gates and out came St. Peter. He said, "What are you doing here! No one is supposed to be here! We are closed for the weekend for remodeling!"

The one nun said, "Well, we're dead and we can't go back."

"Alright," said St. Peter, "what we are going to do is send you back for the weekend as whoever you wish to be and then we'll accept you back into Heaven." He looked at the first nun. "Okay, who do you want to be?" he asked the nun.

"Well, I thought her life was very interesting especially since she gave her life to God, so I want to be Joan of Arc." *Poof!* The first nun became Joan of Arc.

"Okay, You're next," said St. Peter as he looked at the second nun. "Who do you want to be?"

"Well, I thought her life was very interesting and she died a tragic death, so I want to become Marilyn Monroe," pronounced the second nun. *Poof!* The second nun became Marilyn Monroe."

Okay, who do you want to be?" St. Peter asked the third nun.

"I want to be Alice Kapipelean."

"Excuse me!?" asked St. Peter.

"I want to be Alice Kapipelean!" exclaimed the nun.

St. Peter replied, "Pardon me, Sister, we have no record of any Alice Kapipelean being on Earth."

"There is *too* an Alice Kapipelean and I have proof right here!" shouted the nun while she waved a newspaper clipping.

St. Peter takes the news article and reads it. "Oh my, Sister, you have misread this article. This article says that the Alaska Pipeline was laid by 500 men in six months."

* * *

Pedro was driving down the street in a sweat because he had an important meeting and couldn't find a parking place.

Looking up toward heaven, he said, "Lord, take pity on me. If you find me a parking place I will go to Mass every Sunday for the rest of my life and give up tequila."

Miraculously, a parking place appeared. Pedro looked up again and said, "Never mind. I found one."

* * *

Smith climbs to the top of Mt. Sinai to get close enough to talk to God. Looking up, he asks the Lord... "God, what does a million years mean to you?"

The Lord replies, "A minute."

Smith asks, "And what does a million dollars mean to you?"

The Lord replies, "A penny."

"Smith asks, "Can I have a penny?"

The Lord replies, "in a minute."

* * *

A man who has just died finds himself standing at the gates of Heaven. To his right is standing an attractive woman, and to his left is a ladder. The woman speaks, "Come with me through the gate and spend eternity with me, or climb the ladder to success." The man, always eager to get ahead in life, chooses to climb the ladder.

The man finds an even more beautiful woman standing in front of another gate. Next to her is another ladder. The woman says, "Come with me through the gate and all your fantasies will be granted, or climb the ladder to success." This time the man is tempted, but his greed takes over and he climbs the ladder higher.

He again encounters a woman. This woman, however; is the most beautiful woman he has ever seen. She says, "Come with me and I will satisfy your deepest desires forever, or climb the ladder to success." The man can't believe his luck. He decides to take his chances and climbs the ladder.

He comes to another gate. This time there is no woman waiting for him. Suddenly an old overweight man walks up to him. "Are you God?" the man asks.

"No, I'm Sess."

* * *

The Pope had been diagnosed as having a potentially fatal testicular disease and after treatment he was told that he had to have sex with a woman to confirm that the treatment had been fully successful. He called all his Cardinals together and told them what had to be done and they agreed it was necessary. The Pope said he would go ahead with it, but insisted on four conditions.

"Firstly," he said, "the girl has to be blind so she cannot see it's the Holy Father and tell the whole world. Secondly, she must be deaf so that she doesn't recognize the Holy Father's voice and tell the whole world. Thirdly, as a precaution, she has to be dumb so she cannot tell the whole world anyway."

At this point one of the Cardinals stood up and said, "Leave it to me Holy Father, I know just the woman for you."

As the Cardinal was about to leave the Pope said, "Wait a moment, I told you there are four conditions." He beckoned the Cardinal over and as the Cardinal bent down towards him, the Pope whispered in his ear... "Big tits!"

* * *

A married man goes to confessional and says to the priest, "Father, I had an affair with a woman... almost."

"What do you mean almost?" questioned the priest.

"Well, we got undressed and rubbed together, but then I stopped."

"Rubbing together is the same as putting it in," explains the priest. "You're not to go near that woman again. Now, say five Hail Marys and put $50 in the poor box."

The man leaves confessional, says his prayers, and then walks over to the poor box. He pauses for a moment and then turns to leave.

The priest quickly runs over to the man and exclaims, "I saw that... you didn't put any money in the poor box!"

"Well Father, I rubbed the money against it, and, like you said, it's the same as putting it in!"

* * *

One Sunday morning, the priest noticed Little Johnny was staring up at the large plaque that hung in the foyer of the church. It was covered with names, and small American flags were mounted on either side of it. The seven-year old had been staring at the plaque for some time, so the priest walked up, stood beside the boy, and said quietly, "Good morning, Little Johnny."

"Good morning, Father," replied the young man, still focused on the plaque. "Father Scott, what is this?" Little Johnny asked.

"Well, son, it's a memorial to all the young men and women who died in the service." Soberly, they stood together, staring at the large plaque.

Little Johnny's voice was barely audible when he asked, "Which service, the 9:45 or the 11:15?"

* * *

A Catholic, a Baptist, and a Mormon are bragging about the size of their families.

"I have four boys and my wife is expecting another. One more son and I'll have a basketball team!" said the Catholic.

"That's nothing!" said the Baptist. "I have ten boys now, and my wife is pregnant with another child. One more son and I'll have a football team!"

"Big deal," said the Mormon. "I have seventeen wives. One more and I'll have a golf course!"

* * *

A priest and a rabbi are walking down the street together, and they both want a drink, but they have no money on them. The priest says, "I've got an idea how to get us some free drinks." He walks in alone and the rabbi stands at the door and watches. The priest orders a drink, drinks it, and then the bartender gives him his tab. The priest says, "But my son, I've already paid for the drink."

The bartender says, "I'm terribly sorry, father, but it's really busy in here and I must have forgotten."

The rabbi walks in and orders a drink. After he drinks it, the bartender gives him the tab, and the rabbi says, "Son, I paid you when I ordered the drink."

The bartender says, "I'm terribly sorry, rabbi, I don't know what's wrong with me, but that's the second time that happened to me today."

The rabbi says, "That's okay, son, no offense taken. Now, just give me change for the twenty I gave you, and I'll be on my way."

* * *

One day, Heaven is beginning to fill up (of course due to the population explosion), so St. Peter decides to ask each person a question about the Bible before they can enter. Three men stand at the pearly gates, waiting to get into heaven. "How many wise men were there?" St. Peter asks the first man.

"Three," he answers, and the trumpets sound, the gates open, and he enters.

"How long did the flood last?" St. Peter asks the second man.

"Forty days and forty nights," he answers, and the trumpets sound, the gates open and the second man enters.

Seeing how easily the first two answered his trivia questions, St. Peter thinks of a much more difficult one for the third man. Finally, he asks, "What was the first thing Eve said to Adam in the Garden?"

The man thinks and thinks, but can't come up with an answer. "Boy, that's a hard one," he finally says. And the trumpets blow, the gates open, and the last man enters Heaven.

* * *

The new minister's wife had a baby. The minister appealed to the congregation for a salary increase to cover the addition to the family. The congregation agreed that it was only fair, and approved it. When the next child arrived, the minister appealed again and the congregation approved again. Several years and five children later, the congregation was a bit upset over the increasing expense. This turned into a rather loud meeting one night with the minister. Finally, the minister stood and shouted out, "Having children is an Act of God!"

An older man in the back stood and shouted back, "Rain and snow are Acts of God, too, and we wear rubbers for them!"

* * *

There was a priest from a very small church in the backwoods of Alaska. During his first year, he decided to visit two of his most remote parishioners to see how they were doing. The man said that he was getting along, however he couldn't have made it without his Rosary and two martinis each day.

With that, he asked the priest, "Would you like to have a martini with me?"

The priest replied, "Yes, that would be nice."

The man turned around and hollered towards the kitchen, "Rosary, would you fix us two martinis please?"

* * *

A new priest at his first mass was so nervous he could hardly speak.

After mass he asked the monsignor how he had done.

The monsignor replied, "When I am worried about getting nervous on the pulpit, I put a glass of vodka next to the water glass. If I start to get nervous, I take a sip."

So next Sunday he took the monsignor's advice. At the beginning of the sermon, he got nervous and took a drink. He proceeded to talk up a storm.

Upon his return to his office after mass, he found the following note on the door:

1. Sip the vodka, don't gulp.
2. There are 10 commandments, not 12.
3. There are 12 disciples, not 10.
4. Jesus was consecrated, not constipated.
5. Jacob wagered his donkey, he did not bet his ass.
6. We do not refer to Jesus Christ as the late J.C.
7. The Father, Son, and Holy Ghost are not referred to as "Daddy, Junior and Spooky."
8. David slew Goliath, he did not kick the shit out of him.
9. When David was hit by a rock and was knocked off his donkey, don't say he was stoned off his ass.
10. We do not refer to the cross as the "Big T."
11. When Jesus broke the bread at the Last Supper he said, "Take this and eat it for it is my body." He did not say "Eat me."
12. The Virgin Mary is not called "Mary with the Cherry."
13. The recommended grace before a meal is not "Rub-A-Dub-Dub thanks for the grub, yay God."
14. Next Sunday there will be a taffy-pulling contest at St. Peter's, not a peter-pulling contest at St. Taffy's!

* * *

Two priests were taking a piss in the urinals one day and the one priest looks down and sees a nicotine patch on the other guy's dick.

He says, "I'm not really a rocket scientist or anything, but, isn't that supposed to be on your arm?"

And the other priest goes, "Nah, it's working fine. I'm down to two butts a day!"

* * *

Johnny is walking along and a priest is coming the other way. Johnny says, "Hey mister, why are you wearing your collar backwards?"

The priest says, "Because I'm a Father."

Johnny says, "Yeah? Well, my old man's got three kids and he don't wear his collar backwards."

The priest says, "You don't understand, son. I have thousands of children."

Johnny says, "Maybe you should wear your fucking pants backwards."

* * *

A nun and a priest are riding a camel through the desert. After a few days the camel falls over dead. After thinking over the situation the priest figures neither one of them will survive the rest of the journey. The priest asks the nun, "I have never seen a woman's breasts, and at this point it probably wouldn't matter much, so could I see yours?"

The nun agrees and shows him her breasts.

"May I touch them?"

The nun allows him to. The priest comments sincerely on how wonderful they are.

The nun then asks, "Father, I have never seen a man's penis before, could you show me yours?"

The priest drops his drawers.

"May I touch it?"

After she fondles his penis for a minute he sports a huge erection.

The priest says, "You know, if I place my penis in the proper place it can give life!"

"Is that right?" the nun replies.

"Yes," says the priest, quivering with anticipation.

"Then why don't you stick it up that camel's ass and let's get the hell out of here!"

* * *

There was a man put on the reserve list to go to Iraq. When he was told he was going, he fled. He ran about three months before finally ending up on a highway. All he could see were two G.I. men coming from a distance and a nun.

He ran up to the nun and said, "Please help and hide me! I don't want to go to Iraq!" So the nun agreed to let him hide under her dress.

The G.I. men came and went without noticing the nun. When the man crawled out, he said "Thanks for everything, but I do have to say you you've got the most beautiful legs I have ever seen."

The nun replied, "If you looked a little higher, you would have seen my beautiful balls. I don't want to go either!"

* * *

A missionary is sent into the deepest, darkest part of Africa to live with a tribe. He spends years with the people, teaching them to read and write, and preaching to them about the good Christian ways of the white man.

One thing he particularly stresses is the evils of sexual sin: Thou must not commit adultery or fornication!

One day, the wife of one of the tribe's noblemen gives birth to a white baby. The village is shocked and the chief is sent to talk with the missionary.

"You have taught us of the evils of sexual sin, yet here, a black woman gives birth to a white child. You are the only white man who has ever set foot in our village."

The missionary replies, "No, no. You are mistaken. What you have here is a natural occurrence, what is called an albino. Look to thy yonder field. See the flock of white sheep, and yet amongst them, one of them is black. Nature does this on occasion."

"Tell you what," the chief says, "You never mention the sheep again, and I won't say anything about the baby."

* * *

One Sunday, a priest decided to skip church and go hunting in the neighboring forest. So while he was hunting he saw a gigantic grizzly bear that had stopped to get honey from a beehive. The priest thought the bear was good game, so he clumsily shot at it, and he missed. The bear, startled by the shot, jumped up and started charging toward the priest. The priest used his only option: he dropped to his knees and prayed.

"Dear God," he said, "Please let this bear be a good Christian, a better one than I was."

As the bear drew closer, it dropped to its knees and said, "Dear God, thank you for this meal I am about to receive."

* * *

A housewife takes a lover during the day, while her husband is at work.

Not aware that her nine-year-old son was hiding in the closet. Her husband came home unexpectedly, so she hid her lover in the closet. The boy now has company.

Boy: "Dark in here."

Man: "Yes it is."

Boy: "I have a baseball."

Man: "That's nice."

Boy: "Want to buy it?"

Man: "No, thanks."

Boy: "My dad's outside."

Man: "OK, how much?"

Boy: "$250."

In the next few weeks, it happens again that the boy and the mom's lover are in the closet together.

Boy: "Dark in here."

Man: "Yes, it is."

Boy: "I have a baseball glove."

Man: "That's nice."

Boy: "Want to buy it?"

Man: "No, thanks."

Boy: "Ill tell."

Man: "How much?"

Boy: "$750."

Man: "Fine."

A few days later, the father says to the boy, "Grab your glove. Let's go outside and toss the baseball!"

The boy says, "I can't. I sold them."

The father asks, "How much did you sell them for?" The son says, "$1,000."

The father says, "That's terrible to over-charge your friends like that. That is a lot more than those two things cost. I'm going to take you to church and make you confess."

They go to church and the father alerts the priest and makes the little boy sit in the confession booth and closes the door.

The boy says, "Dark in here."

The priest says, "Don't start that shit again!"

* * *

An accountant dies and goes to Heaven. He reaches the pearly gates and is amazed to see a happy crowd all waving banners and chanting his name. After a few minutes, St. Peter comes running across and says, "I'm sorry I wasn't here to greet you personally. God is looking forward to meeting such a remarkable man as you."

The accountant is perplexed. "I've tried to lead a good life, but I am overwhelmed by your welcome," he tells St. Peter.

"It's the least we can do for someone as special as you are. Imagine, living to the age of 160 and still looking so young," says St. Peter.

The man looks even more dumbfounded and replies, "160? I don't know what you mean. I'm only 40."

St. Peter replies, "But that can't be right... we've seen your time sheets!"

* * *

The Pope and one of his Cardinals were on a plane from the Vatican to New York City. It was a long flight, and the Pope was working a crossword puzzle to pass the time.

At one point in the flight, the Pope leaned over to his Cardinal, and asked "Do you know a four letter word for a woman that ends with U-N-T?"

"Of course," replied the Cardinal, "Aunt."

"Do you have an eraser?" asked the Pope.

* * *

A drunken man staggered into a Catholic church, sat down in the Confessional and said nothing. The priest waited and waited. The priest coughed to attract the drunk man's attention, but still the man said nothing. Finally, the priest knocked on the wall three times in a final attempt to get the man to speak.

The drunk replied, "No use knockin', pal. There's no paper."

* * *

John enters the confessional and tells the priest that he's committed adultery.

"Oh, my," the priest says, "Was it with Janice Cook?"

"I'd rather not reveal who it was with," John replies.

"Was it with Cindy Jones?" asks the priest.

"I would rather not say," replies John.

So, the priest grants John absolution and John leaves. As he was leaving the church, John's friend asks him, "Well, did you receive absolution?"

"Yes, and I also received a couple of good leads!" John answers.

* * *

One morning, a parish priest was opening his mail. He took a single sheet of paper out of an envelope and unfolded it. Looking at the paper, he found that only one word had been written… 'Asshole'.

At mass the following Sunday, he announced to his congregation, "I have known many people who have written letters and have forgotten to sign their name. However, this week I received a letter from someone who signed their name, but forgot to write a letter."

* * *

Mother Superior was on her way to late morning prayers when she passed two novices just leaving early morning prayers, on their way to classes. As she passed the young ladies, Mother Superior said, "Good morning ladies."

The novices replied, "Good morning, Mother Superior, may God be with you."

But after they had passed, Mother Superior heard one say to the other, "I think she got up on the wrong side of the bed this morning." This startled Mother Superior, but she chose not to pursue the issue.

A little further down the hall, Mother Superior passed two of the Sisters who had been teaching at the convent for several years. She greeted them with, "Good morning, Sister Martha, Sister Jessica, may God give you wisdom for our students today."

"Good morning, Mother Superior. Thank you, and may God be with you." But again, after passing, Mother Superior overheard, "She got up on the wrong side of the bed today."

Baffled, she started to wonder if she had spoken harshly, or with an irritated look on her face. She vowed to be more pleasant.

Looking down the hall, Mother Superior saw retired Sister Mary approaching, step by step, with her walker. As Sister Mary was rather deaf, Mother Superior had plenty of time to arrange a pleasant smile on her face before greeting Sister Mary. "Good morning, Sister Mary. I'm so happy to see you up and about. I pray God watches over you today, and grants you a wonderful day."

"Ah, Good morning, Mother Superior, and thank you. I see you got up on the wrong side of the bed this morning."

Mother Superior was floored! "Sister Mary, what have I done wrong? I have tried to be pleasant, but three times already today people have said that about me."

Sister Mary stopped her walker, and looked Mother Superior in the face. "Oh, don't take it personally, Mother Superior. It's just that you're wearing Father Murphy's slippers."

* * *

A few minutes after a crowded airliner takes off, a five-year-old boy begins to throw a wild temper tantrum. No matter what his frustrated, embarrassed mother tried to do to calm him down, the boy continued to scream furiously and kick the seats around him.

Suddenly, from the rear of the plane, an elderly priest slowly walks forward up the aisle. Stopping the flustered mother with an upraised hand, the priest leans down and whispers something into the young boy's ear.

Without hesitation, the boy calms down, gently takes his mother's hand, and quietly fastens his seat belt. All the other passengers burst into spontaneous applause.

As the priest begins to make his way back to his seat, one of the flight attendants touches his sleeve. "Pardon me, Father," she says quietly, "but may I ask what magic words you used on that little boy?"

Smiling serenely, the priest gently says, "I told him that if he didn't knock it off, I'd kick the shit out of him."

* * *

Virgin Mary wanted to visit Hell, so she went to God and asked if she might do so. "Yes," God said. "I have only one warning for you. You must stay away from booze, drugs and men. Will you promise me so?"

"Yes," Virgin Mary said.

"And remember to call me every night," God said, before Virgin Mary left.

So, on the first night, the telephone rang in Heaven. "Heaven," God answered.

"Hello, it's Virgin Mary here... I'm sorry to tell you, but I am a bit drunk... I couldn't resist the temptation. Will you forgive me?" asked Virgin Mary.

"Yes I will. Now stay clear of drugs and men, will you? And call me tomorrow," said God.

The following night, the phone rang in Heaven. "Heaven," God answered.

"It's Virgin Mary here. I'm sorry to say, but I'm a bit high... I couldn't resist the temptation. Will you forgive me?" asked Virgin Mary.

"Yes I will. Now stay clear of men, will you. And call me tomorrow," God said.

The next night, the phone rang in Heaven. God answered, "Heaven."

"Mary here."

* * *

A widow named Patricia lived alone in the countryside with her pet dog, which she loved and was totally devoted to. After many years of companionship, her dog died, so she went to see the parish priest.

"Father, my old dog has died and I was wondering if you could say a mass for the dear soul?" Patricia said.

"I'm very sorry to hear about your dog's passing," Father Murphy said. "Unfortunately, we are unable to have services for an animal in the church. There is, however, a new denomination down the road. There's no telling what they believe, so perhaps they'll do something for the animal."

"I'll go there right now," Patricia replied. "By the way, Father, do you think that $500 is enough to donate for the service?"

"Why didn't you tell me your dear dog was a Catholic?" Father Murphy replied.

A man was lying on the sidewalk after being struck by a bus on a busy city street, with a crowd of spectators gathered around him.

"A priest," gasped the man, "Please, someone get me a priest."

A policeman checked the crowd, but there was no priest, no minister, no man of God of any kind.

"A priest, please," the injured man repeated. Suddenly, an elderly man stepped out of the crowd.

"Officer," the old man said, "I'm not a priest, nor am I even a Catholic, but I have lived behind St. Mary's Catholic Church for over fifty years, and I have listened to the Catholic rites every night. Perhaps I can be of some comfort to this man."

The policeman agreed and brought the old man over to the victim. The old man knelt down on the sidewalk, leaned over the injured man, and in a solemn voice said, "B-9, I-21, N-34, G-51, O-68."

* * *

Although they have been the best of friends for years, a priest and a rabbi were always arguing the finer points of their respective theologies.

One day, while they were riding in a car together, they got cut off by a drunk driver. Their car flew off the road, rolled over several times, and came to rest on its roof. The priest and rabbi crawled from the wreckage and were amazed they had survived.

As the priest crossed himself, he noticed the rabbi doing the same.

"Praise Be! You've seen the Light!" exclaimed the priest.

"What?" asked the rabbi.

"You've crossed yourself! You have seen the True Way! This is wonderful!" replied the priest.

"Crossed myself? No, no," explained the rabbi. I was just making sure everything was okay. 'Spectacles, Testicles, Wallet and Watch.'"

* * *

A farmer purchases an old, run-down, abandoned farm with plans to turn it into a thriving enterprise. The fields are grown over with weeds, the farmhouse is falling apart, and the fences are collapsing all around.

During his first day of work, the town preacher stops by to bless the man's work, saying, "May you and God work together to make this the farm of your dreams!"

Several months later, the preacher pays another visit to the farmer. Lo and behold, it's like a completely different place. The farmhouse is completely rebuilt and in excellent condition, there are plenty of cattle and other livestock happily munching on feed in well-fenced pens, and the fields are filled with crops planted in neat rows.

"Amazing!" the preacher says. "Look what God and you have accomplished together!"

"Yes, Reverend," says the farmer, it's quite astounding when you consider what the farm was like when God was working it alone!"

* * *

One morning, two priests head for the showers. It's not until they're undressed and in the showers, that they realize they didn't bring any soap. Father George decides he'll run back for the soap. Rather than taking the time to get dressed, he peaks out into the hallway, sees there's no one around, and decides to make a run for it.

He grabs the two bars of soap, checks the hall before heading back to the showers, sees it's all clear and makes a run for it. Just as he turns the corner to the showers, he spots three nuns walking toward him. With nowhere to go, and hoping that the nuns will think he's a statue, he stands perfectly still, holding the two bars of soap.

The nuns approach and the first nun says, "Oh my, look at that! Isn't that the most life-like statue you've ever seen?" She steps up for a closer look, reaches out and gives a couple of tugs on the priest's pecker. Startled, he drops the first bar of soap.

"Oh Heavens," she exclaims, "I got a bar of soap!"

The second nun is also amazed at how realistic the statue looks, so she steps in for a closer look. She takes a couple of yanks on the priest's pecker, and he drops the other bar of soap.

"My goodness, I too got a bar of soap!" she said.

The third nun, overcome by the miracle statue, walks up to it and gives the priest's pecker a few tugs.

"My God," she says, "liquid soap!"

* * *

George rushed into the confessional with a turkey under his arm. "Forgive me, Father, for I have sinned," he said. "I stole this turkey to feed my family. Please, would you take it and relieve my guilt."

"Certainly not," the priest said. "As penance, you must return it to the one from whom you stole it."

"But I tried and he refused," sobbed George. "Father, what should I do?"

"If what you say is true, then it is all right for you to keep it for your family," the priest said.

"Thank you, Father," George replied, as he rushed off.

When the priest returned to his residence, he entered the kitchen and found that someone had stolen his Thanksgiving turkey.

* * *

A nun entered a liquor store and asked the clerk to give her a pint of brandy.

"I'm sorry, Sister," the clerk replied, "I couldn't do that. I've never sold alcohol to a nun."

"It's for the Mother Superior," the nun explained. "She's constipated and brandy seems to help."

So, the clerk agreed to sell her the brandy.

When he closed the store later that night, he found the nun sitting out on the curb, totally inebriated, singing and laughing to herself.

"Sister, shame on you!" he scolded. "You told me the brandy was for the Mother Superior's constipation."

"It is, young man, it is," replied the nun, slurring her words. "She is constipated and when she sees me, she's gonna shit herself."

* * *

The minister was preoccupied with thoughts of how he was going to ask the congregation to come up with more money than they were expecting for repairs to the church building.

He gave the organist a copy of the service and asked her if she could come up with some kind of inspirational music to play after he made the announcement about the finances to help put the congregation in a giving mood.

"Don't worry, I'll come up with something," she said.

During the service, the minister paused and said, "Brothers and sisters, we find ourselves in great difficulty. The cost of the roof repairs is twice as much as we expected, and we need $4000 more. Any of you who are able to pledge $100 or more, please stand up."

At that moment, the organist began playing, "The Star Spangled Banner."

* * *

During his service, a preacher told his congregation that anything they could possibly think of, old or new, was discussed somewhere in the Bible and that the entirety of the human experience could be found therein.

After the service concluded, he was approached by a woman who said, "Preacher, I don't believe PMS is mentioned anywhere in the Bible."

He told her that he was sure it must be in there somewhere and he would look for it and show her his findings next week.

After his service the following week, the preacher called the woman aside and showed her a passage which read: "And Mary rode Joseph's ass all the way to Bethlehem."

* * *

Being a little nervous about hearing confessions, the new priest asked an older priest to sit in on his sessions. After hearing a few confessions, the older priest asked him to step out of the confessional so he could give him a few suggestions.

"Cross your arms over your chest and rub your chin with one hand," the older priest suggested.

The new priest did as suggested and continued hearing confessions. Again, the older priest took him aside.

The older priest said, "Try saying things like, 'I understand,' 'Yes, I see, please continue,' and 'How do you feel about that?'"

The new priest again did as suggested.

After the new priest's sessions were completed, the older priest said to him, "There now, don't you think that was a little better than chuckling, slapping your knee and saying, 'No shit, what happened next?'"

* * *

Having not seen an elderly church member for a number of years, the priest decided to pay her a visit. After welcoming him and inviting him in, she went into the kitchen to prepare some tea. While he was waiting for her to return, he looked around the room and caught sight of a beautiful oak pump organ with a cut glass bowl sitting on top of it. The bowl was half filled with water and had a condom floating in it.

Astonished and shocked, the priest turned away, but curiosity was getting to him. When the woman came back from the kitchen he asked her about it.

Quite enthusiastically, she explained, "While I was in town about a year ago, I found a package on the sidewalk. I picked it up and read the directions on the back. They said 'Keep wet and put on your organ to prevent disease'. I do believe it works, after all, I haven't had a cold all winter."

* * *

A man had just undergone coronary surgery at Mercy Hospital and was in the recovery room. A Sister of Mercy was at his bedside to reassure him that all went well. "You are going to be fine, Mr. Jones. However, we do need to know how you intend to pay for your hospital stay. Do you have insurance coverage?"

"No, I don't," the groggy man answered.

"Is it possible for you to pay in cash then?" the nun persisted.

"No, I'm afraid that's not possible," he replied.

"Well, do you have any close relatives?" the nun asked. "Only my sister in Texas, but she's a humble spinster nun," said the man.

"Mr. Jones, I must correct you. Nuns are not spinsters for they are married to God," the nun explained.

"Well, in that case, send my bill to my brother-in-law!" he said.

* * *

"The nerve endings," said Gabriel. "How many will I put in her hands?"

"How many did we put in Adam?" asked The Lord.

"Two-hundred, O Mighty One," replied Gabriel.

"Then we shall do the same for this woman," said The Lord.

"How many nerve endings should we put in woman's genitals," inquired Gabriel.

"How many did we put in Adam?" asked The Lord.

"Four-hundred and twenty, O Mighty One," replied Gabriel.

"Of course. We did want Adam to have a means of receiving extra pleasure in his life, didn't we? Do the same for woman," said The Lord.

"Yes, O Great Lord," said Gabriel.

"No, wait!" said The Lord. "Screw it, give her ten-thousand. I want her to scream out my name."

* * *

There was a guy in a bar one night that got really drunk, I mean really, really drunk. When the bar closed he got up to go home.

As he stumbled out the door he saw a nun walking on the sidewalk. So he stumbled over to the nun and punched her in the face.

Well the nun was surprised, but before she could do or say anything he punched her again. This time she fell down and he stumbled over to her and kicked her in the butt, then he picked her up and threw her into a wall.

By this time the nun was pretty weak and couldn't move very much, so then he stumbled over to her, put his face right next to hers and said... "Not so tough tonight, are you Batman?"

* * *

One day, Jesus was doing the rounds in Heaven and decided that this time he would walk around the boundaries of heaven just to see what was going on.

Eventually he came to a big wire fence which surrounded heaven and was very surprised to see an old man on the other side.

"Hello" smiled Jesus, "are you lost or something?"

"I'm not lost," said the old man, "I am looking for my son."

"Perhaps I can help you," said Jesus helpfully, "tell me about him."

"Well, I am a carpenter by trade and my son was born in a stable a long time ago," started the old man.

Jesus eyes looked up in excitement. Surely this could not be. "What other things can you tell me about him old man?"

"My son is easily recognized as he has a hole in each of his hands and each of his feet."

"Daddy, is that... really you?" sobbed Jesus, tears welling up and a lump forming in his throat.

"Pinocchio?"

* * *

Q & A Roundup
God and the Godly

Q What's the definition of suspicion?
A   A nun doing push ups in a cucumber field.

Q How are Christmas trees and Priests alike?
A Their balls are only for decoration.

Q What did Adam say to Eve?
A Stand back, I don't know how big this thing gets!

Q How do you get a nun pregnant?
A Dress her up as an altar boy

Q What's the difference between sin and shame?
A It is a sin to put it in, but it's a shame to pull it out.

Q Did you hear about the new Exorcist movie?
A This time they got the Devil to come in to take the Priest out of the child.

Q What's a priest's love life like?
A Nun.

Q What do you call a nun with a sex change operation?
A A tran-sister.

Q Why did God create man before woman?
A He didn't want any advice.

Lawyers

Like prostitutes, I have very little call to engage these kinds of services. Lawyers aren't like the rest of us. We can't understand them, in much the same way we can't comprehend the thoughts of a hawk or a hyena. Do they sleep or are the lying in wait?

On one of the few occasions when I was forced to retain council, I stared at the attorney's face and pictured one of those discs from the gas meter circulating in and out of his skull, just turning and turning, ticking off charges as it spun. That daydream cost me $1,100.

But lawyers are a necessary evil. You really need them and they often do a good job, but the real question is: Will it cost me more money to win or lose?

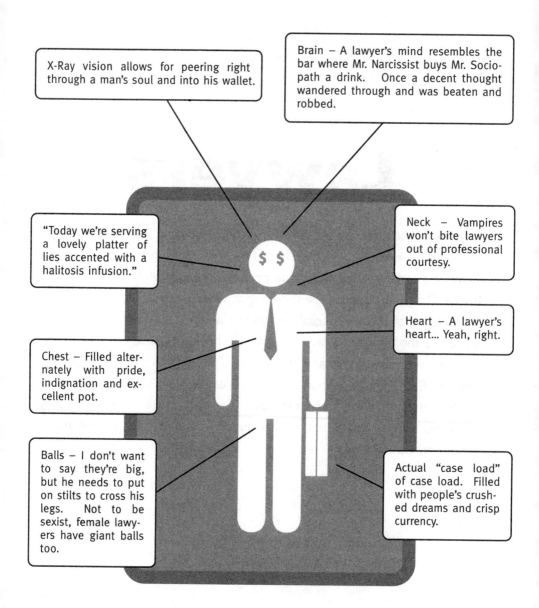

Common Indicators That You Are A

LAWYER

A guy walks into a bar and sees a gorgeous woman nursing a drink. Walking up behind her he says, "Hi there good lookin'. How's it going?"

Having already downed a few power drinks, she turns around, faces him, looks him straight in the eye and says, "Listen up, buddy. I screw anybody, anytime, anywhere, your place, my place, in the car, front door, back door, on the ground, standing up, sitting down, naked or with clothes on, dirty, clean... it doesn't matter to me, I've been doing it ever since I got out of college and I just flat-ass love it."

Eyes now wide with interest, he responds, "No kidding. I'm a lawyer, too. What firm are you with?"

* * *

A man appears before a judge with his lawyer, asking for a divorce. The judge quietly reviews some papers and then says, "Please tell me why you are seeking a divorce."

"Because," the lawyer says, "my client lives in a two-story house."

The judge replies, "What kind of a reason is that? What is the big deal about a two-story house?"

The lawyer answers, "Well Your Honor, one story is 'I have a headache' and the other story is 'It's that time of the month.'"

* * *

A local United Way office realized that it had never received a donation from the town's most successful lawyer. The person in charge of contributions called him to persuade him to contribute.

"Our research shows that out of a yearly income of at least $500,000, you give not a penny to charity. Wouldn't you like to give back to the community?"

The lawyer mulled this over for a moment and replied, "First, did your research also show that my mother is dying after a long illness, and has medical bills that are several times her annual income?"

Embarrassed, the United Way rep mumbled, "Um...no."

"Did your research show that my brother, a disabled veteran, is blind and confined to a wheelchair?"

The stricken United Way rep began to stammer out an apology but was interrupted.

"Did your research show that my sister's husband died in a traffic accident," the lawyer's voice rising in indignation, "leaving her penniless with three children?!"

The humiliated United Way rep, completely beaten, said simply, "I had no idea."

On a roll, the lawyer cut him off once again, "So if I don't give any money to them, why should I give any to you?"

* * *

Two lawyers are in a bank, when, suddenly, armed robbers burst in. While several of the robbers take the money from the tellers, others line the customers, including the lawyers, up against a wall, and proceed to take their wallets, watches, etc. While this is going on lawyer number one jams something in lawyer number two's hand.

Without looking down, lawyer number two whispers, "What is this?"

To which lawyer number one replies, "It's that fifty bucks I owe you."

* * *

"You seem to have more than the average share of intelligence for a man of your background," sneered the lawyer at a witness on the stand.

"If I wasn't under oath, I'd return the compliment," replied the witness.

* * *

A tourist wanders into a back-alley antique shop in San Francisco's Chinatown. Picking through the objects on display he discovers a detailed, life-sized bronze sculpture of a rat. The sculpture is so interesting and unique that he picks it up and asks the shop owner what it costs.

"Twelve dollars for the rat, sir," says the shop owner, "and a thousand dollars more for the story behind it."

"You can keep the story, old man," he replies, "but I'll take the rat."

The transaction complete, the tourist leaves the store with the bronze rat under his arm. As he crosses the street in front of the store, two live rats emerge from a sewer drain and fall into step behind him. Nervously looking over his shoulder, he begins to walk faster, but every time he passes another sewer drain, more rats come out and follow him. By the time he's walked two blocks, at least a hundred rats are at his heels, and people begin to point and shout. He walks even faster, and soon breaks into a trot as multitudes of rats swarm from sewers, basements, vacant lots, and abandoned cars. Rats by the thousands are at his heels, and as he sees the waterfront at the bottom of the hill, he panics and starts to run full tilt.

No matter how fast he runs, the rats keep up, squealing hideously, now not just thousands but millions, so that by the time he comes rushing up to the water's edge a trail of rats twelve city blocks long is behind him. Making a mighty leap, he jumps up onto a light post, grasping it with one arm while he hurls the bronze rat into the San Francisco Bay with the other, as far as he can heave it. Pulling his legs up and clinging to the light post, he watches in amazement as the seething tide of rats surges over the breakwater into the sea, where they drown.

Shaken and mumbling, he makes his way back to the antique shop.

"Ah, so you've come back for the rest of the story," says the owner.

"No," says the tourist, "I was wondering if you have a bronze lawyer."

* * *

A guy walks into a post office one day to see a middle-aged, balding man standing at the counter, methodically placing "Love" stamps on bright pink envelopes with hearts all over them. He then takes out a perfume bottle and starts spraying scent all over them.

His curiosity getting the better of him, he goes up to the balding man and asks him what he is doing. The man says, "I'm sending out 1,000 Valentine cards signed, 'Guess who?'"

"But why?" asks the man.

"I'm a divorce lawyer."

* * *

A man walked into a lawyer's office and inquired about the lawyer's rates.

"Fifty dollars for three questions," replied the lawyer.

"Isn't that awfully steep?" asked the man.

"Yes," the lawyer replied, "and what was your third question?"

* * *

"Doctor," she asks nervously, "can you get pregnant from anal intercourse?"

"Certainly," replies the doctor, "where do you think lawyers come from?"

* * *

A defendant was on trial for murder. There was strong evidence indicating guilt, but there was no corpse. In the defense's closing statement the lawyer, knowing that his client would probably be convicted, resorted to a trick.

"Ladies and gentlemen of the jury, I have a surprise for you all," the lawyer said as he looked at his watch. "Within one minute, the person presumed dead in this case will walk into this courtroom." He looked toward the courtroom door. The jurors, somewhat stunned, all looked on eagerly. A minute passed. Nothing happened.

Finally the lawyer said, "Actually, I made up the previous statement. But, you all looked on with anticipation. I therefore put to you that you have a reasonable doubt in this case as to whether anyone was killed and insist that you return a verdict of not guilty."

The jury, clearly confused, retired to deliberate. A few minutes later, the jury returned and pronounced a verdict of guilty.

"But how?" inquired the lawyer. "You must have had some doubt; I saw all of you stare at the door."

The jury foreman replied, "Yeah, we all looked, but your client didn't!"

* * *

Did you hear about the guy on the beach who found a bottle? He rubbed it and, sure enough, out popped a genie. "I will grant you three wishes," said the genie. "But there's a catch."

The man was ecstatic. "What catch?" he asked.

The genie replied, "Every time you make a wish, every lawyer in the world will receive double what you asked for."

"Well, I can live with that! No problem!" replied the elated man.

"What is your first wish?" asked the genie.

"Well, I've always wanted a Ferrari!" POOF! A Ferrari appeared in front of the man.

"Now, every lawyer in the world has two Ferraris," said the genie. "Next wish?"

"I'd love a million dollars..." replied the man. POOF! One million dollars appeared at his feet.

"Now, every lawyer in the world has two million dollars," said the genie.

"Well, that's okay, as long as I've got my million," replied the man.

"What is your final wish?"

The man thought long and hard, and finally said, "Well, you know, I've always wanted to donate a kidney."

* * *

An investment counselor decided to go out on her own. She was shrewd and diligent, so business kept coming in, and pretty soon she realized that she needed an in-house counsel. She began to interview young lawyers.

"As I'm sure you can understand," she started off with one of the first applicants, "in a business like this, our personal integrity must be beyond question." She leaned forward. "Mr. Peterson, are you an honest lawyer?"

"Honest?" replied the job prospect. "Let me tell you something about honest. Why, I'm so honest that my father lent me $15,000 for my education, and I paid back every penny the minute I tried my very first case."

"Impressive. And what sort of case was that?"

The lawyer squirmed in his seat and admitted, "he sued me for the money."

* * *

A gang of robbers broke into a lawyer's club by mistake. The old legal lions gave them a fight for their life and their money.

The gang was very happy to escape. "It ain't so bad," one crook noted. "We got $25 between us."

The boss screamed: "I warned you to stay clear of lawyers, we had $100 when we broke in!"

* * *

There was a loser who couldn't get a date. He went to a bar and asked this one guy how to get a date.

The guy said, "It's simple. I just say, I'm a lawyer."

So the guy went up to a pretty woman and asked her out. After she said no, he told her that it was probably a good thing because he had a case early in the morning.

She said, "Oh! You're a lawyer?"

He said, "Why yes I am!" So they went to his place and when they were in bed, screwing, he started to laugh to himself.

When she asked what was so funny, he answered, "Well, I've only been a lawyer for fifteen minutes, and I'm already screwing someone!"

* * *

An engineer, a physicist, and a lawyer were being interviewed for a position as chief executive officer of a large corporation.

The engineer was interviewed first, and was asked a long list of questions, ending with "How much is two plus two?"

The engineer excused himself, and made a series of measurements and calculations before returning to the board room and announcing, "Four."

The physicist was next interviewed, and was asked the same questions.

Before answering the last question, he excused himself, made for the library, and did a great deal of research. After a consultation with the United States Bureau of Standards and many calculations, he also announced, "Four."

The lawyer was interviewed last, and was asked the same questions.

At the end of his interview, before answering the last question, he drew all the shades in the room, looked outside the door to see if anyone was there, checked the telephone for listening devices, and asked, "How much do you want it to be?"

* * *

Just before the closing argument, it being apparent that things were not looking good for the defendant, the judge called for a brief adjournment.

"Why don't you take your client aside and give him the benefit of your best advice?" she tactfully suggested to the defense counsel.

When the courtroom was called to order, the judge noted an empty chair next to the lawyer.

"And where is your client?" she inquired.

"On his way to Buenos Ares," was the answer. "That was the best advice I could give him."

* * *

A New York man was forced to take a day off from work to appear for a minor traffic summons. He grew increasingly restless as he waited hour after endless hour for his case to be heard.

When his name was called late in the afternoon, he stood before the judge, only to hear that court would be adjourned for the next day and he would have to return tomorrow.

"What for?" he snapped at the judge.

His honor, equally irked by a tedious day and sharp query roared, "Twenty dollars contempt of court. That's why!"

Then, noticing the man checking his wallet, the judge relented. "That's alright. You don't have to pay now."

The young man replied, "I'm just seeing if I have enough for two more words."

* * *

Taking his seat in his chambers, the judge faced the opposing lawyers. "So," he said, "I have been presented, by both of you, with a bribe."

Both lawyers squirmed uncomfortably. "You, attorney Leon, gave me $15,000. And you, attorney Campos, gave me $10,000."

The judge reached into his pocket and pulled out a check. He handed it to Leon. "Now then, I'm returning $5,000, and we're going to decide this case solely on its merits!"

* * *

A lawyer was walking down the street and saw an auto accident. He rushed over, started handing out business cards, and said, "I saw the whole thing. I'll take either side."

* * *

A man goes to his lawyer and says, "I would like to make a will but I don't know exactly how to go about it."

The lawyer says, "Don't worry, leave it to me."

The man looks somewhat upset, "Well, I knew you were going to take the biggest slice, but I'd like to leave a little to my children too."

* * *

A lawyer goes to the doctor because he is not feeling well. After examining him, the physician says to the lawyer, "Before I tell you anything, I would like for you to be examined by my colleague in the next office, just to get a second opinion."

The lawyer is introduced to the other doctor, then goes through another complete physical examination. When it is over, the physician tells him to sit in the waiting room until the first doctor calls him back into his office.

A few minutes later he is brought in, and as the lawyer takes a seat across from the doctor's desk, he begins to feel a bit nervous. Both doctors are sitting there behind the desk, with very serious looks on their faces.

The first doctor says to the lawyer, "My colleague and I have examined you and we have come to the same conclusion: "You have a very rare incurable disease. You will die in two weeks, and it will be a very slow and painful death."

The other doctor suddenly turns toward the first doctor looking very surprised. "Why did you tell him that?"

"Well," replies the first doctor, "I felt that he had the right to know."

"Yeah," whines the other doctor, "but I wanted to be the one to tell him."

* * *

Two law partners hire a new cute, young secretary, and a contest arises between them as to who can bed her first, even though they're both already married. Eventually one of them scores with her, and his partner is quite eager to hear how things went.

"So what did you think?" he asks.

"Ahh," replies the first lawyer, "my wife is better."

Some time goes by, and then the second lawyer goes to bed with the secretary.

"So," asks the first lawyer, "what did you think?"

The second guy replies, "You were right."

* * *

A guy phones a law office and says, "I want to speak to my lawyer." The receptionist replies, "I'm sorry but he died last week."

The next day he phones again and asks the same question.

The receptionist replies, "I told you yesterday, he died last week."

The next day the guy calls again and asks to speak to his lawyer. By this time the receptionist is getting a little annoyed and says, "I keep telling you, your lawyer died last week. Why do you keep calling?"

The guy says, "because I just love hearing it."

* * *

The devil visited a lawyer's office and made him an offer. "I can arrange some things for you, "the devil said. "I'll increase your income five-fold. Your partners will love you; your clients will respect you; you'll have four months of vacation each year and live to be a hundred. All I require in return is that your wife's soul, your children's souls, and their children's souls rot in Hell for eternity."

The lawyer thought for a moment. "What's the catch?"

* * *

Lawyer: "Judge, I wish to appeal my client's case on the basis of newly discovered evidence."

Judge: "And what is the nature of the new evidence?"

Lawyer: "Judge, I discovered that my client still has $500 left."

* * *

An elderly man of 82, just returned from the doctors only to find he didn't have long to live. So he summons the three most important people in his life to tell, his doctor, his priest, and his lawyer.

"Well today I found out I don't have long to live. So I asked you three here, because your the most important people in my life. And I need to ask a favor. Today I am going to give each of you an envelope with $50,000 dollars in it. When I die, I would ask that all three of you throw the money into my grave."

Well a few days later the man passed on. The doctor said, "I have to admit I kept $10,000 dollars of his money, he owed me lots of medical bills. But I threw the other $40,000 in."

The priest said, "I have to admit I kept $25,000 dollars for the church. It's all going to a good cause. And I threw the rest in."

Well the lawyer just couldn't believe what he was hearing, "I am surprised at you two. I wrote a check for the whole amount and threw it in."

* * *

A police chief, a fire chief, and a lawyer were traveling together by car to a municipal management conference in a distant city. Their car broke down in a rural area, and they were forced to seek shelter for the night at a nearby farmhouse.

The farmer welcomed them in, but cautioned them that there were only two spare beds, and that one of them would have to sleep in the barn with the farm animals. After a short conference, the police chief agreed to take the barn.

Shortly after retiring, a knock was heard on the door of the farmhouse. The party inside answered to find the police chief standing there, complaining that he could not sleep. There were pigs in the barn, he said, and he was reminded of the days when everyone called him a pig.

The fire chief then volunteered to exchange with the police chief.

A short time later, another knock was heard at the door. The fire chief complained that the cows in the barn reminded him of Mrs. O'Leary's cow that started the Great Chicago Fire, and that every time he started to go to sleep, he started to have a fireman's worst nightmare, that of burning to death.

The lawyer, in desperation for sleep, then agreed to sleep in the barn.

This seemed like a good idea until a few minutes later, when another knock was heard at the door. They answered the door; there stood the cows and pigs.

* * *

A doctor, an architect, and an attorney were dining at the country club one day, and the conversation turned to the subject of their respective dogs, which were all quite extraordinary. A wager was placed on who had the most intelligent dog.

The physician offered to show his dog first, and called to the parking lot, "Hippocrates, come!" Hippocrates ran in, and was told by the doctor to do his stuff.

Hippocrates ran to the golf course and dug for a while, producing a number of bones. He dragged the bones into the country club, and assembled them into a complete, fully articulated human skeleton. The physician patted Hippocrates on the head, and gave him a cookie for his efforts.

The architect was only marginally impressed, and called for his dog, "Sliderule, come!" Sliderule ran in, and was told to do his stuff.

The dog immediately chewed the skeleton to rubble, but reassembled the fragments into a scale model of the Taj Mahal. The architect patted his dog and gave him a cookie.

The attorney watched the other two dogs, and called "Bullshit, come!" Bullshit entered and was told to do his stuff.

Bullshit immediately sodomized the other two dogs, stole their cookies, auctioned the Taj Mahal replica to the other club members for a fee, and went outside to play golf.

* * *

The real estate boss got a hot new secretary, and he decided to put some moves on her. But within a few weeks, he is feeling displeased at the way she is working, not caring, coming to work late, and so on. Finally, he pulls her aside, and has a little talk with her. "Listen, baby, we may have gone to bed together a few times, but who said you could start coming in late and slacking off?"

The secretary replied, "My lawyer!"

* * *

In the darkest jungle, two tigers are stalking through the jungle when the one in the rear suddenly reaches out with his tongue and licks the butt of the one in front.

The lead tiger turns and says, "Hey, cut it out!"

The other tiger says, "Sorry." And they continue on their way.

After about five minutes the rear tiger suddenly repeats his action. The front tiger turns angrily and says, "I said don't do that!"

The rear tiger says "sorry" again and they continue.

After about another five minutes, the rear tiger repeats his action. The front tiger turns and says, "What is it with you, anyway? I said to stop."

The rear tiger says, "I really am sorry but I just ate a lawyer, and I'm just trying to get the taste out of my mouth."

* * *

A doctor and a lawyer were talking at a party. Their conversation was constantly interrupted by people describing their ailments and asking the doctor for free medical advice.

After an hour of this, the exasperated doctor asked the lawyer, "What do you do to stop people from asking you for legal advice when you're out of the office?"

"I give it to them," replied the lawyer, "and then I send them a bill." The doctor was shocked, but agreed to give it a try. The next day, still feeling slightly guilty, the doctor prepared the bills. When he went to place them in his mailbox, he found a bill from the lawyer.

* * *

Two West Virginia lawyers hired a secretary from a small town in the hills. She was attractive, but it was obvious that she knew nothing about city life.

One attorney said to the other, "Mary is so young and pretty she might be taken advantage of by some of those fast-talking city guys. Why don't we teach her what's right and what's wrong?"

"Great idea," said the partner. "You teach her what's right."

* * *

A marine was coming home from the Pentagon one day. He noticed that there was a lot more traffic than normal. As he got further up the road all of the traffic had come to a halt. He saw a policeman coming towards his car, so he asked the cop what was wrong.

The cop said, "Man, we are in a crisis situation. George Bush is in the road very upset. He does not have the $33.5 million that he owes his lawyers, and his father has had it with him. He is threatening to douse himself in gasoline and start a fire."

The marine asked the cop, exactly what he was doing there.

The cop said, "I feel sorry for the President so I am going car to car asking for donations."

The marine asked, "How much do you have so far?"

The cop replied, "Well as of right now only 33 gallons, but many people are still siphoning as we speak!"

* * *

Q & A Roundup
Lawyers

Q Why does the Law Society prohibit sex between lawyers and their clients?
A To prevent clients from being billed twice for essentially the same service!

Q What's the difference between a dead dog on the road
and a dead lawyer on the road?
A There are skid marks in front of the dog!

Q You're trapped in a room with a tiger, a rattlesnake and a lawyer.
You have a gun with two bullets, what should you do?
A Shoot the lawyer, twice !!

Q What do you call 20 lawyers skydiving from a plane?
A Skeet.

Q What do you have when 100 lawyers are buried up to their necks in sand?
A Not enough sand.

Q What do lawyers use for birth control?
A Their personalities.

Q What can a goose do, a duck can't, and a lawyer should?
A Stick his bill up his ass.

Q Why did God invent lawyers?
A So that realtors would have someone to look down on.

Q What do you call a lawyer gone bad?
A Your Honor.

Q What do you call a judge gone bad?
A Senator.

Q What's the difference between a good lawyer and a great lawyer?
A A good lawyer knows the law. A great lawyer knows the judge.

Workplace

Okay, I hope you're sitting down; I don't make enough on these books to earn a living. In fact, I don't earn enough doing this to justify doing this, but I really like seeing my name on the shelves of bookstores. I go in and hold the book and people walk by and I think, "They don't know that the name on this book is mine." And then I tell them and they pretend to give a sh*t and I feel like a douche. But I digress. I also work in a... place.

Throughout my life I have worked in everything from a traveling carnival (I left before the dental plan kicked in) to a gig as the first TV "Rap" VJ (nothing whitens up a man faster than trying to say Afrika Bambaataa like you mean it). Each of the 30 some odd jobs I held had one thing in common... a boss.

There is no such thing as the perfect boss. If you are mellow, you're not energizing the staff. If you're peppy, you're a cheer-leading dick. If you're good natured, fun and silly, you're a dick who thinks he's funny. Are you reading this people who happen to work for me at the small company I currently co-own? I am so on to you.

Perpetual thoughts of saving own ass.

Reluctance to stick neck out for someone else's ass.

Stomach – A hellish night-mare out of a Hieronymus Bosch painting. It's a vol-cano of molten gases, roiling with more bad acid than Woodstock.

A boss's socks are never high enough to hide the fish belly white shin section while legs are crossed. The challenge; don't look at it... but you have to don't you? You have to look a that damn white leg – shit, what did he say?

If you think the boss's mind is closed, you should try getting into his wallet!

Ground He Walks On – Something for employees to worship while he's at lunch.

Bosses wear the proper shoe for their profession. Construction supervisors wear work boots, lawyers wear wing tips and doctors wear golf shoes.

Common Indicators That You Are A

BOSS

After the annual office Christmas party blow-out, John woke up with a pounding headache, cotton-mouthed, and utterly unable to recall the events of the preceding evening. After a trip to the bathroom he was able to make his way downstairs, where his wife put some coffee in front of him.

"Louise," he moaned, "tell me what went on last night. Was it bad?"

"Even worse," she assured him in her most scornful tone. "You made a complete ass of yourself, succeeded in antagonizing the entire board of directors, and insulted the chairman of the company to his face."

"He's an arrogant, self-important prick, piss on him!"

"You did. All over his suit," Louise informed him. "And he fired you."

"Well, screw him," said John.

"I did. You're back at work on Monday."

* * *

Three bulls heard via the grapevine that the rancher was going to bring yet another bull onto the ranch, and the prospect raised a discussion among them.

First Bull: "Boys, we all know I've been here five years. Once we settled our differences, we agreed on which 100 cows would be mine. Now, I don't know where this newcomer is going to get *his* cows, but I ain't giving him any of mine."

Second Bull: "That pretty much says it for me, too. I've been here three years and have earned my right to the 50 cows we've agreed are mine. I'll fight him 'till I run him off or kill him, but I'm keeping all my cows."

Third Bull: "I've only been here a year, and so far you guys have only let me have 10 cows to 'take care of.' I may not be as big as you fellows but I am young and virile, so I simply must keep all my cows."

They had just finished their big talk when an eighteen wheeler pulls up in the middle of the pasture with only one animal in it: the biggest bull these guys had ever seen! At 4,700 pounds, each step he took toward the ground strained the steel ramp to the breaking point.

First Bull: "Ahem. you know, it's actually been some time since I really felt I was doing all my cows justice, anyway. I think I can spare a few for our new friend."

Second Bull: "I'll have plenty of cows to take care of if I just stay on the opposite end of the pasture from him. I'm certainly not looking for an argument."

They look over at their young friend, the third bull, and find him pawing the dirt, shaking his horns, and snorting.

First Bull: "Son, let me give you some advice real quick. Let him have some of your cows and live to tell about it."

Third Bull: "Shit, he can have ALL my cows. I'm just making sure he knows I'm a bull!"

* * *

A United State Government employee sits in his office and out of boredom, decides to see what's in his old filing cabinet. He pokes through the contents and comes across an old brass lamp.

"This will look nice on my mantelpiece," he decides, and takes it home with him.

While polishing the lamp, a genie appears and grants him three wishes.

"I wish for an ice cold diet Coke right now!" He gets his Coke and drinks it.

Now that he can think more clearly, he states his second wish. "I wish to be on an island where beautiful nymphomaniacs reside." Suddenly he is on an island with gorgeous females eyeing him lustfully.

He tells the genie his third and last wish. "I wish I'd never have to work ever again."

POOF! He's back in his government office.

* * *

A man came home from work, sat down in his favorite chair, turned on the TV, and said to his wife, "Quick, bring me a beer before it starts."

She looked a little puzzled, but brought him a beer.

When he finished it, he said, "Quick, bring me another beer. It's gonna start."

This time she looked a little angry, but brought him a beer.

When it was gone, he said, "Quick, another beer before it starts."

"That's it!" She blows her top, "You bastard! You waltz in here, flop your fat ass down, don't even say hello to me, and then expect me to run around like your slave. Don't you realize that I cook and clean and wash and iron all day!"

The husband sighed. "Oh shit, it's started."

* * *

A lawyer and an engineer were fishing in the Caribbean.

The lawyer said, "I'm here because my house burned down, and everything I owned was destroyed by the fire. The insurance company paid for everything."

"That's quite a coincidence," said the engineer. "I'm here because my house and all my belongings were destroyed by a flood, and my insurance company also paid for everything."

The lawyer looked somewhat confused. "How do you start a flood?" he asked.

* * *

There are four engineers traveling in a car. One is a mechanical engineer, one a chemical engineer, one an electrical engineer and the other one an engineer from Microsoft. The car breaks down.

"Sounds to me as if the pistons have seized. We'll have to strip down the engine before we can get the car working again," says the mechanical engineer.

"Well," says the chemical engineer, "it sounded to me as if the fuel might be contaminated. I think we should clear out the fuel system."

"I thought it might be a grounding problem," says the electrical engineer, "or maybe a faulty plug lead."

They all turn to the Microsoft engineer who has said nothing. They ask him, "What do you think?"

"Well, I think we should close all the windows, get out, get back in, and open the windows again."

* * *

An engineer dies and goes to heaven. However, when St. Peter meets him at the gate he says, "Wait a second! You're in the wrong place! Beat it!"

So, the engineer goes down to hell, and gets settled in. He soon becomes dissatisfied with conditions there, and begins to make improvements. Before long, there's running water, flush toilets, escalators, and even air conditioning! The engineer is a pretty popular guy.

One day God calls Satan on the telephone and says with a sneer, "So, how's it going down there?"

Satan replies, "Hey, things are going great. We've got air conditioning and flush toilets and escalators, and there's no telling what this engineer is going to come up with next."

God replies, "What! You've got an engineer? That's a mistake, he should never have gone down there. Send him up right away!"

Satan says, "No way! I like having an engineer on the staff. I'm keeping him."

God says, "Send him back up here or I'll sue!"

"Oh, yeah?" Satan replies. "Where are you going to get a lawyer?!"

* * *

An artist asked the gallery owner if there had been any interest in his paintings on display at that time.

"I have good news and bad news," the owner replied. "The good news is that a gentleman inquired about your work and wondered if it would appreciate in value after your death. When I told him it would, he bought all fifteen of your paintings."

"That's wonderful," the artist exclaimed. "What's the bad news?"

"The guy was your doctor."

* * *

A fellow had just been hired as the new CEO of a large tech corporation. The CEO who was stepping down met with him privately and presented him with three numbered envelopes. "Open one of these if you run up against a problem you don't think you can solve," he said.

Things went along pretty smoothly, but six months later, sales took a downturn and the CEO was really catching a lot of heat. About at his wit's end, he remembered the envelopes. He went to his drawer and took out the first envelope.

The message read, "Blame your predecessor."

The new CEO called a press conference and tactfully laid the blame at the feet of the previous CEO. Satisfied with his comments, the press, and Wall Street responded positively, sales began to pick up and the problem was soon behind him.

About a year later, the company was again experiencing a slight dip in sales, combined with serious product problems. Having learned from his previous experience, the CEO quickly opened the second envelope. The message read, "Reorganize."

This he did, and the company quickly rebounded.

After several consecutive profitable quarters, the company once again fell on difficult times. The CEO went to his office, closed the door and opened the third envelope.

The message said, "Prepare three envelopes."

* * *

So you want a day off? Let's take a look at what you are asking for!

There are 365 days this year.

There are 52 weeks per year in which you already have two days off per week, leaving 261 days available for work.

Since you spend 16 hours each day away from work, you have used up 170 days, leaving only 91 days available.

You spend 30 minutes each day on coffee break. That accounts for 23 days each year, leaving only 68 days available.

With a one hour lunch period each day, you have used up another 46 days, leaving only 22 days available for work.

You normally spend two days per year on sick leave. This leaves you only 20 days available for work.

We are off for five holidays per year, so your available working time is down to 15 days.

We generously give you 14 days vacation per year which leaves only one day available for work and I'll be damned if you're going to take that day off!

* * *

A man who had been in a mental home for some years finally seemed to have improved to the point where it was thought he might be released.

The head of the institution, in a fit of commendable caution, decided to interview him first.

"Tell me," said he, "if we release you, as we are considering doing, what do you intend to do with your life?"

The inmate said, "It would be wonderful to get back to real life and if I do, I will certainly refrain from making my former mistake. I was a nuclear physicist, you know, and it was the stress of my work in weapons research that helped put me here. If I am released, I shall confine myself to work in pure theory, where I trust the situation will be less difficult and stressful."

"Marvelous," said the head of the institution.

"Or else," ruminated the inmate. "I might teach. There is something to be said for spending one's life in bringing up a new generation of scientists."

"Absolutely," said the head.

"Then again, I might write. There is considerable need for books on science for the general public. I might even write a novel based on my experiences in this fine institution."

"An interesting possibility," said the head.

"And finally, if none of these things appeals to me, I can always continue to be a tea kettle."

* * *

Jerry was removing some engine valves from a car on the lift when he spotted the famous heart surgeon, Dr. Samuel Kaiser, who was standing off to the side, waiting for the service manager.

Jerry, who was somewhat of a loud mouth, shouted across the garage, "Hey Kaiser, is that you? Come over here a minute."

The famous surgeon, a bit surprised, walked over to where Jerry was working on the car. Jerry, in a loud voice that all could hear, said argumentatively, "So, Mr. fancy doctor, look at this work. Like you, I too take valves out, grind them, put in new parts, and when I'm finished, this baby will purr like a kitten. So how come you get the big bucks, when you and I are doing basically the same work?"

Dr. Kaiser, very embarrassed, shook his head and replied, "Try doing your work with the engine running."

* * *

The boss called one of his employees into the office. "Rob," he said, "you've been with the company for a year. You started off in the post room, one week later you were promoted to a sales position, and one month after that you were promoted to district manager of the sales department.

Just four short months later, you were promoted to vice-chairman. Now it's time for me to retire, and I want you to take over the company. What do you say to that?"

"Thanks, Dad."

* * *

A man is flying in a hot air balloon and realizes he is lost. He reduces height and spots a man down below. He lowers the balloon further and shouts, "Excuse me, can you tell me where I am?"

The man below says, "Yes. You're in a hot air balloon, hovering 30 feet above this field."

"You must work in Information Technology," says the balloonist.

"I do," replies the man. "How did you know?"

"Well," says the balloonist, "everything you have told me is technically correct, but it's of no use to anyone."

The man below says, "you must work in business."

"I do," replies the balloonist, "but how did you know?"

"Well," says the man, "you don't know where you are, or where you're going, but you expect me to be able to help. You're in the same position you were before we met, but now it's my fault."

* * *

Two gas company servicemen, a senior training supervisor and a young trainee were out checking meters in a suburban neighborhood. They parked their truck at the end of the alley and worked their way to the other end.

At the last house, a woman looking out her kitchen window watched the two men as they checked her gas meter.

Finishing the meter check, the senior supervisor challenged his younger co-worker to a foot race down the alley and back to the truck to prove that an older guy could outrun a younger one.

As they came running up to the truck, they realized the lady from that last house was huffing and puffing right behind them. They stopped and asked her what was wrong.

Gasping for breath, she replied, "When I see two gas men running as hard as you two were, I figured I'd better run too!"

* * *

Steve, Bob and Jeff are all working on some very high scaffolding.

Suddenly, Steve falls off and is killed instantly. After the ambulance leaves with Steve's body, Bob and Jeff realize they'll have to inform his wife. Bob says he's good with this sort of sensitive stuff, so he volunteers to do it.

After two hours, he returns carrying a six-pack of beer.

"So, did you tell her?" asks Jeff.

"Yep," replies Bob.

"Hey, where did you get the six-pack?"

"She gave it to me."

"What?!" Exclaims Jeff. "You just told her that her husband died, and she gave you a six-pack?!"

"Sure. When she answered the door, I asked her whether she was Steve's widow."

"Widow?" she said. "No, no. I'm not a widow. You must be mistaken."

So I said, "Wanna bet a six-pack?"

* * *

A young businessman rented a beautiful office and furnished it with antiques. However, no business was coming in. Sitting there, worrying, he saw a man come into the outer office. Wanting to look busy, he picked up the phone and pretended he was negotiating a big deal. He spoke loudly about big figures and huge commitments.

Finally, he put down the phone and asked the visitor, "Can I help you?"

The man said, "I've come to install the phone."

* * *

An Indian walks into a cafe with a shotgun in one hand pulling a male buffalo with the other, and says to the waiter, "Want coffee."

The waiter says, "Sure chief, coming right up." He gets the Indian a tall mug of coffee. After drinking the coffee down in one gulp, the Indian turns and blasts the buffalo with the shotgun, then just walks out.

The next morning the man returns. He has his shotgun in one hand pulling another male buffalo with the other. He walks up to the counter and says to the waiter, "Want coffee."

The waiter says, "Whoa, Buddy! We're still cleaning up your mess from yesterday. What the heck was all that about, anyway?"

The Indian smiles and proudly says, "Training for upper management position. Come in, drink coffee, shoot the bull, leave mess for others to clean up, disappear for rest of day."

* * *

The union workers at the Federal Mint went on strike today.
They are demanding to make less money!

* * *

UPS and Fed-Ex are merging. There going to call it Fed-Up

* * *

A store manager overheard one of his salesmen talking to a customer. "No sir," said the salesman, "we haven't had any for awhile and it doesn't look like we'll be getting any soon."

The manager was horrified and yelled after the departing customer, "Come back next week. We're sure to have whatever it is you need."

Irate, he turned to his salesman, "Never tell a customer we're out of anything! Now, what did he want?"

"Rain."

* * *

A man has a toothache, so he goes to see his dentist. After examining the tooth, the dentist tells the man he is going to have to give him an injection for the pain.

The man says, "No way! I don't want an injection."

The dentist replies, "OK, I'll give you gas."

"Noooo!" shrieks the man. "I don't want any gas."

"Fine," says the dentist, "I'm going to give you some Viagra!"

"Viagra?" exclaims the man. "What for?"

"You're going to need something to hang on to when I pull your tooth!"

* * *

A Texas oil magnate stormed into his lawyer's office demanding that divorce proceedings begin at once against his young bride.

"What's the problem?" the lawyer inquired.

"I want to hit that adulterin' bitch for breach of contract," snapped the oil magnate.

"I don't know if that will fly," the lawyer replied. "Your wife isn't a piece of property. You don't own her!"

"Damn right," the tycoon snarled, "but I sure as hell expect exclusive drillin' rights!"

* * *

Members of a health club were having their first meeting. The director of the group said, "Now, I'd like each of you to give the facts of your daily routine."

Several people spoke, admitting their excesses, and then one obviously overweight member said, "I eat moderately, I drink moderately, and I exercise frequently."

"Hmm?" said the director. "And are you sure you have nothing else to add?"

"Well, yes," said the member. "I lie extensively."

* * *

The world was shocked and saddened this morning, to learn of the death of the Energizer Bunny.

Best known as the irritating pink bunny that kept going and going and going, 'Pinkie,' as he was known to his closest friends and relatives, was six years old and alone at the time of his death.

An autopsy was performed earlier today and Chief Medical Examiner, Dr. Dura Cell, concluded that the cause of death was acute cardiac arrest induced by sexual over-stimulation. It appears that someone had put Pinkie's batteries in backwards, causing him to keep coming, and coming, and coming...

* * *

It was the Christmas season and the judge was in a cheerful mood. "What are you charged with?" he asked the defendant.

"Doing my Christmas shopping early, Your Honor," replied the defendant.

"Well, that certainly isn't a crime," the judge said. "How early were you doing this shopping?"

"Before the store opened!" the defendant replied.

* * *

The graduate with a Science degree asks, "Why does it work?"
The graduate with an Engineering degree asks, "How does it work?"
The graduate with an Accounting degree asks, "How much will it cost?"
The graduate with a Liberal Arts degree asks, "Do you want fries with that?"

* * *

Handicapped

The designation "handicapped" is a bit confusing. For instance, in the case of parking, it is perfectly acceptable. Even many perfectly healthy, if unscrupulous, people will happily accept the moniker if it gets them a good parking space. I will frequently use the handicapped bathroom in large facilities because I like the space and privacy even though I assume those who see me enter wonder what's wrong with me. I don't want your urine splash-back anywhere near my leg is what's wrong with me.

But I have met 'little people' (midget is the n-word of the extremely short, so watch it) who, if referred to as 'handicapped,' would head butt you right in the balls. Also, as they are quick to point out, their dick still may be bigger than yours, so there's that.

It may seem heartless or rude to include the handicapped in a collection of this kind, but I think they've had a free ride for too long. Alright not free, but I think the fares are sharply discounted. But, c'mon already, they get to board flights first, ride in private elevators, even their Olympics are special. Then there's the marketplace. Every company needs to have some token special needs folks in the upper echelons to help make them look less like vampires. Did you ever consider that it's your fitness that's holding you back? Relax, it's not; your failing on your own.

Common Indicators That You Are

HANDICAPPED

Why Beer is Better than Retarded People

Beer doesn't drool.

Beer stains wash out easier than drool.

Beer will wait patiently in the car.

Beer is never late.

You don't have to limit yourself to bisyllabic words in discourse with beer.

Beer doesn't cry if you forget it.

Beer doesn't vote.

Beer never answers your phone.

Beer doesn't work your crossword puzzles in ink.

Beer doesn't demand that you watch cartoons.

Beer won't ask loud, embarrassing questions in public.

If the head's too big on your beer you can blow it off.

If the head's too small on your beer you can get another.

Beer doesn't have to be sterilized.

* * *

A tourist in Vienna is going through a graveyard and, all of a sudden, he hears some music. No one is around, so he starts searching for the source. He finally locates the origin and finds it is coming from a grave with a headstone that reads "Ludwig van Beethoven, 1770-1827." Then he realizes that the music is the Ninth Symphony and it is being played backward!

Puzzled, he leaves the graveyard and persuades a friend to return with him. By the time they arrive back at the grave, the music has changed. This time it is the Seventh Symphony, but like the previous piece, it is being played backward.

Curious, the men agree to consult a music scholar. When they return with the expert, the Fifth Symphony is playing, again backward. The expert notices that the symphonies are being played in the reverse order in which they were composed, the 9th, then the 7th, then the 5th.

By the next day the word has spread and a crowd has gathered around the grave. They are all listening to the Second Symphony being played backward. Just then the graveyard's caretaker ambles up to the group.

Someone in the group asks him if he has an explanation for the music.

"Don't you get it?" The caretaker says incredulously "He's decomposing."

* * *

"Doctor, doctor, I keep thinking I'm a dog."

"Sit down and tell me all about it."

"I can't, I'm not allowed on the furniture."

* * *

A young conservative Jew left his office during Passover to have lunch in the park. He sat down on a bench beneath a tree and removed several pieces of matzoh, as well as several plastic containers filled with charoset, and various fishes in spread form. As he was eating, a blind man walked along and sat down on the bench next to him.

In the spirit of the holiday, the young Jew turned to the blind man and asked, "Would you like to share my lunch with me?"

The blind man replied, "That's very kind of you. I would be honored."

Gently, the young Jew took the blind man's hands and placed a piece of matzoh. A few moments later, he asked the blind man, "So... how does it taste?"

The blind man paused a moment then said, "Taste?! I'm still trying to figure out what it says!"

* * *

One weekend, there was a costume party at a mental hospital, and the theme of the party was "war".

The first patient comes up onto the stage and says, "I am an atomic bomb." He gets his applause and steps down.

The second person comes up and says, "I am a hydrogen bomb." Again, there is a round of applause and he steps down.

And then a naked little man comes up to the stage and says, "I'm dynamite." Everybody in the audience runs away hysterically.

When one of the mental patients was asked why they all ran away, he replied, "Didn't you see how short his fuse was?"

* * *

Knowing that Bill was in the hospital near death, the family called the priest to be with them. As the priest stood next to the bed, Bill's condition started to deteriorate and he motioned frantically for a piece of paper to write on. The priest handed him pen and paper and using his last bit of energy, Bill scribbled his message and died.

Thinking it best not to read the note at that time, the priest tucked it into his jacket pocket.

As he was finishing the service at Bill's funeral, the priest realized he was wearing the same jacket as when Bill died. He said, "Bill handed me this note just before he died. I haven't looked at it but knowing Bill, I'm sure it's a wonderful message."

With that, he opened the note and read, "Get off my oxygen tube!"

* * *

There was an earthquake at the monastery and it was leveled. All fifty brothers were transported to heaven at the same time. At the pearly gates, St Peter said,

"Let's go through the entry test as a group. Now, first question: How many of you have played around with little boys?"

Forty-nine hands went up.

"Right!" said St Peter. "You forty-nine can go down to hell. Oh, and take that deaf bastard with you!"

* * *

One day at a busy airport, the passengers on a commercial airliner are all seated, waiting for the cockpit crew to show up so they can get under way. The pilot and co-pilot finally appear in the rear of the plane, and begin walking up to the cockpit along the center aisle. Both appear to be blind. The pilot is using a white cane, bumping into passengers left and right as he stumbles down the aisle, and the copilot is using a guide dog. Both are wearing huge sunglasses to cover their eyes. At first the passengers do not react, thinking that it must be some sort of practical joke. After a few minutes the engines start revving and the airplane starts moving down the runway. The passengers look at each other with some uneasiness. They start whispering among themselves and desperately look to the flight attendants for reassurance. Then, the airplane starts accelerating rapidly and the passengers begin panicking. Some passengers are praying, and as the plane gets closer and closer to the end of the runway, the voices are becoming more and more hysterical. When the airplane has less than 20 feet of runway left, there is a sudden change in the pitch of the shouts as everyone screams all at once. At the very last moment the airplane lifts off and is airborne. All the passengers breath a sigh of relief and laugh nervously at their fears.

In the cockpit, the copilot turns to the pilot and says: "You know, one of these days the passengers aren't going to scream, and we're all gonna get killed!"

* * *

A midget went to the corner bar one night and ordered the strongest drink available. Once he had finished the drink, he asked who the strongest man in the room was. When the bartender pointed the man out, the midget approached the man, picked a fight, and whipped him.

The next night he returned. Again, he ordered the strongest drink, picked a fight with the strongest man and won. Concerned about the loss of business, the bartender decided he needed to take some kind of measures to end this guy's visits. He had a large, mean, gorilla delivered and placed in the men rest room.

That night after the midget had finished his drink, the bartender told him the strongest was in the rest room. There were painful moans and loud noises echoing from the rest room just shortly after the midget had entered.

Then, he came out, walked up to the bartender and said, "Whenever that guy wakes up, tell him I put his fur coat in the trash can."

* * *

A doctor at the asylum decided to take his inmates to a baseball game. For weeks in advance, he coached his patients to respond to his commands.

When the day of the game arrived, everything seemed to be going well. As the national anthem started, the doctor yelled, "Up nuts!" And the inmates complied by standing up.

After the anthem he yelled, "Down nuts!" And they all sat. After a home run he yelled, "Cheer nuts!" And they all broke into applause and cheers.

Thinking things were going very well, he decided to go get a beer and a hot dog, leaving his assistant in charge. When he returned there was a riot in progress. Finding his assistant, he asked what happened.

The assistant replied, "Well, everything was fine until some guy walked by and yelled, "PEANUTS!"

* * *

A man goes to a psychiatrist. To start things off, the psychiatrist suggests they start with a Rorschach test. He holds up the first inkblot and asks the man what he sees.

"A man and a woman making love in a park," the man replies.

The psychiatrist holds up the second picture and asks the man what he sees.

"A man and a woman making love in a boat."

He holds up the third picture.

"A man and a woman making love at the beach."

This goes on for the rest of the set of pictures; the man says he sees a man and a woman making love in every one of the pictures. At the end of the test, the psychiatrist looks over his notes and says, "It looks like you have a preoccupation with sex."

And the man replies, "Well, you're the one with the dirty pictures."

* * *

Two deaf people get married. During the first week of marriage, they find that they are unable to communicate in the bedroom when they turn off the lights because they can't see each other using sign language.

After several nights of fumbling around and misunderstandings, the wife decides to find a solution.

"Honey," she signs, "why don't we agree on some simple signals? For instance, at night, if you want to have sex with me, reach over and squeeze my left breast one time. If you don't want to have sex, reach over and squeeze my right breast one time."

The husband thinks this is a great idea and signs back to his wife, "Great idea, now if you want to have sex with me, reach over and pull on my penis one time."

"If you don't want to have sex, reach over and pull on my penis 100 times."

* * *

There once was a blind man who decided to visit Texas.

When he arrived on the plane, he felt the seats and said, "Wow, these seats are big!"

The person next to him answered, "Everything is big in Texas."

When he finally arrived in Texas, he decided to visit a bar. Upon arriving in the bar, he ordered a beer and got a mug placed between his hands.

He exclaimed, "Wow, these mugs are big!"

The bartender replied, "Everything is big in Texas."

After a couple of beers, the blind man asked the bartender where the bathroom was located.

The bartender replied, "Second door to the right."

The blind man headed for the bathroom, but accidentally skipped the second door. Instead, he entered the third door, which lead to the swimming pool, and fell in.

Scared to death, the blind man started shouting, "Don't flush, don't flush!"

* * *

A man was about to tee off on the golf course when he felt a tap on his shoulder and a man handed him a card that read "I am mute. I am not able to speak. May I play through, please?"

The first man angrily gave the card back, and communicated that "No, he may not play through, and that his handicap did not give him such a right." He whacked the ball onto the green and left to finish the hole.

Just as he was about to put the ball into the hole he was hit in the head with a golf ball, laying him out cold. When he came to a few minutes later, he looked around and saw the mute sternly looking at him, holding up four fingers.

* * *

Coming home from work a few hours early, Mr. Johnson caught his wife in bed with a dwarf. After kicking the man out of his house, Mr. Johnson angrily confronted his wife, "I thought we were over this already! After all that money I've spent for the therapy sessions to cure you of your nymphomania, here you are in bed with some guy! You're absolutely hopeless!"

A contrite Mrs. Johnson said, "I am cutting down."

* * *

One morning a man entered the church on crutches. He stopped in front of the holy water, placed some on each leg, then threw away his crutches. An alter boy witnessed this and ran into the rectory to tell the priest what he had seen.

"My son," the priest said, "you have witnessed a miracle. Where is this man now?"

"He's flat on his ass over by the holy water," the alter boy replied.

* * *

Two morons stand on a cliff with their arms outstretched. One has some budgies lined up on each arm, the other has parrots lined up on his arms.

After a couple of minutes, they both leap off the cliff and fall to the ground.

Laying next to each other in intensive care at the hospital, one moron says to the other, "I don't think much of this budgie jumping."

The other moron replies, "Yeah, I'm not too keen on this paragliding either."

* * *

A champion jockey is about to enter an important race on a new horse. The horse's trainer meets him before the race and says, "All you have to remember with this horse is that every time you approach a jump, you have to shout, 'alllleee ooop!' really loudly in the horse's ear. If you do that, you'll be fine."

The jockey thinks the trainer is mad but promises to shout the command. The race begins and they approach the first hurdle. The jockey ignores the trainer's ridiculous advice and the horse crashes straight through the center of the jump.

They carry on and approach the second hurdle. The jockey, somewhat embarrassed, whispers 'Alee oop' in the horse's ear. The same thing happens, the horse crashes straight through the center of the jump.

At the third hurdle, the jockey thinks, "It's no good, I'll have to do it," and yells, "ALLLEEE OOOP!" really loudly. Sure enough, the horse sails over the jump with no problems. This continues for the rest of the race, but due to the earlier problems the horse only finishes third.

The trainer is fuming and asks the jockey what went wrong. The jockey replies, "Nothing is wrong with me, it's this bloody horse. What is he, deaf or something?"

The trainer replies, "Deaf? He's not deaf, he's blind!"

* * *

A blind man was describing his favorite sport, skydiving. When asked how this was accomplished, he said that things were all done for him. "I am placed in the door and told when to jump," he said. "My hand is placed on my release ring for me, and out I go."

"But how do you know when you are going to land?" he was asked.

"I have a very keen sense of smell and I can smell the trees and grass when I am 300 feet from the ground," he answered.

"But how do you know when to lift your legs for the final arrival on the ground?" he was again asked.

He quickly answered, "Oh, my dog's leash goes slack."

* * *

Okay, I don't feel good about this, but I'll do it for the kids. Here are some of the classic Helen Keller jokes that were so popular when I was a boy. This is so wrong.

Q & A Roundup
The Handicapped

Q What is Helen Keller's favorite color?
A Corduroy.

Q How did Helen Keller burn the side of her face?
A She answered the iron.

Q How did she burn the other side of her face?
A They called back.

Q Why was Helen Keller's leg wet?
A Her dog was blind too.

Q Why does Helen Keller masturbate with one hand?
A She needs the other to moan with.

Q How did she burn her fingers?
A Reading the waffle iron.

Q What did she do when she fell down the well?
A She screamed and screamed until her hands turned blue.

Q How come she didn't scream when she fell off the cliff?
A She was wearing mittens.

Q How come Helen Keller can't have kids?
A Because she's dead.

Q How did Helen Keller drive herself crazy?
A Trying to read a stucco wall.

Q What did Helen Keller's parents do to punish her?
A Rearranged the furniture. *or...*
A Left the plunger in the toilet bowl. *or...*
A Put Saran Wrap on the toilet. *or...*
A Put her in a round room and told her there was a penny in the corner. *or...*
A Washed her hands out with soap. *or...*
A Sprinkled bird-seed on her books. *or...*
A Glued doorknobs to the walls.

Q Why can't Helen Keller drive a car?
A She's a woman.

Q What's the name of Helen Keller's favorite book?
A "Around the Block in 80 Days."

Q Define true love.
A Helen Keller and Stevie Wonder playing tennis.

Q How did Helen Keller drive her car?
A One hand on the wheel; the other on the road.

Q How did Helen Keller meet her husband?
A On a blind date!

Q How did Helen Keller pierce her ear?
A Answering the stapler.

Q Why didn't Helen Keller change her baby's diaper?
A So she could always find him.

Q Why did Helen Keller have yellow fingers?
A From whispering sweet-nothings in her boyfriends ear.

Q If Helen Keller is playing the piano with one hand, what is she doing with the other?
A Singing.

Q Did you hear about the new Helen Keller doll?
A You wind her up and she bumps into the furniture.

Q What did Helen Keller name her dog?

A Ughgaaaaaauuuuuuggg

Q How did Helen Keller burn her face?

A Bobbing for french fries.

Q Why were Helen Keller's fingers purple?

A She heard it thru the grapevine.

Q What's Helen Keller's favorite color?

A Black

Kids

I don't really like kids. That's not entirely true, but it *is* close. I tend to like them for about five minutes and then I thank my lucky stars that I can walk away. The problem is, as parents will tell you, they are all insane little freaks. They are hyper-active, mood-swinging little attention junkies. Which can be pretty damn entertaining... for five minutes.

Children are like mosquitoes; you're never relaxed when they're flying near you. When I see children on a plane, I immediately hate their parents... and their grandparents whose prolonged life has probably inspired the trip. They cannot, no, *will* not be controlled. It would seem that in a world where dosing the very young with legal dope like Ritalin is perfectly acceptable, one should at least be able to administer a safe effective kiddie-tranquilizer. But, no. And with the threat of water-boarding off the table, coercion is out of the question as well. Only the one they call, "Gameboy" seems to fill the breech. God bless him.

Of course there are exceptions. Some children are absolutely perfect little angels who, even at their worst, are just demonstrating levels of curiosity and intelligence unlike any other child on Earth. It is clear that these small wonders are being brilliantly raised by sensitive, clever people who can more easily be identified as, say, any friends of mine who have kids and happen to be reading this book.

Otherwise; they're f#@king monkeys.

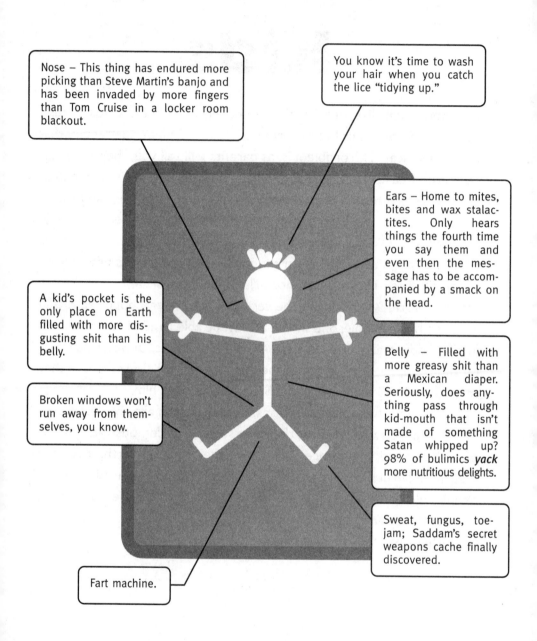

Nose – This thing has endured more picking than Steve Martin's banjo and has been invaded by more fingers than Tom Cruise in a locker room blackout.

You know it's time to wash your hair when you catch the lice "tidying up."

Ears – Home to mites, bites and wax stalactites. Only hears things the fourth time you say them and even then the message has to be accompanied by a smack on the head.

A kid's pocket is the only place on Earth filled with more disgusting shit than his belly.

Belly – Filled with more greasy shit than a Mexican diaper. Seriously, does anything pass through kid-mouth that isn't made of something Satan whipped up? 98% of bulimics *yack* more nutritious delights.

Broken windows won't run away from themselves, you know.

Sweat, fungus, toe-jam; Saddam's secret weapons cache finally discovered.

Fart machine.

Common Indicators That You Are A

KID

I was walking in the park one bright sunny Sunday afternoon, when I noticed a cute little girl out walking her dog. As she approached me on the path, she looked about nine years old, all dressed up in her Sunday best, and her freshly scrubbed face, just gleaming with cutesiness. Tugging on her leash was a well groomed terrier.

As we met on the path, I greeted her, "Hi there. My, aren't you pretty today? And what a fine looking dog you have."

"Thank you, sir," she said. "And what a nice day this is, isn't it?"

"Yes it is" I answered, "My, what a polite little girl you are, and what a pretty dress you're wearing."

"Oh, thank you, sir. My mother taught me to always be polite and she made this dress for me, isn't it pretty?" she said with a beaming smile.

"Yes, very pretty," I answered, "by the way, what's your dog's name?"

"Oh, sir, my dog's name is Porky. Isn't that cute?"

"Well, it certainly is an unusual name for a dog. Why do you call him Porky?"

"Because he fucks pigs!"

* * *

A teacher was having a tasting day where she would put candy in the kids' mouth and they would guess what it was. She went to the first little boy and put a Hershey's Kiss in his mouth.

"Can you guess what it is?"

"I don't know," said the boy.

"I'll give you a hint. It's something your daddy asks your mommy for every morning."

The girl next to the boy says, "Don't eat it. It's a piece of ass."

* * *

"Mommy, my turtle is dead," Little Johnny sorrowfully told his mother, holding the turtle out to her in his hand.

The mother kissed him on the head, then said, "That's all right, dear. We'll wrap him in tissue paper, put him in a little box, and have a nice burial ceremony in the back yard. After that, we'll go out for an ice cream soda, and then get you a new pet." Her voice trailed off as she noticed the turtle move. "Little Johnny, you're turtle is not dead after all."

"Oh," the disappointed Little Johnny said. "Can I kill it?"

* * *

The teacher wrote on the blackboard: "I ain't had no fun in months." Then asked the class, "How should I correct this sentence?"

Little Johnny raised his had and replied, "Get yourself a new boyfriend."

* * *

The boss of a big company needed to call one of his employees about an urgent problem with one of the main computers. He dialed the employee's home phone number and was greeted with a child's whispered, "Hello?"

Feeling put out at the inconvenience of having to talk to a youngster the boss asked, "Is your Daddy home?"

"Yes," whispered Little Johnny.

"May I talk with him?" the man asked.

To the surprise of the boss, Little Johnny whispered, "No."

Wanting to talk with an adult, the boss asked, "Is your Mommy there?"

"Yes," came the answer.

"May I talk with her?" Again Little Johnny whispered, "No."

Knowing that it was not likely that a young child would be left home alone, the boss decided he would just leave a message with the person who should be there watching over the child. "Is there anyone there besides you?" the boss asked the child.

"Yes," whispered Little Johnny, "A policeman."

Wondering what a cop would be doing at his employee's home, the boss asked, "May I speak with the policeman?"

"No, he's busy," whispered Little Johnny.

"Busy doing what?" asked the boss.

"Talking to daddy and mommy and the fireman," came the whispered answer.

Growing concerned and even worried as he heard what sounded like a helicopter through the ear piece on the phone the boss asked, "What is that noise?"

"A hello-copper," answered the whispering Little Johnny.

"What is going on there?" asked the boss, now alarmed.

In an awed, whispering voice Little Johnny answered, "The search team just landed the hello-copper!"

Alarmed, concerned and more than just a little frustrated the boss asked, "Why are they there?"

Still whispering, Little Johnny replied along with a muffled giggle, "They're looking for me!"

* * *

One evening a mom and dad and two sons are watching TV. The dad gives the mom a look, and they head upstairs. The two little boys wonder what they are doing, so they go up to take a peek.

"Well," said the older boy, "Remember this when Mom gets on your case for sucking your thumb."

* * *

Little Suzy raised her hand during a biology lesson and asked if her grandmother could have a baby. The teacher was a bit surprised at the question, but answered that the grandmother was too old to have babies.

"So what about my mother?" asked Little Suzy.

The teacher said that it was possible, but that her mother was probably getting too old to be having babies as well.

"Well, then could I have a baby?" she wanted to know.

"Goodness no!" said the teacher, "you are much too young."

"See!" yelled Little Johnny from the back of the classroom, "I told you that you didn't have anything to worry about!"

* * *

A small boy was unfortunately lost, so the kid went up to a policeman and said, "I have lost my Daddy!"

The cop asked the lad, "What's he like?"

The little boy replied, "Beer and women!"

* * *

Three Boy Scouts, a lawyer, a priest, and a pilot are in a plane that's about to crash. The pilot says, "Well, we only have three parachutes, let's give them to the three Boy Scouts. They are young and have their whole lives in front of them."

The lawyer says, "Fuck the Boy Scouts!"

The priest says, "Do we have time?"

* * *

The kindergarten class had a homework assignment to find out about something exciting and relate it to the class the next day. When the time came for the little kids to give their reports, the teacher was calling on them one at a time. She was reluctant to call upon little Johnnie, knowing that he sometimes could be a bit crude. But eventually his turn came. Little Johnnie walked up to the front of the class, and with a piece of chalk, made a small white dot on the blackboard, then sat back down.

Well the teacher couldn't figure out what Johnnie had in mind for his report, so she asked him just what that was.

"It's a period," reported Johnnie.

"Well I can see that," she said, "but what is so exciting about a period?"

"Damned if I know," said Johnnie, "but this morning my sister said she missed one. Then Daddy had a heart attack, Mommy fainted and the man next door shot himself."

* * *

On Christmas morning a cop on horseback is sitting at a traffic light and next to him is a kid on his shiny new bike.

The cop says to the kid, "Nice bike you got there. Did Santa bring that to you?"

The kid says, "Yeah."

The cop says, "Well, next year tell Santa to put a tail-light on that bike." The cop then proceeds to issue the kid a $20 bicycle safety violation ticket.

The kid takes the ticket and before he rides off says, "By the way, that's a nice horse you got there. Did Santa bring that to you?"

Humoring the kid, the cop says, "Yeah, he sure did."

The kid says, "Well, next year tell Santa to put the dick underneath the horse, instead of on top."

* * *

An old man sitting on his front porch down in Louisiana watching the sun rise, sees the neighbor's kid walk by carrying something big under his arm. He yells out "Hey boy, whatcha got there?"

The boy yells back, "Roll of chicken wire."

The old man says, "What you gonna do with that?"

The boy says, "Catch some chickens."

Old man yells, "You damn fool, you can't catch chickens with chicken wire!"

Boy just laughs and keeps walking. That evening at sunset the boy comes walking by and to the old man's surprise he is dragging behind him the chicken wire with about 30 chickens caught in it. Same time next morning the old man is out watching the sun rise, and he sees the boy walk by carrying something kind of round in his hand.

Old man yells out, "Hey boy, whatcha got there?"

Boy yells back, "Roll of duck tape."

Old man says, "What you gonna do with that?"

Boy says back, "Catch me some ducks."

Old man yells back, "You damn fool, you can't catch ducks with duct tape!"

Boy just laughs and keeps walking. That night around sunset the boy walks by coming home, and to the old man's amazement he is trailing behind him the unrolled roll of duct tape with about 35 ducks caught in it. Same time next morning the old man sees the boy walking by carrying what looks like a long reed with something fuzzy on the end.

Old man says, "Hey boy, whatcha got there?"

Boy says, "It's a pussy willow."

Old man says, "I'll get my hat."

* * *

A little boy and his grandfather are raking leaves in the yard. The little boy finds an earthworm trying to get back into its hole. He says, "Grandpa, I bet I can put that worm back in that hole."

The grandfather replies, "I'll bet you five dollars you can't. It's too wiggly and limp to put back in that little hole."

The little boy runs into the house and comes back out with a can of hair spray. He sprays the worm until it is straight and stiff as a board. Then he puts the worm back into the hole.

The grandfather hands the little boy five dollars, grabs the hair spray, and runs into the house. Thirty minutes later the grandfather comes back out and hands the little boy another five dollars.

The little boy says, "Grandpa, you already gave me five dollars."

The grandfather replies, "I know. That's from your grandma."

* * *

One day Little Johnny was playing with his toy train and it was going round and round when he stopped it he said, "All you sons of bitches getting on get on, and all you sons of bitches getting off get off."

His mother comes in and says, "What did you say young man? Go to your room and think about what you said."

So after four hours his mother comes and says, "Come eat some supper and then you can play with your train again."

After supper Little Johnny goes back to his train and says, "All you sons of bitches getting on get on, and all you sons of bitches getting off get off, and all you sons of bitches pissed off about the delay, talk to the bitch in the kitchen!"

* * *

The pretty teacher was concerned with one of her eleven-year-old students. Taking him aside after class one day, she asked, "Little Johnny, why has your school work been so poor, lately?"

"I'm in love," the boy replied.

Holding back an urge to smile, she asked, "With whom?"

"With you," he said.

"But Johnny," she said gently, "don't you see how silly that is? It's true that I would like a husband of my own someday. But I don't want a child."

"Oh, don't worry," the boy said reassuringly, "I'll use a rubber."

* * *

What is the difference between acne and a catholic priest?
Acne doesn't come on a boy's face until he turns twelve.

* * *

One day Little Johnny comes home from school and his mom asks him how his day was. He replies, "Mom, today I had sex with the teacher!"

Immediately she was angry. She said, "just wait 'till your dad gets home, he's going to be very mad at you. Go to your room!"

So the boy goes to his room and finally his dad is home and comes up to the room. The boy tells his dad and the dad is proud of the boy.

"Great job son! How old are you 12? 13? How about we go down to the store and get that shiny red bicycle you wanted?"

So, they go to the store and the dad buys the bike for his son. Then he says, "Well Johnny, do you want to ride the bike home?"

The boy answers, "No, that's okay Dad, my ass is still sore!"

* * *

A girl comes home from school and asks her mother "Is it true what Rita just told me? Babies come out of the same place where boys put their dicks?"

"Yes dear," replies her mother, pleased that the subject had finally come up and she wouldn't have to explain it to her daughter.

"But then when I have a baby," responded the teenager "won't it knock my teeth out?"

* * *

A little girl runs out to the backyard where her father is working, and asks him, "Daddy, what's sex?"

Her father sits her down, and tells her all about the birds and the bees. He tells her about conception, sexual intercourse, sperms and eggs. He goes on to tell her about puberty, menstruation, erections, wet-dreams... and he thinks, what the hell, and goes on to tell her the works.

He covers a wide and varied assortment of sub-topics and by the time he's finished, his daughter is somewhat awestruck with this sudden influx of bizarre new knowledge.

Her father finally asks, "So what did you want to know about sex for?"

"Oh, mommy said to tell you lunch would be ready in a couple of secs..."

* * *

A cute little girl goes into a pet store and asks, "Do you sell little rabbits?"

The store manager kneels down, to be at her level and replies, "Yes, darlin'. I have a very cute black bunny, a friendly brown bunny with long ears, and a very lovable white bunny. Which would you prefer?"

The little girls puts her hands on her knees, leans forward and says, "I really don't think my python gives a fuck."

* * *

A little boy is talking to his guidance counselor after having problems at home. The counselor asks him if he would like to go live with his father.

The boy says, "no, he beats me."

"How about your aunt?"

"No, she beats me too."

"Where do you want to live?"

The boy thinks long and hard and says, "I want to go live with the Cleveland Browns. They don't beat anybody."

* * *

One day, the teacher asked her class, "What vegetable makes you cry?"

Little Johnny replies, "A turnip."

"No Johnny," says the teacher, "onions make you cry, not turnips."

"No Miss," says Johnny, "have you ever been hit in the balls with a turnip?"

* * *

The teacher had asked the class to write an essay about an unusual event that happened during the past week.

Little Johnny got up to read his. It began, "My daddy fell in a well last week."

"Good Lord!" the teacher exclaimed. "Is he okay?"

"He must be," said Little Johnny. "He stopped calling for help yesterday."

* * *

Little Johnny's teacher says, "Class, today we are going to learn multi-syllable words. Does anybody have an example of a multi-syllable word?"

Little Johnny raises his hand, "Me, Miss Finch!"

Miss Finch turns towards the eager young lad, "All right, Little Johnny, what is your multi-syllable word?"

Little Johnny says, "Mas-tur-bate."

Miss Finch smiles and says, "Well, Little Johnny, that sure is a mouthful!."

Little Johnny says, "No, Miss Finch, you're thinking of a blowjob."

* * *

Little Johnny walked into his dad's bedroom one day only to catch him sitting on the side of his bed putting a condom onto his penis in preparation of sex with his wife.

Johnny's father in attempt to hide his full erection with a condom on it, bent over, as if to look under the bed.

Little Johnny asked curiously, "Whatcha doin Daddy?"

His father quickly replied, "I thought I saw a rat go underneath the bed."

To which Little Johnny replied, "Whatcha gonna do, fuck him?"

* * *

Little Johnny and Little Lisa are only ten years old, but they know that they are in love. One day they decide that they want to get married, so Johnny goes to Lisa's father to ask for his blessing.

Johnny bravely walks up to him and says, "Mr. Jones, me and Lisa are in love and I want to ask you for your blessing."

Thinking that this was the cutest thing, Mr. Jones replies, "Well Johnny, you're only ten. Where will you two live?"

Without even taking a moment to think about it, Johnny replies, "In Lisa's room. It's bigger than mine and we can both fit there nicely."

Still thinking this is just cute, Mr. Jones says, "Okay then how will you live? You're not old enough to get a job. How will you afford food and rent?"

Again, Johnny instantly replies, "With our allowance. Lisa gets five bucks a week and I get ten bucks a week. That's about sixty bucks a month, and that should do us just fine."

By this time Mr. Jones is realizing that Johnny has put much thought into this. So, he thinks for a moment trying to come up with something that Johnny won't have an answer to.

He then says, "Well Johnny, it seems like you've got everything all figured out. I just have one more question for you. What will you do if the two of you should have kids of your own?"

Johnny shrugs his shoulders and says, "We've been lucky so far..."

* * *

Little Johnny was doing his math homework. He said to himself, "Two plus five, that son of a bitch is seven. Three plus six, that son of a bitch is nine." His mother heard what he was saying and gasped, "What are you doing?"

The little boy answered, "I'm doing my math homework."

"And this is how your teacher taught you to do it?" the mother asked.

"Yes," he answered.

Infuriated, she called Little Johnny's teacher the next day, "What are you teaching my son in class?"

The teacher replied, "Right now, we are learning addition."

The mother asked, "And are you teaching them to say two plus two, that son of a bitch is four?"

After the teacher stopped laughing, she answered, "What I taught them was, two plus two, the sum of which is four."

* * *

Little Johnny's mother decided to give her son an anatomy lesson one day, so she took off all of her clothes and pointed to her vagina, saying, "Johnny, this is where you came from."

Johnny went to school the next day smiling and insisting that all his friends now refer to him as "Lucky Johnny."

"Why?" one asked.

Johnny held his fingers an inch apart and said, "Because I came this close to being a turd."

* * *

The only way the couple could have a Sunday afternoon quickie with their eight year old son in the apartment was to send him out on the balcony with a Popsicle, and tell him to report on all the neighborhood activities.

He began his commentary as his parents put their plan into operation:

"There's a car being towed from the parking lot," he shouted.

A few moments passed. "An ambulance just drove by."

A few moments later, "Looks like the Anderson's have company," he called out.

"Matt's riding a new bike."

A few moments later, "Looks like the Sanders are moving."

"Jason is on his skate board"

A few more moments, "The Allen's are having sex!"

Startled, mother and dad shot up in bed. Dad cautiously asked, "How do you know they are having sex?"

"Jimmy Allen is standing on his balcony with a Popsicle too."

* * *

Little Nancy was in her garden shoveling dirt back into a fairly large hole when her neighbor looked over the fence.

Interested in what the girl was doing, he politely asked, "What are you up to there, Nancy?"

"My goldfish died," replied Nancy tearfully, without looking up, "and I've just buried him."

The neighbor was concerned and asked, "That's an awfully big hole for a goldfish isn't it?"

Nancy patted down the last heap of earth then replied, "that's because he's inside your fucking cat."

* * *

A guy is walking down the street and sees Little Johnny smoking a cigarette. He says, "Kid, you're too young to smoke. How old are you?"

Johnny says, "Six."

The guy says, "Six? When did you start smoking?"

Johnny says, "Right after the first time I got laid."

The guy says, "Right after the first time you got laid? When was that?"

Johnny says, "I don't remember. I was drunk."

* * *

A little boy walks into his parents' room to see his mom on top of his dad bouncing up and down. The mom sees her son and quickly dismounts, worried about what her son has seen. She dresses quickly and goes to find him.

The son sees his mom and asks, "What were you and dad doing?"

The mother replies, "Well you know your dad has a big tummy and sometimes I have to get on top of it to help flatten it."

"You're wasting your time," said the boy.

"Why is that?" asked his mom, puzzled.

"Well when you go shopping the lady next door comes over and gets on her knees and blows it right back up."

* * *

A man and his young wife were in divorce court, but the custody of their children posed a problem. The mother leaped to her feet and protested to the judge that since she brought the children into this world, she should retain custody of them. The man also wanted custody of his children, so the judge asked for his justification.

After a long silence, the man slowly rose from his chair and replied, "Your Honor, when I put a dollar in a vending machine and a Pepsi comes out, does the Pepsi belong to me or the machine?

Q & A Roundup
Kids

Q What's the best part of having sex with 28 year olds?
A There's 20 of them.

Q What's red, bubbly, and scratches at glass?
A A baby in a microwave.

Q What's the difference between a baby and a trampoline?
A You take your boots off when you jump on a trampoline.

Q What gets louder as it gets smaller?
A A baby in a trash compactor.

Q What sits in the kitchen and keeps getting smaller and smaller?
A A baby combing its hair with a potato peeler!

Q What's funnier than a dead baby?
A A dead baby in a clown costume!

Q How do you know when a baby is a dead baby?
A The dog plays with it more.

Q How do you get 100 babies into a bucket?
A With a blender.

Q How do you get them out again?
A With tortilla chips.

Q What's the difference between a truck full of bowling balls
and a truck full of dead babies?
A You can't unload a truck full of bowling balls with a pitchfork.

Q What is pink and red and sits in a corner?
A A baby chewing on razor blades.

Q What is green and sits in a corner?
A The same baby, six weeks later.

Old People

If we are lucky, we will all get old. Many people claim to be afraid of getting old, but I don't believe them. I think they're afraid of getting dead... and getting old is one of the sure signs you're getting close.

One of things that has always amazed me about old people is their pace. They move through the world unhurried and slow. It would seem the less time we have, the more time we have! Sometimes slower isn't better, like on the highway. There's about twelve miles per hour separating "caution" from "obstruction." I am one of those people who believe that our driving should be regularly re-tested. There are people out there who should not have a license at all, never mind retaining it even when physical factors are clearly compromising their control and rendering the driver all but murderous, but here we are talking about the Asians again.

I once saw a documentary about a senior living facility. It would seem old people are doing a lot of f#@king.

Need a minute?

This is, of course, good news and bad news. The good news is that we can all look forward to a lifetime of sexual pleasure. The bad news is we'll be f#@king old people. To better prepare yourself for the future, try this: bang an old person. You can find plenty of them at restaurants all over your town at around 4:00 p.m. Just look for one dining alone and send over a milkshake, old people really don't give a damn what they eat any more. Follow one around for a day; they eat like a nine-year-old celebrating their birthday at a carnival. Next start a conversation. Give them something to complain about. Ask if their neighbors have any pets and they'll handle the rest. Then somewhere about ten minutes in say, "Let's go." They'll ask where and you say, "To my place to have sex. You said you wanted to about six minutes ago." They won't want to admit their memory is shot and you're in. Remember, in the heat of passion you don't want to shout out the name of the wrong old person, like, say, "Grandma!"

Common Indicators That You Are

OLD

The family wheeled Grandma out on the lawn in her wheelchair where the activities for her 100th birthday were taking place. Grandma couldn't talk very well, but she could write notes fairly well when she needed to communicate.

After a short time out on the lawn, Grandma started leaning off to the right and some family members grabbed her, straightened her up and stuffed pillows on her right.

A short time later she started leaning off to her left and again the family grabbed her and stuffed pillows on her left.

Soon she started leaning forward and the family members again grabbed her and tied a pillow case around her waist to hold her up. A nephew who arrived late came running up to Grandma and said, "You're looking good, how are they treating you?"

Grandma took out her little notepad and slowly wrote a note to her nephew, "They won't let me fart."

* * *

An old man decided his old wife was getting hard of hearing. So he called her doctor to make an appointment to have her hearing checked.

The doctor said he could see her in two weeks, and meanwhile there's a simple, informal test the husband could do to give the doctor some idea of the dimensions of the problem.

"Here's what you do. Start about 40 feet away from her, and speak in a normal conversational tone and see if she hears you. If not, go to 30 feet, then 20 feet, and so on until you get a response."

So that evening she's in the kitchen cooking dinner, and he's in the living room, and he says to himself, "I'm about 40 feet away, let's see what happens."

"Honey, what's for supper?" No response.

So he moves to the other end of the room, about 30 feet away. "Honey, what's for supper?" No response.

So he moves into the dining room, about 20 feet away. "Honey, what's for supper?" No response.

On to the kitchen door, only 10 feet away. "Honey, what's for supper?" No response.

So he walks right up behind her. "Honey, what's for supper?"

"For the fifth time, CHICKEN!!!!"

* * *

A little old lady was in the kitchen one day, washing the dishes when suddenly a little genie appeared beside her.

"You've led a long and good life," the genie said, "I have come to reward you by granting you three wishes. Ask for anything you want and I will make it happen."

The old lady was surprised but cynical. Not really believing that anything would happen she decided to play along for a minute. "Okay," she said, "turn all those dirty dishes into money." With that there was a big Poof! and the dishes had turned into a big pile of cash.

"My," said the old lady, staggered that it had actually worked, "Perhaps you could make me look young and beautiful again?" There was another big poof and the woman now looked a lot younger and was very good looking. Excitedly she carried on, "Can you turn my dear old cat into a handsome young man?"

Once more there was a big Poof, and the cat was replaced by a handsome young man. Smiling devilishly she turned to the young man and said, "At last! Now I want to make love with you for the rest of the day and all night too!"

The young man just looked at her for moment then replied in a high pitched voice, "Well you should have thought about that before you took me to the vet's!"

* * *

An old lady in a nursing home is wheeling up and down the halls in her wheelchair making sounds like she's driving a car. As she's going down the hall, an old man jumps out of a room and says, "Excuse me ma'am but you were speeding. Can I see your driver's license?" She digs around in her purse a little, pulls out a candy wrapper, and hands it to him. He looks it over, gives her a warning and sends her on her way.

Up and down the halls she goes again. Again, the same old man jumps out of a room and says, "Excuse me ma'am but I saw you cross over the center line back there. Can I see your registration please?" She digs around in her purse a little, pulls out a store receipt and hands it to him. He looks it over, gives her another warning and sends her on her way.

She zooms off again up and down the halls weaving all over. As she comes to the old man's room again, he jumps out. He's stark naked and has an erection! The old lady in the wheel chair looks up and says, "Oh, no, not the breathalyzer again!"

* * *

A older guy is out to dinner with his wife to celebrate her fortieth birthday. He says, "So what would you like, Julie? A Jaguar? A sable coat? A diamond necklace?"

She says, "Bernie, I want a divorce."

"Oh," he says, "I really wasn't planning on spending that much."

* * *

A small tourist hotel was all abuzz about an afternoon wedding where the groom was 95 and the bride was 23. The groom looked pretty feeble and the feeling was that the wedding night might kill him, because his bride was a healthy, vivacious young woman.

But lo and behold, the next morning, the bride came down the main staircase slowly, step by step, hanging onto the banister for dear life. She finally managed to get to the counter of the little shop in the hotel. The clerk looked really concerned, "Whatever happened to you, honey? You look like you've been wrestling an alligator!"

The bride groaned, hung on to the counter and managed to speak, "Oh God! He told me he'd been saving up for 75 years and I thought he meant his money!"

* * *

An elderly man was quite unhappy because he had lost his favorite hat. Instead of buying a new one, he decided he would go to church and swipe one out of the vestibule. When he got there, an usher intercepted him at the door and took him to a pew where he had to sit and listen to the entire sermon on "The Ten Commandments." After church, the man met the preacher in the vestibule doorway, shook his had vigorously, and told him, "I want to thank you, Preacher, for saving my soul today. I came to church to steal a hat and after hearing your sermon on the Ten Commandments, I decided against it."

The preacher asks, "You mean the commandment 'Thou shalt not steal' changed your mind?"

The old man answers, "No, the one about adultery did. As soon as you said that I remembered where I left my old hat!"

* * *

"Oh John, do you remember, the last time we were up here was 25 years ago and we made love for the very first time near an old barn. I wonder if we could find it again."

"I don't think it'd be here after all this time," he said, "but we'll go and have a look."

Surprisingly enough, the barn was still there. "Look Doreen, I sat you on that fence over there and we made love, let's do it again." She agreed and he sat her on the fence and began the business.

Doreen went completely wild, thrashing her arms in the air and waving her feet around. "Wow, Doreen, you didn't do that last time."

"I know" she stammered, "but it wasn't electrified then."

* * *

An old man, Mr. Smith, resided in a nursing home. One day he went into the nurses' office and informed Nurse Jones that his penis died. Nurse Jones, realizing that Mr. Smith was old and forgetful decided to play along with him.

"It did? I'm sorry to hear that," she replied.

Two days later, Mr. Smith was walking down the halls at the nursing home with his penis hanging outside his pants.

Nurse Jones saw him and said, "Mr. Smith, I thought you told me your penis died?"

"It did," he replied. "Today is the viewing!"

* * *

Three old men are talking about their aches, pains and bodily functions.

The 70-year-old man says, "I have this problem. I wake up every morning at seven and it takes me twenty minutes to pee."

The 80-year-old man says, "My case is worse. I get up at eight and I sit there and grunt and groan for half an hour before I finally have a bowel movement."

The 90-year-old man says, "At seven I pee like a horse, and at eight I crap like a cow."

"So what's your problem?" ask the others.

"I don't wake up until nine!"

* * *

An old man was having trouble with his memory. He couldn't remember anything and his wife was having trouble with her memory, too.

The man read in the paper one evening about a memory doctor who could help restore memory. He called his wife over and told her to read the ad.

She thought it sounded pretty good and said, "I think we ought to see that doctor." So, they went to see the memory doctor.

After seeing the doctor for about six weeks, the old man and his wife ran into one of their old friends. The friend said, "I understand you're going to the memory doctor."

"Yes, that's right; we're both going."

His friend asked, "Is he any good?"

"Is he any good?" said the man. "He's the best doctor we've ever been to, he's really good!"

His friend said, "You know, I'm having trouble with my memory, too. I think I ought to see that doctor. What's the doctor's name?"

The man hesitated, "What's the doctor's name... what's the doctor's name?" He said, "Look, there's a flower with a real long stem, the stem has little green leaves and there are thorns sticking out of the stem. At the top of the stem is a big bulb flower that comes in all different colors. What do you call that?"

His friend said, "Why, that's a rose."

"Yeah, that's right, rose." He turned to his wife and said, "Hey, Rose, what's the name of that doctor we've been going to?"

* * *

An elderly gentleman went to the local drug store and asked the pharmacist for Viagra.

The pharmacist said, "That's no problem. How many do you want?"

The man answered, "Just a few, maybe 4, but cut each one in 4 pieces."

"That won't do you any good."

"That's all right," the elderly gentleman said. "I don't need them for sex any-more, as I'm over 80 years old. I just want it to stick out far enough so I don't pee on my shoes."

* * *

One day two old ladies met up for a small lunch, one of the ladies said to the other, "Did you come on the bus?"

The other lady replied, "Yeah but I made it look like an asthma attack."

* * *

An elderly couple (who lived in an old folks home) had had feelings for one another for quite some time.

Then one day they had a chance to meet up as the rest of the old folks were going out on a day trip.

The two complained of some sort of illness and the caretakers told them to stay put.

When the bus with the elders in had pulled away the couple made sure the coast was clear before slipping into the man's bedroom.

As soon as they'd taken their clothes off and got into bed the man asked the women what she liked done to her.

"I love to be licked down below!" came the reply.

So the man ventured downwards.

After five minutes the man came back up.

"What is wrong?" asked the women.

"Well yes there's a horrible smell and it tastes quite bad down there," said the man.

"Oh," said the women. "That must be my arthritis."

"In your vagina?" enquired the man.

"No," answered the women. "The arthritis is in my shoulder so I can't wipe my ass."

* * *

A old game hunter was telling a couple of his cronies about the tragedy that befell him while scouting the woods that weekend prior to the opening of deer season. "I was going through the woods," he said, "When, turning behind a big tree, I came face to face with a huge grizzly."

"Wow!" said one of the friends, "that must've been really scary."

"Yeah," said the man telling the story, "the grizzly reared up like this." The old man stood up, raising both hands in front with hands clawed and roared, "GRRRRRRRRRRRRRR!!! I just shit all over myself."

"But of course," says one of the cronies, "I would have shit all over myself as well had a bear done that to me."

"No, no," said the teller, "I didn't mean, then. I meant, just now, when I reared up and screamed GRRRRRRRRRRRRRRRR!"

* * *

A senior citizen decided to visit the Social Security office to sign up for his benefits. Upon his arrival the clerk asked for proof of his age. When he reached for his wallet the embarrassed man realized he had left it home. After explaining his problem to the clerk, she replied, "Don't worry, just open your shirt, and if your chest hair is gray you will qualify." The senior citizen opened up his shirt and was soon signed up for his benefits.

Upon arriving home, he related the story to his wife. She looked at him, smiled and said, "Too bad you didn't drop your pants. You would have qualified for disability too!"

* * *

An older gent goes to his doctor for a check up. The doc said, "I'm sorry, buddy. You've got terminal cancer and maybe six months to live."

The fellow calls his adult son and asks him to meet at the corner tavern for some bad news.

Upon finding out, the son said, "Well, Dad, you should call your drinking buddies down here and tell them too."

A short time later a dozen or so of the man's best friends arrive at the bar. The gent said, "Fellas, I've got some really bad news. The doc said I have AIDS and I'll be dead in around six months."

The son leans over and whispers, "Dad, I thought the doctor said you've got cancer?"

The old man replied, "Yeah, that's right son. But I don't want these guys going over to the house and trying to screw your mom after I'm gone."

* * *

An old man was eating in a truck stop when three bikers walked in.

The first walked up to the old man, pushed his cigarette into the old man's pie and then took a seat at the counter. The second walked up to the old man, spit into the old man's milk and then he took a seat at the counter. The third walked up to the old man, turned over the old man's plate, and then he took a seat at the counter. Without a word of protest, the old man quietly left the diner.

Shortly thereafter, one of the bikers said to the waitress, "Humph, not much of a man, was he?"

The waitress replied, "Not much of a truck driver either. He just backed his truck over three motorcycles."

* * *

One morning, a woman and her baby were taking a bus. As she entered the bus the driver says, "Wow, that is one ugly baby." The woman was deeply hurt. She continued to get on to the bus and found a seat next to an elderly man.

The man asked her, "What's wrong? You look mad."

She replied, "I am. That bus driver just insulted me."

"You shouldn't take that from him," the man replied. "He's a public worker and should give you respect. If I was you I would take his badge number and report him."

"You're right sir, I think I will report him."

The elderly man says, "You go on up there and get his badge number. I'll hold your monkey for you."

* * *

A group of senior citizens were exchanging notes about their ailments.

"My arm is so weak I can hardly hold this coffee cup."

"Yes, I know. My cataracts are so bad I can't see to pour the coffee."

"I can't turn my head because of the arthritis in my neck."

"My blood pressure pills make my dizzy."

"I guess that's the price we pay for getting old."

"Well, it's not all bad. We should be thankful that we can still drive."

* * *

A fit old man was giving a lecture to a class of young people. "Look at me!" he boasted. "I'm as fit as a fiddle! And would you like to know why? It's because I don't drink, I don't smoke, I don't stay up late, and I don't chase after women."

He smiled at them and with a twinkle in his eyes, added, "And tomorrow, I'm going to celebrate my 90th birthday!"

"Really?" muttered one of the young people, "How?!?"

* * *

Three sons left home, went out on their own and prospered. Getting back together, they discussed the gifts they were able to give their elderly mother.

The first said, "I built a big house for our mother."

The second said, "I sent her a Mercedes with a driver."

The third smiled and said, "I've got you both beat. You remember how Mom enjoyed reading the Bible? And you know she can't see very well any more. I sent her a remarkable parrot that recites the entire Bible. It took elders in the church 12 years to teach him. He's one of a kind. Mama just has to name the chapter and verse, and the parrot recites it."

Soon thereafter, Mom sent out her letters of thanks, "Milton," she wrote one son, "the house you built is so huge. I live in only one room, but I have to clean the whole house."

"Gerald," she wrote to another, "I am too old to travel any more. My eyesight isn't what it used to be. I stay most of the time at home, so I rarely use the Mercedes. And the driver is so rude!"

"Dearest Donald," she wrote to her third son, "you have the good sense to know what your mother likes. The chicken was delicious!"

* * *

An elderly woman contacted her telephone company to report that her telephone failed to ring when her friends called, and that on the few occasions when it did ring, her dog always moaned right beforehand. A telephone company repairman proceeded to the scene, curious to see this psychic dog or the senile elderly woman. He climbed a nearby telephone pole, hooked in his test set, and dialed the subscriber's house.

The phone didn't ring right away, but then the dog moaned loudly and the telephone began to ring. Climbing down from the pole, the telephone repairman found:

1. The dog was tied to the telephone system's ground wire via a steel chain and collar.

2. The wire connection to the ground rod was loose.

3. The dog was receiving 90 volts of signaling current when the phone number was called.

4. After a couple of such jolts, the dog would start moaning and then urinate on himself and the ground.

5. The wet ground would complete the circuit, thus causing the phone to ring.

Which demonstrates that some problems *can* be fixed by pissing and moaning.

* * *

There is a merry family gathering with all generations around the table.

The children (naughty little rascals) sneak a Viagra tablet into Grandpa's drink.

After a while, Grandpa excuses himself because he has to go to the bathroom. When he returns, however, his trousers are wet all over.

"What happened, Grandpa?" asked his concerned children.

"Well," he answers, "I had to go to the bathroom to pee. So I took it out, but then I saw that it wasn't mine, so I put it back."

* * *

A man was suffering from impotence, so he went to see a specialist. The doctor gave him a prescription that he was to take faithfully three times a day, and always with food.

A couple of days later, the man was at a formal banquet and didn't want any of the other guests to spot and possibly identify his pink and purple capsule of medication. So, he instructed the waiter to empty the capsule into his soup, thinking he could eat his soup openly with everyone else, take his medication, and preserve his privacy all at the same time.

However, when the soup was served everyone received a bowl of it but the man, who began feeling conspicuous and angry. He confronted the waiter and asked why he hadn't been served his 'special' soup.

"Well, sir, I poured your medication into your bowl as instructed. Since then, I have been waiting for the noodles to lie down."

* * *

A aging actor found he had a serious problem, he could no longer remember his lines. After many years of searching, he finally found a theater where they were willing to give him a chance to shine again.

"This is the most important part of the play," the director said, "and it consists of only one line. You must walk onto the stage carrying a rose. You must hold the rose to your nose with only one finger and your thumb, sniff it deeply, and then recite the line, 'Ah, the sweet aroma of my mistress.'"

The actor was thrilled. For the entire day prior to the play he practiced his line, over and over again. Finally, the big day came.

The curtain was raised and the actor walked onto the stage. With the greatest of passion, he delivered his line, "Ah, the sweet aroma of my mistress."

Suddenly, the audience burst into laughter and the director was fuming. "You damn fool!" cried the director. "You've ruined me!"

Bewildered, the actor asked, "What? What happened? I didn't forget my line did I?"

"No, you fool!" the director screamed. "You forgot the fucking rose!"

* * *

Women

Ah, sweet mystery. Let's start with physicality. As the magazine covers teach us, nothing demands attention like the image of an attractive female. They are like a police car; they flash like the lights, attracting our eyes; like a siren they set off alerts in our very hormones and, in the case of your girlfriend, have a back seat full of gang bangers.

I remember being on vacation in Italy and seeing Michelangelo's Statue of David. There was a beautiful, young woman there, let's say she was French, and I had trouble keeping my eyes on the statue. Here you have arguably the most revered piece of art in history. It makes Italians feel proud, Jews feel brave and Asians feel hung. But, I am hard wired by forces far beyond my own comprehension, a fact that Victoria's Secret and my wife exploit with impudence.

Then there is the mind of the woman. Listening to her, learning and understanding her feelings, empathizing with each of her thoughts; this is the way into her castle of pleasure. Her mind is the mote and the drawbridge must be lowered before you can enter the magical kingdom of Metaphoreforgettinyourselfsomeiswaytoolongia. Or you can get her drunk.

A woman's hair is a very important symbol of who she is. If it's long she could be glamorous or a hippy chick. If it's short she could be sassy or... lesbian. If she has a receding hairline that shows a great deal of forehead but still has enough volume to give a kind of dashing effect, she's me, so please be gentle if you fuck her.

Eyebrows – Hair Removal Zone #1 on our tour. We will be passing through all kinds of Hair Removal Zones (or HRZ) on our tour. This one is generally performed with plucking. Let's move on.

Armpits – With the thought of having some Guatemalan slather hot wax on your armpit and yank out all the hair, let's look at HRZ #3. *Wooof.*

Upper lip – HRZ #2 though sometimes hair is lightened with bleach instead. Ah, the bleach mustache. Got Chlorine? Top lip can also be pumped up with collagen in case your man wants to see what it's like to kiss Steven Tyler.

Vagina – That's right, vagina, and HRZ #4. Okay, I'm not going to beat around the bush here: Brazilian wax. I'm just saying. If you are unfamiliar, it is a... please, everybody is familiar. What I didn't know is that at the conclusion of the Brazilianing, the Brazilianer proceeds to carefully pluck out the remaining hairs. This is either incredibly hot or wildly degrading... for both parties!

Legs are the low man on the shaving totem pole, and the last stop on our HRZ tour. No Guatemalans, no Brazilians, just a woman in a hurry and a blade at the end of its career.

Okay, listen up; it's all about the feet. Take off a woman's shoes and give her a good, long foot rub and she will invariably blow you. Not at the same time of course, unless she's with Cirque Du Soliel, but not long after, I promise.

Common Indicators That You Are A
WOMAN

Three guys are discussing women. "I like to watch a woman's tits best," the first guy says.

The second says, "I like to look at a woman's ass." He asks the third guy, "What about you?"

"Me? I prefer to see the top of her head."

* * *

A woman who had outlived no less than eight husbands finally passed away. Old friends and enemies alike gathered at the grave site and consoled or bitched with each other, as is so often the way. "Oh well, at least they'll be together again," sighed one of the departed lady friends.

"Yes," replied a childhood friend with a sob, "but with which husband?"

"No silly," said the snide friend, "I meant her legs."

* * *

A woman went to her doctor for a follow up visit after the doctor had prescribed testosterone for her. She was a little worried about some of the side effects she was experiencing.

"Doctor, the hormones you've been giving me have really helped, but I'm afraid that you're giving me too much. I've started growing hair in places that I've never grown hair before."

The doctor reassured her. "A little hair growth is a perfectly normal side effect of testosterone. Just where has this hair appeared?"

"On my balls."

* * *

A group of guys and one girl are sitting together at a ball game. During the game the guys notice that the girl knows just as much about the game as themselves, and are really impressed.

After the game they ask her, "how is it that you know so much about baseball?"

She says, "Well, I used to be a guy and got a sex change."

The guys are amazed, but very curious about the process. "What was the most painful part of the process? Was it when they cut off your penis?"

"That was very painful, but was not the most painful part."

"Was it when they cut off your balls?"

"That was very painful, but was not the most painful part."

"What was the most painful part?"

"The part that hurt the most was when they scooped half my brain out!"

* * *

A Los Angeles policeman pulled alongside a speeding car on the freeway. Glancing at it, he was astounded to see that the woman at the wheel was knitting! The cop cranked down his window and yelled, "PULL OVER!"

"NO," the woman yelled back, "IT'S A CARDIGAN!"

* * *

A woman went into a store to buy her husband a pet for his birthday. After looking around, she found that all the pets were very expensive. She told the clerk she wanted to buy a pet, but she didn't want to spend a fortune.

"Well," said the clerk, "I have a very large bullfrog. They say it's been trained to give blowjobs!"

"Blowjobs," the woman replied.

"It hasn't been proven, but we've sold 30 of them this month," he said.

The woman thought it would be a great gag gift, and what if it's true... no more blowjobs for her! She bought the frog. When she explained froggy's ability to her husband, he was extremely skeptical and laughed it off.

The woman went to bed happy, thinking she may never need to perform this less than riveting act again.

In the middle the night, she was awakened by the noise of pots and pans flying everywhere, making hellacious banging and crashing sounds. She ran downstairs to the kitchen, only to find her husband and the frog reading cookbooks.

"What are you two doing at this hour?" she asked.

The husband replied," If I can teach this frog to cook, your ass is gone."

* * *

A brunette, redhead, and a blonde are talking when the brunette says, "I was looking through my daughter's purse and I found cigarettes. I didn't even know that she smoked."

The redhead then says, "Well I was looking through my daughters purse and I found a joint. I didn't even know she did drugs."

Lastly, the blonde says, "Well I was looking through my daughters purse and I found condoms. I didn't even know that she had a dick!"

* * *

There once was a blonde who was very tired of blonde jokes and insults directed at her intelligence. So she cut and dyed her hair, got a make-over, got in her car, and began driving around in the country. Suddenly, she came to a herd of sheep in the road. She stopped her car and went over to the shepherd who was tending to them.

"If I can guess the exact number of sheep here will you let me have one?" she asked. The shepherd, thinking this was a pretty safe bet, agreed.

"You have 171 sheep," said the blonde in triumph.

Surprised, the shepherd told her to pick out a sheep of her choice. She looked around for a while and finally found one that she really liked.

She picked it up and was petting it when the shepherd walked over to her and asked, "If I can guess your real hair color, will you give me my sheep back?"

The blonde thought it was only fair to let him try.

"You're a blonde! Now give me back my dog."

* * *

TI went to a psychiatrist because I was having severe problems with my sex life. The psychiatrist asked me a lot of questions, but didn't seem to be getting a clear picture of my problems.

Finally he asked, "Do you ever watch your girlfriend's face while you're having sex?"

"Well, yes, I did once."

"Well, how did she look?"

"Oh boy... she looked *very* angry!"

At this point the psychiatrist felt that he was really getting somewhere and he said, "Well that's very interesting, we must look into this further. Now tell me, you say that you have only seen your girlfriend's face once during sex; that seems somewhat unusual; how did it occur that you saw her face that time?"

"She was watching us through the window."

* * *

A man and a woman were waiting at the hospital donation center.

Man: "What are you doing here today?"

Woman: "Oh, I'm here to donate some blood. They're going to give me $5 for it."

Man: "Hmm, that's interesting. I'm here to donate sperm, myself. But they pay me $25."

The woman looked thoughtful for a moment and they chatted some more before going their separate ways.

Several months later, the same man and woman meet again in the donation center.

Man: "Oh, hi there! Here to donate blood again?"

Woman: [shaking her head with mouth closed] "Unh unh."

* * *

Three nurses arrive at the pearly gates. St. Peter asks the first why he should admit her.

She replies that she has been an emergency room nurse and has saved thousands and thousands of lives.

"OK," he says, "Come on in!"

The second reports that he has been an ICU nurse and he, too, has saved thousands and thousands of lives.

St. Peter lets him in, too. St. Peter asks the third nurse the same question.

She replies that she has been a managed care nurse and has saved thousands and thousands of dollars for the insurance company.

St. Peter replies, "OK. Come on in. But you can only stay three days."

* * *

This husband and wife are staying in a hotel, and after a romantic evening wining and dining they go off to bed. However, as soon as they settled down, the man (not quite ready for slumber) leans over and whispers softly, "Hey snuggle boopy boops, your lickle hubby wubby isn't quite ready for bye-byes yet."

The wife takes the hint and says, "Okay, but I have to use the bathroom first." So off she goes but on her way back she trips over a piece of carpet and lands flat on her face.

Her husband jumps up and exclaims in a concerned tone "Oh my little honey bunny, is your nosey-wosey all right?"

No harm is done, so she jumps into bed and they have mad passionate sex for three hours. Afterwards, the wife goes off to the bathroom again, but on her way back she trips over the same piece of carpet and again lands flat on her face on the floor.

Her husband looks over and grunts, "Clumsy bitch."

* * *

Luke's wife bought a new line of expensive cosmetics guaranteed to make her look years younger.

After a lengthy sitting before the mirror applying the "miracle" products she asked, "Darling, honestly what age would you say I am?"

Looking her over carefully, Luke replied, "Judging from your skin: twenty... your hair: eighteen... and your figure: twenty-five."

"Oh, you flatterer!" she gushed.

"Hey, wait a minute!" Luke interrupted. "I haven't added them up yet."

* * *

A very flat-chested woman finally decided she needed a bra and set out to the mall in search of one in her size.

She entered an upscale department store and approached the saleslady in lingerie, "Do you have a size 28AAAA bra?"

The clerk haughtily replied in the negative, so she left the store and proceeded to another department store where she is rebuffed in much the same manner.

After a third try at another department store in the mall, she had become disgusted. Leaving the mall, she drove to K-Mart.

Marching up to the sales clerk, she unbuttoned and threw open her blouse, yelling, "Do you have anything for these?"

The lady looked closely at her and replied, "Have you tried Clearasil?"

* * *

Two Southern belles, one of whom was from Texas, were seated on the porch swing of a large white-pillared mansion talking. The first woman, who was not from Texas, said, "When my first child was born, my husband had this beautiful mansion built for me."

"That's nice," commented the lady from Texas.

"When my second child was born," the first woman continued, "he bought me that fine Cadillac automobile you see parked in the drive."

Again, the lady from Texas commented, "That's nice."

"Then, when my third child was born," boasted the first woman, "he bought me this very exquisite diamond and emerald bracelet."

Once more, the lady from Texas commented, "That's nice."

"What did your husband buy for you when you had your first child?" asked the first woman.

"My husband sent me to charm school," answered the lady from Texas.

"Charm school!" exclaimed the first woman. "What on earth for?"

"So that instead of saying 'Who gives a shit,' I learned to say 'That's nice!'" replied the lady from Texas.

* * *

A man is in a hotel lobby and wants to ask the clerk a question.

As he turns to go to the front desk, he accidentally bumps into a woman beside him and his elbow pokes her in the breast. They are both quite startled.

The man turns to her and says, "Ma'am, if your heart is as soft as your breast, I know you'll forgive me."

She replies, "If your cock is as hard as your elbow, I'm in room 436."

* * *

The wife approaches her husband wearing the exact same sexy little negligee she wore on their wedding night.

She looks at her husband and says, "Honey, do you remember this?"

He looks up at her and replies, "Yes dear, I do, you wore that same negligee the night we were married."

"That's right." she replied, "And do you remember what you said to me that night?"

He nods and says, "Yes dear, I still remember."

"Well, what was it?"

He responds, "Well honey, as I remember, I said, "Ohhhhhhh, baby, I'm going to suck the life out of those big tits and screw your brains out!"

She giggles and says, "Yes, That was it. That was exactly what you said. And now it's 50 years later, I'm in the same negligee I wore that night. What do you have to say tonight?"

Again, he looks up at her and looks her up and down and says, "Mission Accomplished."

* * *

A guy starts a new job, and the boss says, "If you marry my daughter, I'll make you a partner, give you an expense account, a Mercedes, and a million dollar annual salary."

The guy says, "What's wrong with her?" The boss shows him a picture, and she's hideous.

The boss says, "It's only fair to tell you, she's not only ugly, she's as dumb as a wall."

The guy says, "I don't care what you offer me, it ain't worth it."

The boss says, "I'll give you a five million dollar salary and build you a mansion on Long Island."

The guy accepts, figuring he can put a bag over her head when they have sex. About a year later, the guy buys an original Van Gogh and he's about to hang it on the wall. He climbs a ladder and yells to his wife, "Bring me a hammer."

She mumbles, "Get the hammer. Get the hammer," and she fetches the hammer.

The guy says, "Get me some nails." She mumbles, "Get the nails. Get the nails," and she gets him some nails.

The guys starts hammering a nail into the wall, he hits his thumb, and he yells, "Fuck!"

She mumbles, "Get the bag. Get the bag."

* * *

The newlyweds entered the elevator of their Miami Beach hotel. The operator, a magnificent blonde, looked at them in surprise and said, "Why, hello Teddy, how are you?"

A frosty silence prevailed until the couple reached their room, when the piqued bride demanded: "Who was that woman?!"

"Take it easy, honey," said the groom, "I'm going to have trouble enough explaining you to her."

* * *

A fellow and his wife are on a golf outing. Since she is a novice, he warns her not to stand in front of him when he swings or she might be hit by the ball. Later, the wife forgot the warning and was accidently struck in the head by the ball, killing her instantly. At the coroner's inquest, the District Attorney said, "Sir, the autopsy found that your wife died as the result of the flying golf ball striking her in the head. We believe that event to be an accident and you will not be charged with a crime." The attorney added, "However, during the examination of your wife's body, the pathologist found a golf ball stuck in her rectum. Can you explain that?"

The fellow replied, "Sure. That was my Mulligan!"

* * *

Two young boys were discussing their parents, when one realized he really knew very little about his mother. Arriving home that evening, he began to interrogate her.

"How old are you, Mom?" he asked.

"None of your business," replied his mother.

"Okay, then how much do you weigh?"

"That's none of your business either, young man," she said.

The boy thought for a minute, then delivered his final bombshell. "Well then, can you tell me why you and Daddy got divorced?"

Shocked and appalled, mom sent him to bed without supper.

The next day, the kid reported his failure to his friend. "I know!" said his buddy. "Just look at her driver's license in her purse. It'll tell you everything you want to know."

Later that day, the mom found her son next to her disemboweled purse, holding her driver's license. "Just what the heck do you think you are doing?" she snapped.

"Well, you wouldn't tell me what I wanted to know," explained the junior detective, "but my friend said it's all right here. See, you're 43 years old... you weigh 135 pounds... and Daddy divorced you because you got an 'F' in Sex."

* * *

A man went to see his priest and stated in a very serious tone, "Father, something horrible is happening and I must talk to you about it."

"What is wrong, my son?" asked the priest.

"My wife is poisoning me," stated the man.

The priest, very shocked by this, asked, "How can that be?"

"I'm telling you, Father, I'm positive she's poisoning me. What should I do?" the man pleaded.

"Tell you what. Let me talk to her. I'll see what I can find out and I'll let you know," said the priest.

A few days later, the priest called the man and said, "Well, I have spoken with your wife. We spoke on the phone for almost four hours. Do you want my advice?"

The man anxiously replied, "Yes."

"Take the poison!" said the priest.

* * *

A young girl is walking up the stairs in a church just as the priest is walking by. He looks up and is shocked to see the girl isn't wearing any panties.

He calls to the girl, gives her $25 and says, "Young lady, it's not proper to walk around without any panties on. Take this money and buy yourself some panties."

The girl goes home and gives the money to her mother and asks her to buy some panties for her. The mother asks her daughter where she got the money from and the girl explains what happened.

After learning how her daughter got the money, the mother rushes to her room, whips off her panties, puts on the shortest skirt she has and runs to the church.

As soon as she sees the priest approaching, she starts to walk up the stairs. The priest notices her and calls her down.

Not wanting the priest to think she's expecting anything, she calmly walks back down the stairs to where he is waiting.

The priest hands the woman $1 and says, "Lady, take this and for goodness sake, go buy yourself a razor!"

* * *

A college "Creative Writing" class was asked by the professor to write a concise essay containing the following four elements:

Religion, Royalty, Sex, Mystery

The writer of the best essay would be given a bookstore gift certificate. The winning essay read:

"My God!" said the Queen. "I'm pregnant. I wonder who did it?"

* * *

A third grade teacher asks her students to use the word 'contagious' in a sentence.

Cathy stands up and says, "Last summer I had the mumps and my mother said it was contagious."

"Very good, Cathy," the teacher says. "Does anyone else have a sentence?"

Julie, a sweet little girl in the front row, stands up and says, "My grandmother says there's a bug going around and it's contagious."

"Excellent, Julie," says the teacher, as she looks around the class and sees Little Johnny waving his hand impatiently. "Yes, Little Johnny, do you have a sentence?"

Little Johnny quickly jumps up and says, "The lady next door was painting her porch with a one inch brush and my dad said it would take the contagious."

* * *

The big game hunter walked into the bar and bragged to everyone about his hunting skills. The man was undoubtedly a good shot and none could dispute that. But then he said they could blindfold him and he would recognize any animal's skin from it's feel, and if he could locate the bullet hole he would even tell them what caliber bullet it was that killed the animal.

The hunter said that he was willing to prove it if they would put up the drinks, and so the bet was on.

They blindfolded him carefully and took him to his first animal skin. After feeling it for a few moments, he announced "ring brook." Then he felt the bullet hole and declared, "Shot with a .308 rifle." He was right.

They brought him another skin, one that someone had in their car trunk. He took a bit longer this time and then said, "Kalahari Lion. Shot with a .416 rifle." He was right again.

Through the night, he proved his skills again and again, every time against a round of drinks. Finally he staggered home, drunk out of his mind, and went to sleep.

The next morning he got up and saw in the mirror that he had one hell of a shiner. So he said to his wife, "I know I was drunk last night, but not drunk enough to get in a fight and not remember it. Where did I get this black eye?"

His wife angrily replied, "I gave it to you. You got into bed and put your hand down my panties. Then you fiddled around a bit and loudly announced, "Skunk, killed with an axe."

* * *

There was this Eskimo chick who spent the night with her boyfriend. Next morning she found out she was six months pregnant.

* * *

A guy stood over his tee shot for what seemed an eternity, looking up, looking down, measuring the distance, figuring the wind direction and speed. He was driving his partner nuts. Finally his exasperated partner says, "What's taking so long? Hit the blasted ball!"

The guy answers, "My wife is up there watching me from the clubhouse. I want to make this a perfect shot."

"Forget it, man," said his partner, "you don't stand a snowball's chance in hell of hitting her from here!"

* * *

A woman came up behind her husband while he was enjoying his morning coffee and slapped him on the back of the head.

"I found a piece of paper in your pants pocket with the name 'Marylou' written on it," she said, furious. "You had better have an explanation."

"Calm down, honey," the man replied. "Remember last week when I was at the dog track? That was the name of the dog I bet on."

The next morning, his wife snuck up on him and smacked him again.

"What was that for?" he complained.

"Your dog called last night."

* * *

Q & A Round Up
Women

Q What is the difference between a woman and a magnet?
A Magnets have a positive side!

Q What do you do when a blonde throws a pin at you?
A Run like hell....she's got a hand grenade in her mouth.

Q What is the difference between a wife and a girlfriend?
A About 45 pounds!!

Q Why are hurricanes normally named after women?
A When they come they're wild and wet, but when they go they take your house and car with them.

Q Why don't witches wear panties?
A Better grip on the broom.

Q Why did cavemen drag their women back to the cave by the hair?
A If they dragged them by the ankles, they would fill up with dirt!

Q Why are married women heavier than single women?
A Single women come home, see what's in the fridge and go to bed. Married women come home, see what's in bed and go to the fridge.

Q What do you call a woman who knows where her husband is every night?
A A Widow.

Q Why did God give man a penis?
A So we'd have at least one way to shut a woman up!

Q What are the small bumps around a woman's' nipples for?
A It's Braille for "suck here."

Q Why do women close their eyes during sex?
A They can't stand seeing a man have a good time.

Q What's the difference between your wife and your job?
A After 5 years your job will still suck.

Q How is a woman like a condom?
A Both of them spend more time in your wallet than on your dick.

Q Why don't women blink during foreplay?
A They don't have time!

Q How do you get a nun pregnant?
A You fuck her.

Q Why do women take longer than men to reach orgasm?
A Who cares?

Q Why do women wear make up and perfume?
A Because they're ugly and they stink.

Q What is the difference between a sorority girl and a bowling ball?
A You can't fit a sorority girl inside a bowling ball.

Q Why do women have periods?
A Because they deserve them.

Q What's the difference between a paycheck and a penis?
A You don't have to beg your girlfriend to blow your paycheck.

Q What's the difference between a whore and a bitch?
A A whore screws everyone; a bitch screws everyone except you.

Q Why don't men trust women?
A Would you trust anything that bled for five days and didn't die?

Q What's the difference between a boyfriend and a husband?
A 45 minutes.

Q How can you tell if your wife is dead?
A The sex is the same but the dishes pile up.

Q How can you tell if your husband is dead?

A The sex is the same but you get the remote.

Q If your wife keeps coming out of the kitchen to nag you, what have you done wrong?

A Made her chain too long.

Q How many men does it take to change a light bulb?

A None, they just sit there in the dark and complain.

Q What's the fastest way to a man's heart?

A Through his chest with a sharp knife.

Q What's the difference between a new husband and a new dog?

A After a year, the dog is still excited to see you.

Q A brunette, a blonde, and a redhead are all in third grade. Who has the biggest tits?

A The blonde, because she's 18.

Q Why do men take showers instead of baths?

A Pissing in the bath is disgusting.

Q Why don't pygmies wear tampons?

A They keep stepping on the strings.

Q Did you hear about the guy who finally figured out women?

A He died laughing before he could tell anybody.

Q How does a single woman in New York get rid of cockroaches?

A She asks them for a commitment.

Q Do you know why women fake orgasm?

A Because men fake foreplay.

Men

If I were a woman, I would be a lesbian. Not for the obvious reasons: my love of the ladies, my soft, desk-jockey hands or my propensity for wearing a strap-on; but because I don't seem to get along well with men.

By "men," I don't mean anybody with a penis, though that does seem to cover it, I mean "manly" men. For instance I don't care for sports, watching or participating, I don't hunt and I don't resent women for castrating me into some kind of lifestyle I find untenable.

This is probably due to my having some kind of testosterone deficiency, I grant you, but "a night out with the guys" watching the game, sounds gay to me. Inspecting a herd of strapping young bucks chasing each other around various types of enclosures wearing a variety of numbered uniforms pushes the gay envelope, but when they score a point and start bouncing their sweaty chests against one another's or exchanging playful spankings, well, that turns the envelope over and licks it closed!

It also seems that when the "guys" get together, all they really do is deal with the fact that there are no women! They talk about women; maybe they'll go to a titty bar or a regular bar to, um, hit on women! Why not have a few along in the first place?!

What I really think is this: guys would always want women around if they weren't already stuck with the wrong woman! The most important decision a man will ever make in his life is his choice of a mate. Guys who want a night out with the boys have not only made the wrong choice, they hang out with other guys who made the wrong choice. My friends and I seem to have done a good job of picking fun girly-humans with happy vaginas to mate with. I'm not gloating, I'm just saying.

Here's the easiest way to test whether or not you're with the right woman: If you act *any* differently when she is around than you do when your buddies are around YOU HAVE GOT THE WRONG GIRL!!!

I need you to trust me on this. It's important.

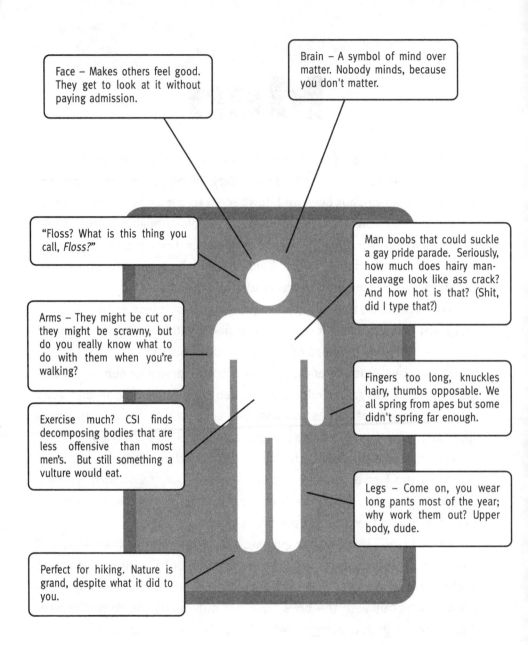

Face – Makes others feel good. They get to look at it without paying admission.

Brain – A symbol of mind over matter. Nobody minds, because you don't matter.

"Floss? What is this thing you call, *Floss?*"

Man boobs that could suckle a gay pride parade. Seriously, how much does hairy man-cleavage look like ass crack? And how hot is that? (Shit, did I type that?)

Arms – They might be cut or they might be scrawny, but do you really know what to do with them when you're walking?

Fingers too long, knuckles hairy, thumbs opposable. We all spring from apes but some didn't spring far enough.

Exercise much? CSI finds decomposing bodies that are less offensive than most men's. But still something a vulture would eat.

Legs – Come on, you wear long pants most of the year; why work them out? Upper body, dude.

Perfect for hiking. Nature is grand, despite what it did to you.

Common Indicators That You Are A

MAN

A guy says to his buddy, "I don't know what to get my wife for her birthday. She has everything, and besides, she can afford to buy anything she wants. So, I'm stumped."

His buddy said, "I have an idea. Why don't you make up a certificate that says she can have two hours of great sex, any way she wants it. She'll probably be thrilled!" So the first guy did just that. The next day his buddy asked, "Well, did you take my suggestion? How did it turn out?"

"She loved it. She jumped up, thanked me, kissed me on the mouth, and ran out the door yelling, 'I'll see you in two hours.'"

* * *

There was a middle-aged couple who had two stunningly beautiful teenaged daughters. They decided to try one last time for the son that they always wanted.

After months of trying, the wife became pregnant and sure enough, nine months later delivered a healthy baby boy. The joyful father rushed to the nursery to see his new son. He took one look and was horrified to see the ugliest child he had ever seen.

He went to his wife and said that there was no way he could be the father of that child. "Look at the two beautiful daughters I fathered." Then he gave her a stern look and asked, "Have you been fooling around on me?"

The wife just smiled sweetly and said, "Not this time."

* * *

The policeman had stopped a man for obvious drunken driving, but since the guy had a clean record, he made him park the car and took him home in the patrol car. "Are you sure this is your house?" the cop asked as they drove into a rather fashionable neighborhood.

"Shertainly!" said the drunk, "and if you'll just open the door f'me, I can prove it to ya." Entering the living room, he said, "You shee that piano? Thash mine. You shee that giant television set? Thast mine too. Now follow me."

The police officer followed the man as he shakily negotiated the stairs to the second floor. The drunk pushed open the first door they came to. "Thish ish my bedroom," he announced. "Shee the bed there? Thast mine! Shee that woman lying in the bed? Thash my wife. An' see that guy lying next to her?"

"Yeah?" the cop replied suspiciously. Beginning at this point to seriously doubt the man's story.

"Well, thash me!"

* * *

A man called home to his wife and said, "Honey, I have been asked to go fishing up in Canada with my boss and several of his friends. We'll be gone for a week. This is a good opportunity for me to get that promotion I've been wanting so could you please pack enough clothes for a week and set out my rod and fishing box? We're leaving from the office and I will swing by the house to pick my things up. Oh! Please pack my new blue silk pajamas."

The wife thinks this sounds a bit fishy but being the good wife she is, did exactly what her husband asked.

The following weekend he came home a little tired but otherwise looking good. The wife welcomed him home and asked if he caught many fish.

He said, "Yes! Lots of salmon, some bluegill, and a few swordfish. But why didn't you pack my new blue silk pajamas like I asked you to do?"

The wife replied, "I did. They're in your fishing box!"

* * *

This guy is stranded on a desert island, all alone for ten years. One day, he sees a speck in the horizon. He thinks to himself, "Too small to be a ship."

The speck gets a little closer and he thinks, "Too small to be a boat."

The speck gets even closer and he thinks, "Too small to be a raft."

Then, out of the surf comes this gorgeous woman, wearing a wet suit and scuba gear. She comes up to the guy and says, "How long has it been since you've had a cigarette?"

"Ten years!" he says. She reaches over and unzips a waterproof pocket on her left sleeve and pulls out a pack of fresh cigarettes. He takes one, lights it, takes a long drag, and says, "Man, oh man! Is that good!"

Then she asked, "How long has it been since you've had a drink of whiskey?"

He replies, "Ten years!" She reaches over, unzips her waterproof pocket on her right sleeve, pulls out a flask and gives it to him.

He takes a long swig and says, "Wow, that's fantastic!"

Then she starts unzipping this long zipper that runs down the front of her wet suit and she says to him, "And how long has it been since you got to play around?"

And the man replies, "My God! Don't tell me that you've got golf clubs in there!"

* * *

A man takes the day off of work and decides to go out golfing. He is on the second hole when he notices a frog sitting next to the green. He thinks nothing of it and is about to shoot when he hears, "Ribbit, nine iron."

The man looks round and doesn't see anyone so he tries again. "Ribbit, nine iron." He looks at the frog and decides to prove the frog wrong, puts his other club away, and grabs a nine iron. Boom! he hits a birdie. He is shocked.

He says to the frog, "Wow that's amazing. You must be a lucky frog, eh?"

The frog replies, "Ribbit. Lucky frog. Lucky frog."

The man decided to take the frog with him to the next hole. "What do you think frog?" the man asks.

"Ribbit, three wood," was the reply.

The guy takes out a three wood and Boom! Hole in one. The man is befuddled and doesn't know what to say. By the end of the day, the man golfed the best game of golf in his life and asks the frog,

"Okay where to next?"

The frog replies, "Ribbit, Vegas."

They go to Las Vegas and the guy says, "Okay frog, now what?"

The frog says, "Ribbit, Roulette."

Upon approaching the roulette table the man asks, "What do you think I should bet?"

The frog replies, "Ribbit, $3000 black six." Now, this is a million to one shot that this would win but after the golf game, the man figures what the heck. Boom! Tons of cash comes sliding back across the table.

The man takes his winnings and buys the best room in the hotel. He sits the frog down and says, "Frog, I don't know how to repay you. You won me all this money and I am forever grateful."

The frog replies, "Ribbit, Kiss Me."

He figures why not, since after all the frog did for him he deserves it.

All of a sudden the frog turns into a gorgeous 16-year-old girl.

"...and that, your honor, is how the girl ended up in my room."

* * *

On preparing to return home from an out of town trip, a man got a small puppy as a present for his son. Not having time to get the paperwork to take the puppy on board, the man just hid the pup down the front of his pants and sneaked him on board the airplane.

About 30 minutes into the trip, a stewardess noticed the man shaking and quivering. "Are you okay, sir?" asked the stewardess.

"Yes, I'm fine," said the man.

Later, the stewardess noticed the man moaning and shaking again. "Are you sure you're alright sir?"

"Yes," said the man, "but I have a confession to make. I didn't have time to get the paperwork to bring a puppy on board, so I hid him down the front of my pants."

"What's wrong?" asked the stewardess. "Is he not house trained?"

"No, that's not the problem. The problem is he's not weaned yet!"

* * *

One evening this drunk walks into a bar, sits down, and happens to notice a 12-inch-tall man standing on the bar. Astonished, the man asks the guy next to him; "What the hell is that?"

The guy next to him replied, "He's a musician."

To which the drunk replied, "Horseshit! You're pulling my leg."

So the guy next to him picks up the little man and brings him to the piano. Sure enough, this little man started hammering out all the favorite tunes of the bars' patrons.

Stunned, the drunk asks, "That little guy is cool, where the hell did you get him?"

The guy told the drunk how he had found a genie bottle out in the alley, rubbed it until a genie appeared, and was granted one wish. All of a sudden the drunk hauls ass out the back door, finds the bottle, and starts rubbing it. When suddenly a genie pops out and grants him one wish.

In a slur, the drunk asks, "I wish for a million bucks." All of a sudden, the sky turns black and overhead a million ducks come flying overhead shitting all over him.

Angrily, the drunk runs back inside, slams the door and begins cursing, "You son of a bitch, I found that genie bottle and wished for a million bucks and all of a sudden there are a million ducks shitting all over my new suit."

The guy started laughing and wildly exclaimed, "You don't really think I wished for a 12-inch pianist do you?"

* * *

This guy walks into a bar on the top of a very tall building. He sits down, orders a huge beer, chugs it, walks over to the window, and jumps out.

Five minutes later, the guy walks into the bar again, orders another huge beer, chugs it, walks over to the window, and jumps out again.

Five minutes later, he re-appears and repeats the whole thing.

About half an hour later, another guy at the bar stops the first guy and says, "Hey, how the heck are you doing that?!"

The first guy responds, "Oh, it's really simple physics. When you chug the beer, it makes you all warm inside and since warm air rises, if you just hold your breath you become lighter than air and float down to the sidewalk."

"Wow!" exclaims the second man, "I gotta try that!" So he orders a huge beer, chugs it, goes over to the window, jumps out, and splats on the sidewalk below.

The bartender looks over to the first man and says, "Superman, you're an asshole when you're drunk."

* * *

A man was having problems with premature ejaculation so he decided to go to the doctor. He asked the doctor what he could do to cure his problem.

In response the doctor said, "When you feel like you are getting ready to ejaculate try startling yourself."

That same day the man went to the store and bought himself a starter pistol. All excited to try this suggestion out he runs home to his wife. At home his wife is in bed, naked and waiting on her husband.

As the two begin, they find themselves in the '69' position. The man, moments later, feels the sudden urge to come and fires the starter pistol. The next day, the man went back to the doctor.

The doctor asked, "How did it go?"

The man answered, "Not that well. When I fired the pistol my wife crapped on my face, bit three inches off my penis and my mailman came out of the closet naked with his hands in the air!"

* * *

A golfer and his buddies were playing a big round of golf for $200. At the eighteenth green the golfer had a ten foot putt to win the round, and the $200. As he was lining up his putt, a funeral procession started to pass by. The golfer set down his putter, took his hat off, placed it over his chest, and began to wait for the funeral procession to pass. After it passed, he picked up his putter and returned to lining up his putt.

One of his buddies said, "That was the most touching thing I have ever seen. I can't believe you stopped playing, possibly losing your concentration, to pay your respects."

"Well," he said, "we were married for 25 years."

* * *

One day, back in the olden days, a cowboy was crossing the desert to do some trading and came upon an Indian. The Indian was laying on his back and had an erection that stuck straight up in the air.

The cowboy asked the Indian what he was doing.

The Indian replied, "Me tell-um time." This made sense to the cowboy, he was using his penis as a sundial.

A few days later, after completing his trading, the cowboy came across the same Indian. This time the Indian was laying on his back vigorously masturbating.

The cowboy asked what he was doing this time.

The Indian said, "Me wind-um watch."

* * *

Joe, a notoriously bad golfer, hits his ball off the first tee and watches as it slices to the right and disappears through an open window. Figuring that's the end of it, he gets another ball out of his bag and plays on. On the eighth hole, a police officer walks up to Joe on the course and says, "Did you hit a golf ball through a window back there?"

Joe says, "Yes I did."

"Well," says the police officer, "it knocked a lamp over, scaring the dog, which raced out of the house onto the highway. A driver rammed into a brick wall to avoid the dog, sending three people to the hospital. And it's all because you sliced the ball."

"Oh my goodness," says Joe, "is there anything I can do?"

"Yes there is," the cop says. "Try keeping your head down and close up your stance a bit."

* * *

Sherlock Holmes and Dr. Watson went on a camping trip. After a good meal and a bottle of wine, they were exhausted and went to sleep.

Some hours later, Holmes awoke and nudged his faithful friend.

"Watson, look up at the sky and tell me what you see."

Watson replied, "I see millions and millions of stars."

"What does that tell you?" Holmes asked.

Watson pondered for a minute. "Astronomically, it tells me that there are millions of galaxies and potentially billions of planets. Astrologically, I observe that Saturn is in Leo. Time-wise, I deduce that the time is approximately a quarter past three. Theologically, I can see that The Lord is all-powerful and that we are small and insignificant. Meteorologically, I suspect that we will have, a beautiful day tomorrow. What does it tell you?"

Holmes was silent for a minute, then spoke. "Watson, you idiot, some asshole stole our tent."

* * *

The Lone Ranger and Tonto were riding on the range one day. The two came to a stop, where Tonto jumped off his horse and put his head on the ground to listen to see if anyone was coming.

After a few seconds he rose and said, "Buffalo come."

The Lone Ranger was amazed and proclaimed "Damn you Indians are smart, how the hell did you know there were buffaloes coming?"

Tonto replied, "Face sticky."

* * *

Morris was in his usual place in the morning sitting at the table, reading the paper after breakfast. He came across an article about a beautiful actress that was about to marry a football player who was known primarily for his lack of IQ and common knowledge.

He turned to his wife Sherry, with a questioning look on his face. "I'll never understand why the biggest schmucks get the most attractive wives."

His wife replies, "Why thank you, dear!"

* * *

A women accompanied her husband to the doctor's office. After his checkup, the doctor called the wife into his office alone.

He said: "If you don't do the following, your husband will surely die.

1. Each morning , fix him a healthy breakfast.

2. Be pleasant and make sure he is in a good mood.

3. For lunch, make him a nutritious meal.

4. For dinner, prepare him an especially nice meal.

5. Don't burden him with chores as he probably had a hard day.

6. Don't discuss your problems with him.

7. And most importantly, have sex with him several times a week."

On the way home, the husband asked his wife what the doctor said to her. She replied, "He said you're not going to make it."

* * *

If a man says something and there is not a woman around to hear it, is he still wrong?

* * *

A wife went in to see a therapist and said, "I've got a big problem doctor. Every time we're in bed and my husband climaxes, he lets out this earsplitting yell."

"My dear," the shrink said, "that's completely natural. I don't see what the problem is."

"The problem is," she complained, "it wakes me up."

* * *

Two women were digging in the garden. One pulls out a two-foot carrot. She says, "This one reminds me of my husband's."

The second woman says, "Your husband's is that long?"

"No that dirty."

* * *

Bernie was invited to his friend's home for dinner. Morris, the host, preceded every request to his wife by endearing terms, calling her Honey, My Love, Darling, Sweetheart, Pumpkin, etc.

Bernie looked at Morris and remarked, "That is really nice. After all these years that you have been married, you keep calling your wife those pet names."

Morris hung his head and whispered, "To tell the truth, I forgot her name three years ago."

*　*　*

A divorced man meet's his ex-wife's new husband at a party. After knocking back a few drinks, he goes over to the new guy and asks him: "So, how do you like using second hand stuff?"

To which the new husband replied, "It isn't that bad. Past the first three inches, it's all brand new!"

*　*　*

When the Ark's door was closed, Noah called a meeting with all the animals. "Listen up!" Noah said with a demanding voice. "There will be NO SEX on this trip! All of you males take off your penises and hand them in to my sons. I will sit over there and write you a receipt. After we see land, you can get your penises back."

After about a week Mr. Rabbit stormed into his wife's cage and was very excited. "Quick!" he said, "Get on my shoulders and look out the window to see if there is any land out there!"

Mrs. Rabbit got onto his shoulders, looked out the window, and said, "Sorry, no land yet."

"Darn it!", exclaimed Mr. Rabbit.

This went on every day until Mrs. Rabbit got fed up with him. Mrs. Rabbit asked, "What is the matter with you? You know it will rain for forty days and nights. Only after the water has drained will we be able to see land. But why are you acting so excited every day?"

"Look!" said Mr. Rabbit with a sly expression, as he held out a piece of paper, "I got the horse's receipt!"

*　*　*

While out one morning in the park, a jogger found a brand new tennis ball, and seeing nobody around, he slipped it into the pocket of his shorts. Later, on his way home, he stopped at a pedestrian crossing, waiting for the lights to change. A girl standing next to him eyed the large bulge in his shorts. "What's that?" she asked, her eyes gleaming with lust.

"Tennis ball," came the breathless reply.

"Oh," said the girl sympathetically, "that must hurt. I had tennis elbow once."

Q & A Round Up
Men

Q Why are men like laxatives?
A They irritate the shit out of you

Q Why did God create man?
A Because vibrators don't mow lawns

Q Why is it hard for a women to find men who are sensitive, caring and good looking?
A Because those men already have boyfriends

Q Why do men fall asleep immediately after sex?
A So women can masturbate and finish the job off properly!

Q Why do men want to marry virgins?
A They can't stand criticism.

Q What do you have when you have two little balls in your hand?
A A man's undivided attention.

Q Why do men name their penises?
A Because they want to be on a first-name basis with the thing that makes all their decisions.

Q What is gross stupidity?
A 144 men in one room.

Q What is a man's view of safe sex?
A A padded headboard.

Q What's the difference between a clitoris and a bar?
A Nine out of ten men can find a bar.

Q How many men does it take to change a light bulb?
A Four. One to actually change it, and three friends to brag to about how well he screws.

Q How many honest, intelligent, caring men in the world does it take to do the dishes?

A Both of them.

Q Why did the man cross the road?

A He heard the chicken was a slut.

Q Why does it take one million sperm cells to fertilize one egg?

A They won't stop to ask directions.

Q What do men and sperm have in common?

A They both have a one-in-a-million chance of becoming a human being.

Q How does a man show that he is planning for the future?

A He buys two cases of beer.

Q What is the difference between men and government bonds?

A The bonds mature.

Q Why are blond jokes so short?

A So men can remember them.

Q How many men does it take to change a roll of toilet paper?

A We don't know; it has never happened.

Q How did Pinocchio find out he was made of wood?

A His hand caught fire.

Q How do you get a man to do sit-ups?

A Put the remote control between his toes.

Q What is the one thing that all men at singles bars have in common?

A They are married.

Q What do a clitoris, an anniversary, and a toilet have in common?

A Men always miss them.

Q What have men and floor tiles got in common?

A If you lay them properly the first time, you can walk all over them for life.

Q What makes men chase women they have no intention of marrying?

A The same urge that makes dogs chase cars they have no intention of driving.

Q What is the biggest problem for an atheist?

A No one to talk to during orgasm.

Q Who is the most popular guy at the nudist colony?

A The guy who can carry a cup of coffee in each hand and a dozen donuts.

Q Who is the most popular girl at the nudist colony?

A She is the one who can eat the last donut!

Q How do men sort their laundry?

A "Filthy," and "filthy, but wearable."

Q Why do men snore when they lay on their backs?

A Because their testicles fall over their anus and they vapor-lock.

Gays

See "Men" foreword (or backward...) and replace all references to anything female with "anus."

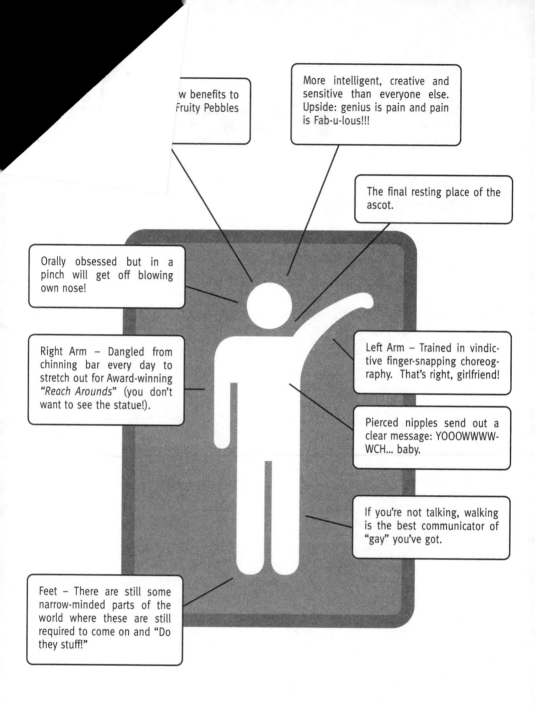

w benefits to Fruity Pebbles

More intelligent, creative and sensitive than everyone else. Upside: genius is pain and pain is Fab-u-lous!!!

The final resting place of the ascot.

Orally obsessed but in a pinch will get off blowing own nose!

Right Arm – Dangled from chinning bar every day to stretch out for Award-winning *"Reach Arounds"* (you don't want to see the statue!).

Left Arm – Trained in vindictive finger-snapping choreography. That's right, girlfriend!

Pierced nipples send out a clear message: YOOOWWWW-WCH... baby.

If you're not talking, walking is the best communicator of "gay" you've got.

Feet – There are still some narrow-minded parts of the world where these are still required to come on and "Do they stuff!"

Common Indicators That You Are

GAY

Two young guys were picked up by the cops for smoking dope and appeared in court before the judge. The judge said, "You seem like nice young men, and I'd like to give you a second chance rather than jail time. I want you to go out this weekend and try to show others the evils of drug use and get them to give up drugs forever. I'll see you back in court Monday."

Monday, the two guys were in court, and the judge said to the first one, "How did you do over the weekend?"

"Well, your honor, I persuaded 17 people to give up drugs forever."

"Seventeen people? That's wonderful. What did you tell them?"

"I used a diagram, your honor. I drew two circles and told them the big circle is your brain before drugs and the small circle is your brain after drugs."

"That's admirable," said the judge. "And you, how did you do?" the judge said to the second boy.

"Well, your honor, I persuaded 156 people to give up drugs forever."

"156 people! That's amazing! How did you manage to do that?"

"Well, I used a similar approach. I also used two circles. I pointed to the small circle and said, "This is your asshole before prison..."

* * *

One day a nun was standing on the side of the road waiting for a cab. A cab stopped and picked her up. During the ride she noticed that the driver was staring at her.

When she asked him why, he said, "I want to ask you something, but I don't want to offend you."

She said, "You can't offend me. I have been a nun long enough that I have heard just about everything."

The cab driver then said, "Well, I've always had a fantasy to have a nun give me a blow job."

She said, "Well, perhaps we can work something out under two conditions. You have to be single, and you have to be Catholic."

Immediately the cab driver said, "Oh, yes! I'm single and I'm Catholic!"

The nun said, "Okay, pull into that alley."

The cab driver pulled into the alley and the nun went to work. Shortly afterwards, the cab driver started crying.

The nun said, "My child, what's the matter?"

He said tearfully, "Sister, I have sinned. I lied, I lied... I'm married and I'm Jewish!"

The nun replied, "That's okay. My name's Bruce and I'm on my way to a costume party!"

* * *

Three gay men died, and were going to be cremated. Their lovers happened to be at the funeral home at the same time, and were discussing what they planned to do with the ashes.

The first man said, "My Ryan loved to fly, so I'm going up in a plane and scatter his ashes in the sky."

The second man said, "My Ross was a good fisherman, so I'm going to scatter his ashes in our favorite lake."

The third man said, "My Jack was such a good lover, I think I'm going to dump his ashes in a pot of chili, so he can tear my ass up just one more time."

* * *

As he drove along the highway, a guy kept seeing billboards with beautiful, tanned people and the words: Visit the Garden of Hedon. His curiosity got the best of him and he turned off the road at the entrance to the place a few miles down the road. He went inside a building marked "Registration" and saw an attractive woman sitting at a desk.

"Exactly what do you do here?" he asked.

"It's quite simple," said the receptionist. "This is a nudist camp. We take off all our clothes and commune with nature."

"Cool," said the guy, "count me in!" So he paid his membership fee, took off his gear and strolled off. As he walked along a path, he saw a big sign which read, "Beware of Gays." A little further along he saw another sign which read the same thing: "Beware of Gays."

He continued walking until he came to a small clearing which had a bronze plaque set in the ground. He bent over to read the plaque and it said, "Sorry, you've had two warnings!"

* * *

Lesbian goes into a brothel and asks for the prettiest, youngest girl available. The owner replies, "Sorry, we don't sell minors to lickers."

* * *

Two gay guys are going at it. After they finish, one turns to the other and says, "Hey, I feel something in my ass... see if you can feel anything."

So his boyfriends puts his finger in his ass and feels around. "I don't feel anything," the boyfriend says.

So the first guy says, "No deeper... I'm sure I feel something."

So the boyfriend put his hand in the guys ass and feels around. "I'm telling you there is nothing there," says the boyfriend.

"No really," the guys says, "I can feel it, look deeper." So the boyfriend puts his whole arm in the guys ass and is feeling around when he touches something.

"Hey, I found something," says the boyfriend.

"Well take it out," says the guy. The boyfriend pulls his hand out of the guys ass, looks at it and see's it is a Rolex. The guy starts singing, "Happy Birthday to you, Happy birthday to you..."

* * *

Three friends, two straight guys and a gay guy, and their significant others were on a cruise. A tidal wave came up and swamped the ship; they all drowned, and next thing you know, they're standing before St. Peter.

First came one of the straight guys and his wife. St. Peter shook his head sadly. "I can't let you in. You loved money too much. You loved it so much, you even married a woman named Penny."

Then came the second straight guy. "Sorry, can't let you in, either. You loved food too much. You loved to eat so much, you even married a woman named Candy."

The gay guy turned to his boyfriend and whispered nervously, "It doesn't look good, Dick."

* * *

In a small cathedral a janitor was cleaning the pews between services when he was approached by the minister. The minister asked the janitor, "Could you go into the confessional and listen to confessions for me? I really have to go to the bathroom and the Widow McGee is coming. She tends to go on but never really does anything worthy of serious repentance, so when she's done just give her ten Hail Mary's and I'll be right back."

Being the helpful sort, the janitor agreed. Just as expected the Widow McGee came into the booth and started her confession. "Oh Father, I fear I have done the unforgivable. I have given into carnal thoughts and have had oral sex."

Stunned, the janitor had no idea how to handle this situation. Surely ten Hail Mary's would not do. So, in a moment of desperation the janitor peered his head out of the confessional and asked an altar boy, "Son, what does the minister give for oral sex?"

In reply the altar boy said, "Two Snickers bars and a Coke."

* * *

A guy decides that maybe he'd like to have a pet and goes to a pet shop.

After looking around he spots a parrot sitting on a little perch. It doesn't have any feet or legs. The guy says out loud, "Geez, I wonder what happened to this parrot?"

"I was born this way," says the parrot. "I'm a defective parrot."

"Ha, ha," the guy laughs. "It sounded like this parrot actually understood what I said and answered me."

"I understand every word," says the parrot. "I am a highly intelligent and thoroughly educated bird."

"Yeah?" the guy asks. "Then answer this: how do you hang onto your perch without any feet?"

"Well," the parrot says, "this is a little embarrassing, but since you asked, I will tell you. I wrap my little parrot penis around this wooden bar, kind of like a little hook. You can't see it because of my feathers."

"Wow," says the guy, "you really can understand and answer, can't you?"

"Of course. I speak both Spanish and English. I can converse with reasonable competence on almost any subject: politics, religion, sports, physics, philosophy. And I am especially good at ornithology. You should buy me; I am a great companion. I should tell you, though, I am gay."

No problem," said the guy, "I am, too."

The guy looks at the $200 price tag. He says. "I can't afford that."

"Pssst," the parrot hisses, motioning the guy over with one wing. "Nobody wants me because I don't have any feet. You can get me for $20. Just make an offer."

The guy offers twenty dollars and walks out with the parrot. Weeks go by and the parrot is sensational. He's funny; he's interesting; he's a great pal, he understands everything, sympathizes, and gives good advice. The guy is delighted.

One day the guy comes home from work and the parrot says, "Pssst," and motions him over with one wing. The guy goes up close to the cage. "I don't know if I should tell you this or not," says the parrot, "but it's about your lover and the mailman."

"What?" asks the guy.

"Well," the parrot says, "when the mailman came to the door today, your lover greeted him in a pair of briefs that showed everything and kissed him on the mouth."

"What happened then?" asks the guy.

"Then the mailman came into the house and put his hand on your lovers crotch and began petting him all over," reports the parrot.

"My God!" the guy says. "Then what?"

"Then he pulled down the briefs, got down on his knees and began to lick him, starting with his chest, slowly going down and down." The parrot pauses for a long time.

"What happened? What happened?" says the frantic guy.

"That's what pisses me off. I don't know." said the parrot. "I got a hard-on, and fell off my fucking perch."

* * *

Construction worker on the fifth floor of a building needed a handsaw. So he spots another worker on the ground floor and yells down to him, but he can't hear him. So the worker on the fifth floor tries sign language. He pointed to his eye meaning "I", pointed to his knee meaning "need", then moved his hand back and forth in a hand saw motion. The man on the ground floor nods his head, pulls down his pants, whips out his schlong and starts masturbating.

The worker on fifth floor gets so pissed off he runs down to the ground floor and says, "What the fuck is your problem!!! I said I needed a hand saw!"

The other guy says, "I knew that! I was just trying to tell you, I'm coming!"

* * *

Three guys go to see a witch doctor about their problems.

One has a smoking problem, one is an alcoholic, and one is gay but wants to change.

The doctor puts a curse on them so that if any of them indulge their habits again they will die.

Two days later the alcoholic dies because he gave in and had to drink.

The next day the gay guy and the smoker are walking down the street together. The smoker sees a cigarette lying on the ground and stops to stare at it.

The gay guy looked at him and said, "If you bend over and pick that up we are both fucked."

* * *

Four gay guys walk into a bar and start arguing over who's penis is longer. Well the bartender finally got sick of hearing them arguing, so told them he had a way to solve this problem.

He told them to stick their penises on the bar and he'd tell them who's was bigger.

Well just as they put them up there, another gay guy walks in and says, "How nice, a buffet!"

* * *

An employee of USAir with the last name of Gay boarded a USAir flight with a free travel voucher. Soon after he sat down, someone else came and claimed he had the same seat assignment, so Mr. Gay moved down to an empty seat. Soon after that the airplane began to fill up. The rule with the USAir employee vouchers is that if a paying customer needs your seat, you have to surrender it. So when the flight became completely full and still more needed to get on, a flight attendant went to the original seat of Mr. Gay and said the man now sitting there, "Excuse me, are you Gay?" The man, somewhat stunned, said, "Well, yes, as a matter of fact I am!" The flight attendant said, "I'm sorry, but you'll have to get off the plane."

At this point Mr. Gay, who had been watching all of this, jumped up and said, "Excuse me, you've made a mistake. I'm Gay!"

Finally, another man jumped up and said, "Well, hell, I'm gay too! They can't throw us all off!"

* * *

A plane's cabin was being served by an obviously gay flight attendant who was just as obviously enjoying himself. He came swishing down the aisle and announced to the passengers, "Captain Marvey has asked me to announce that he'll be landing the big scary plane shortly, lovely people, so if you could just put up your trays that would be fab." On his trip back up the aisle, he noticed that a woman hadn't moved a muscle. "Perhaps you didn't hear me over those big, noisy brute engines. I asked you to raise your tray-z-poo so that El Capitan can put us on the ground."

She calmly turned her head and said, "In my country, I am called a Princess. I take orders from no one."

To which the flight attendant replied, without missing a beat, "Well, sweet-cheeks, in my country, I'm called a queen, so I outrank you. Put the tray up, bitch!"

* * *

Two lesbian frogs just finished having sex with each other when one turned to the other and said, "See? We *do* taste like chicken!"

* * *

Two firefighters are buttfucking in a smoke filled room. The fire chief walks in and says, "What the hell is going on in here?!!"

One of the firefighters says, "Well sir, this man has got smoke inhalation."

The chief says, "Why didn't you give him mouth to mouth?"

The firefighter says, "How do you think this shit got started?"

* * *

A farmer rears 25 young hens and one old cock. As the old cock could no longer handle his job efficiently, the farmer buys one young cock from the market and puts it in the pen with the old cock and the hens.

The old cock says, "Welcome to the farm. We'll work together towards productivity."

The young cock says, "Whattya mean? As far as I know, you are old and should be retired."

The old cock says, "young boy, there are 25 hens here, can't I help you with some?"

The young cock says, "No! Not even one. All of them will be mine."

The old cock asks, " If I challenge you to a competition and, if I win, will you let me have one hen? If I lose you have them all."

The young cock says, "Okay. What kind of competition?"

The old cock suggests, "A 50-yard dash. From here to that tree. But due to my age, I hope you allow me to start off the first 10 yards."

The young cock says, "No problem! We race tomorrow morning."

Confidently, the following morning, the young cock allows the old cock to start off and when the old cock crosses the 10-yard mark, the young cock chases him with all his might. He was right behind the old cock in a matter of seconds and – BANG!

Before he can overtake the old cock, he is shot dead by the farmer, who sighs and says, "Damn. That's the fifth gay rooster I bought this week."

* * *

On the first day of school, a teacher decided to get to know the kids by asking them their names and what their fathers did for a living.

The first little girl said: "My name is Mary and my daddy is a postman."

The next little boy said: "I'm Andy and my dad is a mechanic."

Then another little boy said: "My name is Jimmy and my father is a striptease dancer in a cabaret for gay men."

The teacher gasped and quickly changed the subject, but later in the schoolyard the teacher approached Jimmy privately and asked if it was really true that his dad danced nude in a gay bar.

The kid blushed and said, "I'm sorry, but my dad is an advisor to the president. I was just too embarrassed to say so."

* * *

By the time a Marine pulled into a little town, every hotel room was taken. "You've got to have a room somewhere," he pleaded. "Or just a bed, I don't care where."

"Well, I do have a double room with one occupant... a Navy guy," admitted the manager. "He might be glad to split the cost. But to tell you the truth, he snores so loudly that people in adjoining rooms have complained in the past. I'm not sure it would be worth it to you."

"No problem," the tired Marine assured him. "I'll take it." The next morning the Marine came down to breakfast bright-eyed and bushy-tailed.

"How did you sleep?" asked the manager.

"Never better," replied the Marine.

The manager was impressed. "No problem with the other guy snoring, then?"

"Nope, I shut him up in no time," said the Marine.

"How did you manage that?" asked the manager.

"He was already in bed, snoring away, when I came in the room," the Marine explained. "I went over, gave him a kiss on the cheek and said, 'Goodnight, beautiful,' and he sat up all night watching me."

* * *

Two Marines were sitting around talking one day.

The first Marine asked the second Marine, "If we found out they were gonna drop an a-bomb on us, what would be the first thing you would do?"

The second Marine said, "I would screw the first thing that moved. What would you do?"

The first Marine replied, "Stand very still!"

* * *

A traveling salesman finds himself stranded in the tiniest town in Australia. He knocks on the door of a little hotel. "Sorry, we don't have a spare room," says the manager, "but you are welcome to share with a little red-headed schoolteacher, if that's okay with you."

"Oh, that'll be great," says the salesman, grinning from ear to ear. "And don't worry, I'll be a real gentleman."

"Just as well," says the manager. "So will the little red-headed schoolteacher!"

* * *

When Matthew answered the door late in the evening, one day after he had lost his lover in a scuba diving accident, he was greeted by two grim-faced policemen.

"We're sorry to call on you at this hour, sir, but we have some information about your, um, boyfriend."

"So, tell me." Matthew demanded.

The policeman said, "We have some bad news, some pretty good news, and some really great news. Which do you want to hear first?"

Fearing the worst, Matthew said, "Give me the bad news first."

So the policeman said, "I'm sorry to tell you sir, but we found his body this morning in the San Francisco Bay."

"Oh, my God," said Matthew, overcome by emotion. Then, remembering what the policeman had said, he asked, "What's the good news?"

"Well," said the policeman, "When we pulled him up he had two five-pound lobsters and a dozen good-sized dungeness crabs eating him."

"What? Huh?" Matthew said, not understanding. "So, what's the great news?"

The policeman smiled, licked his chops, and said, "We're going to pull him up again tomorrow morning."

* * *

A few years ago, a man who was openly gay was elected as mayor of Key West, Florida. After the election results were in, a horde of reporters surrounded him and began asking him questions on how he won. A young reporter walked up to him and said, "Mr. Mayor, I understand that you used a basic grass-roots campaign to win, met lots of people, shook lots of hands, kissed lots of babies. I even heard that you kissed a parakeet."

The mayor replied, "That's right, young man. I brought the campaign to the people. But I must correct you on one point, I did not kiss a parakeet. I kissed a cock-or-two."

* * *

Three women at the doctors office. The first one goes in to see the doctor. When the doctor goes to examine her he notices a big "Y" on her chest. The doctor asks, "Why do you have a big "Y" on your chest?"

She replies, "Well, my boyfriend went to Yale and when we make love he likes to wear his college sweater."

The doctor nods and continues on with the next patient. When he examines her he notices a big "H" on her chest. Again, the doctor asks, "How did you get a big "H" on your chest?"

The woman replies, "My husband went to Harvard and when we make love he likes to wear his college sweater."

The doctors just nods his head and continues on with the last patient. As he examines her he notices once again that this woman also has a letter on her chest. A large "M." He says, "Don't tell me, your boyfriend went to Michigan?"

"No," replies the patient. "But my girlfriend went to Wisconsin."

* * *

In a small Midwestern town, two gay guys die in a car accident. The mortician was terribly homophobic and refused to prepare the bodies for burial. So, finally, in desperation, the hospital called on the local taxidermist. He said, "Sure, bring 'em on over, I'll take care of 'em." So an ambulance driver carts the bodies off to the taxidermist's shop. When he arrives, the taxidermist asks the ambulance driver "Do you want them mounted?"

To which the driver replies. "Nah, just holding hands..."

* * *

Frank had just come to terms with his homosexuality and decided to come out of the closet. His plan was to tell his mother first. So on his next home visit, he went into the kitchen where his mother was busying herself stirring her chicken soup. Rather nervously, Frank explained to her that he had realized he was gay.

Without looking up from her stirring, his mother said, "You mean, homosexual?"

"Well, yes." he answers.

Still without looking up she asks, "Does that mean you suck men's penises?" Caught off guard, Frank eventually managed to stammer an embarrassed affirmative, whereupon his mother turned to him and brandishing the wooden spoon threateningly under his nose, snapped, "Don't you ever complain about my cooking again!"

* * *

Bill and his sidekick walk into a bar, not realizing it's a gay bar. They take a table and sit down. Some guy walks over and leans on the table, saying, "Hey, you guys wanna play butt football?" Not really knowing what that is, Bill asks the bartender.

The bartender says, "Oh, you just chug a beer; that's the touchdown; then you pull down your pants and boxers, bend over and moon the room and fart; that's the extra point."

Bill looks at his friend and says, "Why not? Sounds like a whole lot of fun!" Bill's sidekick chugs a beer, pulls down his pants, moons the room, and farts.

Bill chugs his beer, pulls down his pants, bends over and is just about to moon the room when another guy walks up behind him, sticks his dick up Bill's ass, and yells, "Block that kick!"

* * *

A gay man is in a bar, on all fours, trying to pick up some money he dropped.

A big bouncer says, "Hey, you! Move it or I'll give you a foot up the ass!"

The gay man looks around and says, "I think you're bragging, but I'm game if you are."

* * *

A lesbian goes to a gynecologist and the gynecologist says, "I must say, this is the cleanest twat I've seen in ages."

"Thanks," said the lesbian. "I have a girl in twice a week."

* * *

Two gay men were visiting a zoo, when they found themselves at the gorilla cage. The gorilla was sitting there with a huge erection. Unable to contain himself one of the men reaches in to touch it. As soon as his arm goes into the cage, the gorilla grabs him, and pulls him into the cage, slams him to the floor and screws him senseless. A few days later in hospital the boyfriend visits and asks his partner if he is hurt.

His lover responded, "Hurt? Hurt?! You bet I'm hurt. He hasn't phoned, he hasn't written..."

* * *

Two gay guys were talking when one of them happened to mention that he had got circumcised last week.

"Can I see it?" asked his friend. So the guy dropped his pants.

"Ohhhhh!" said the friend, "You look ten years younger!"

* * *

Two condoms walking past a gay bar. One turns to the other and says "Wanna go get shit faced?"

* * *

Two lesbians were out playing golf. They tee off and one drive goes to the right and one drive goes to the left. One of them finds her ball in a patch of buttercups. She grabs a club and takes a mighty swing at the ball. She hits a beautiful second shot, but in the process she hacks the hell out of the buttercups.

Suddenly a woman appears out of nowhere. She blocks her path to her golf bag and looks at her and says, "I'm Mother Nature, and I don't like the way you treated my buttercups. From now on, you won't be able to stand the taste of butter. Each time you eat butter you will become physically ill to the point of total nausea."

The mystery woman then disappears as quickly as she appeared. Shaken, the woman calls out to her partner, "Hey, where's your ball?"

"It's over here in the pussy willows."

She screams back, "Don't hit the ball! Don't hit the ball!"

* * *

One day these three friends went hunting in the forest. As they are walking along they are ambushed by a primitive tribe. They were all taken back to the camp and one by one tied to three separate trees.

Then the "big chief" comes out of his mudhut and stares each guy in the face, he then turns to the tribe and says, "Death or Bongo!"

There is a fierce uproar and the tribe begins to chant, "Bongo, Bongo, Bongo!"

The chief then turns to the men and asks the first one, "Death or Bongo?"

The first man replies "I don't like the sound of death, so it will have to be Bongo"

So ten men come out of the tribe and begin to bugger him up the ass!

The chief then turns to the second man and asks the same question. He replies, slightly hesitantly, "Bongo."

So thirty men come and bugger him up the ass!

The third man, who is now quite distressed decided that he would rather die than be subjected to this horrible ordeal.

So the chief asks him, "Death or Bongo?"

"Death!" he says defiantly.

The chief then smiled and replied, "So be it, death by Bongo!"

* * *

Q & A Roundup
Gays

Q What does one gay guy say to another gay guy going on vacation?
A Can I help you pack your shit?

Q How do you know when you're in a gay church?
A Only half the congregation kneels to pray!

Q What does a gay man call his testicles?
A Mud flaps.

Q What do you call a gay dinosaur?
A Mega-sore-ass.

Q What's the difference between a refrigerator and a gay guy?
A The fridge doesn't fart when you pull the meat out!

Q What do you have if you put 50 government employees
and 50 lesbians in the same room?
A 100 people who don't do dick.

Q Did you hear about the two gay lawyers?
A They wanted to try each other.

Q Did you hear about the lesbian who took Viagra?
A She couldn't get her tongue back in her mouth for a week.

Q How can you tell when your house has been burglarized by gays?
A When you come home, you discover that your jewelry is missing,
and all your furniture has been tastefully rearranged.

Q Did you hear about the three gay guys who attacked a woman?
A Two held her down while the other did her hair.

Q How many gay men does it take to put in a light bulb?
A Only one, but it takes an entire emergency room to remove it!

Part 2

Ethnicities

Jews

The Jew thing is strange. For instance, in spite of my godlessness and the fact that the only Jewish ceremony I ever participated in took a sharp blade to my dick, I am a Jew. It's not a nationality, it's not quite a religion, but it's a little like a club.

Because I am genetically Jewish, there is a base of knowledge I am supposed to possess. The introduction of this cultural data is very crafty; food. Throughout the early Jewish life, we are brought to the homes of our grandparents where flavorless, greasy food is served up with a side of Yiddish and other Jewy stuff. So, by the time we go to, say, a Jewish-leaning day camp. We are equipped to communicate with other little Jewlettes that have been similarly socialized. Through this we gain some kind of pride in our exclusive little "thing."

Not so much pride, however, that if we are mistaken for Italian, we aren't thrilled to death. Italians mistaken for Jews have a very different reaction!

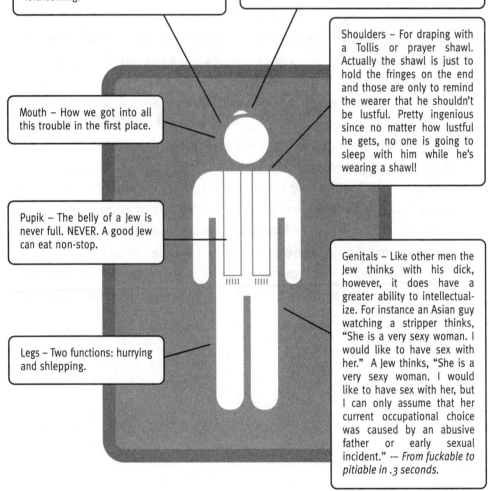

The Jewish nose is legendary. It is celebrated in art, surgery, and the low rent jokes of lederhosen bedecked Bavarians and beer addled incestuous love children alike, and in a couple of the jokes forthcoming.

The beanie thing. There are other hats as well. The guys who wear the big and furry ones are seriously big-time Jews. There are two reasons I can figure for the hats: one, it tells everyone who sees you, Hey, I am way more religious than you, bee-atch, and two, male pattern baldness is very common among Jews. The design of even the smallest yarmulke places it right over the bald spot. Think about it.

Shoulders – For draping with a Tollis or prayer shawl. Actually the shawl is just to hold the fringes on the end and those are only to remind the wearer that he shouldn't be lustful. Pretty ingenious since no matter how lustful he gets, no one is going to sleep with him while he's wearing a shawl!

Mouth – How we got into all this trouble in the first place.

Pupik – The belly of a Jew is never full. NEVER. A good Jew can eat non-stop.

Genitals – Like other men the Jew thinks with his dick, however, it does have a greater ability to intellectualize. For instance an Asian guy watching a stripper thinks, "She is a very sexy woman. I would like to have sex with her." A Jew thinks, "She is a very sexy woman. I would like to have sex with her, but I can only assume that her current occupational choice was caused by an abusive father or early sexual incident." -– *From fuckable to pitiable in .3 seconds.*

Legs – Two functions: hurrying and shlepping.

Common Indicators That You Are A

A Jewish traveler, carrying a huge suitcase, has been riding a New Jersey train for twenty miles along its route, all the while attempting to avoid the ticket collector. Finally, the conductor manages to corner him and tells him to pay up. "You've been on for twenty miles, and that'll be $10 please, and $3 for your suitcase."

The traveler responds, "I have not; I just got on a moment ago." They begin to argue, and the ticket collector become more and more enraged and finally, as the train is passing over a bridge, he grabs the traveler's suitcase, and hurls it out of the train.

It lands in the river and sinks without a trace.

The Jewish traveler stands shocked for a moment and says to the ticket collector, "Not only are you trying to overcharge me for the ticket, but now you've gone and drowned my son."

* * *

God offered his tablet of commandments to the world.

He first approached the Italians. "What commandments do you offer?" they asked.

He answered, "Thou shalt not murder."

They answered, "Sorry, we are not interested."

Next he offered it to the Romanians.

"What commandments do you offer?" they said.

He answered, "Thou shalt not steal."

They answered, "Sorry, we are not interested."

Next he offered them to the French.

"What commandments do you offer?" they asked.

"Thou shalt not covet they neighbors wife."

"Sorry we are not interested," they answered.

Finally he approached the Jews.

"How much is a commandment?" they asked.

"It's free," he answered.

"We'll take ten of them!"

* * *

A Jewish boy asked his father, "Dad, can I have five dollars to buy a guinea pig?"
The father replied, "Here's ten dollars. Go find yourself a nice Irish girl."

* * *

A young Jewish boy starts attending public school in a small town. The teacher of the one-room school decides to use her position to try to influence the new student. She asks the class, "Who was the greatest man that ever lived?"

A girl raises her hand and says, "I think George Washington was the greatest man that ever lived because he is the father of our country."

The teacher replies, "Well... that's a good answer, but that's not the answer I am looking for."

Another young student raises his hand and says, "I think Abraham Lincoln was the greatest man that lived because he freed the slaves and helped end the Civil War."

"Well, that's another good answer, but that is not the one I was looking for."

Then the new Jewish boy raises his hand and says, "I think Jesus Christ was the greatest man that ever lived."

The teacher's mouth drops open in astonishment. "Yes!" she says, "that's the answer I was looking for." She then brings him up to the front of the classroom and gives him a lollipop.

Later, during recess, another Jewish boy approaches him as he is licking his lollipop. He asks, "why did you say, 'Jesus Christ?'"

The boy stops licking his lollipop and replies, "I know it's Moses, and YOU know it's Moses, but business is business."

* * *

The Harvard School of Medicine did a study of why Jewish women like Chinese food so much. The study revealed that this is due to the fact that Wonton spelled backwards is Not Now.

* * *

There's a big controversy on the Jewish view of when life begins. In Jewish tradition, the fetus is not considered viable until after it graduates from medical school.

* * *

When the doctor called Mrs. Liebenbaum to tell her that her check came back, she replied, "So did my arthritis."

* * *

Short summary of every Jewish Holiday: They tried to kill us, we won, let's eat.

* * *

A priest and a rabbi are walking through the park. The priest says, "Look at that ten-year-old boy over there. I'd sure like to screw him."

The rabbi replies, "out of what?"

* * *

Two old Jewish men are strolling down the street one day when they happen to walk by a Catholic church. They see a big sign posted that says, "Convert to Catholicism and get $10.00." One of the Jewish men stops walking and stares at the sign.

His friend turns to him and says, "Murray, what's going on?"

"Abe," replies Murray, "I'm thinking of doing it."

Abe says, "Are you, crazy?"

Murray thinks for a minute and says, "Abe, I'm going to do it."

With that, Murray strides purposefully into the church and comes out twenty minutes later with his head bowed.

"Well?" asks Abe, "did you get your ten dollars?"

Murray looks up at him and says, "Is that all you people ever think about?"

* * *

Three Texans are sitting together on an airplane. Two are hardy, tall men wearing cowboy boots and 10 gallon hats. The third is a little old Jewish man wearing a yalmuke, short pants, and high black socks with sandals.

The first Texan says, "My name is Roger, I have 2,000 acres and 3,000 head of cattle. I call my place "The Jolly Roger."

The second Texan says: "My name is Gene. I own 5,000 acres and 5,000 head. I call my place "Gene's Ranch Estate."

The little old Jewish man says: "I own 200 acres and got no cattle."

"And what do you call your place?" asks Roger sarcastically.

"Downtown Dallas," says the old Jewish man.

* * *

Abe and Golda are on their honeymoon. Golda turns to Abe in bed and says, "Please be gentle, I'm still a virgin."

Shocked, Abe asks, "How can you be a virgin? I'm your fourth husband, you were married three times before!"

Golda responds, "My first husband, Max, was a gynecologist and all he wanted to do was examine it. My second husband, Hymie, was a psychiatrist, and all he wanted to do was talk about it. And my third husband, Izzy, was a stamp collector and all he wanted to do was... Oy! I miss Izzy!"

* * *

Sylvia looks out the picture window and says to Becky, "What a husband you have! He just pulled up and he's carrying a bouquet of roses!"

"Oy!" says Becky. "That means I'll just have to spend the night with my legs in the air!"

"Why," says Sylvia, "don't you have a vase?"

* * *

A woman enters a kosher butcher shop and tells the kid behind the counter, "I would like a Long Island duck!"

The kid runs in the back and brings out a duck. She immediately sticks her index finger up the duck's tuchas, and twirls it. She then looks at the kid and yells, "This is a New Jersey duck. I said a Long Island duck, dummy!" The kid runs in the back and comes out with a second duck. After sticking her finger is the second duck she yells, "This is a Rhode Island duck. I said a Long Island duck. How dumb can you be?"

The kid runs in the back again, and comes out with a third duck and says, "I hope this is what you want lady. It's the last duck we have."

After sticking her finger up the behind of the third duck she says, "Ah! This is a Long Island duck. I'll take it! Wrap it up!"

As the kid is wrapping the duck, she says "You're not too bright, are you! You're new around here. Where are you from, any way?"

The kid bends down with his tuchas toward her and says, "Here lady! You tell me!"

* * *

A totally naked woman jumps into Moish Goldberg's taxi and says, "Take me to Brooklyn."

Moish looks at her and says, "Lady, how are you going to pay for the ride. You're totally naked and don't even have a pocketbook."

The woman points between her legs and says, "How about with this?"

Moish replies, "Got anything smaller?"

* * *

Cohen went into the showroom of his factory one Sunday and found the fashion model taking all the money out of the safe.

"I'm going to send for the police."

"Please, Mr. Cohen don't send for the police."

"You were going to rob me, I must send for the police."

"Mr. Cohen please, I'll do anything but don't send for the police."

"Anything?"

"Yes anything."

"Go down to the basement where there's that bed, take your clothes off, I'll be down after I've locked the safe."

He tried for three quarters of an hour to finish making love to her, but he was an old man and he failed. Wearily he climbed off her.

"It's no good. I'll have to send for the police."

* * *

An old man walks into a church, and goes for confession.

The priest pulls back the window, and the old man says, "Forgive me father, for I have sinned."

The priest says, "Tell me, my son."

The old man explains, "I am 80 years old, and I have recently started a relationship with a woman of 25. She is absolutely gorgeous, and we have been having unbelievable sex three or four times a day, every day, I can almost not catch my breath, it's a mind-blowing experience"

The priest then asks, "How long has this relationship been going on?"

"About two months."

The priest then asks, "When was the first time that you confessed this relationship?"

"Today."

The priest asks, "Why is this the first time?"

The old man explains, "Actually this is my first ever confession. Actually, I'm Jewish."

The priest is exasperated. "In that case, why are you telling me?!"

The old man says, "I'm telling everybody!"

* * *

Monica Lewinsky was walking on the beach when she found a lantern washed up on the shore. She started to rub it and out popped a genie. "Oh goodie, now I will get three wishes!" she exclaimed.

"No," said the genie, "You have been very bad, and because of this, I can only give you one wish."

"Let's see," says Monica, "I don't need fame, because I have plenty of that due to all of the media coverage. And I don't need money, because after I write my book, and do all my interviews, I'll have all the money I could ever want. I would like to get rid of these love handles, though. Yes, that's it, for my one wish I would like my love handles removed."

Poof! And just like that, her ears were gone.

* * *

A policeman stops a Jewish driver. He tells him, "Excuse me Sir, there seems to be a problem."

He replies, "Yes, Officer, how can I help."

The policeman says, "I'm afraid I've got some bad news for you."

The driver replies, "Oh no, please tell me."

The policeman says, "I'm sorry to tell you that your wife fell out of the car about a mile back."

The driver says, "Oh, thank God for that, I thought I'd gone deaf."

* * *

A Jewish family invited their Gentile neighbors for holiday dinner.

The first course was set in front of them and the Jewish couple announced, "This is matzoh ball soup."

On seeing the two large matzoh balls in the soup, the Gentile man was hesitant to taste this strange looking brew. Gently, the Jewish couple pressed the Gentile man. "Just have a taste. If you don't like it, you don't have to finish it."

Finally he agrees. He digs his spoon in, first picking up a small piece of matzoh ball with some soup in the spoon, and tasting it gingerly.

The usual "mmmmmmm" sound can be heard coming from somewhere deep in his chest, and he quickly finished the soup.

"That was delicious," he said. "Can you eat any other parts of the matzoh?"

* * *

The line in front of the butcher shop in Warsaw is long, and the people grow ever more weary, of the wait.

Eventually an official comes out and announces, "We are very low on meat. All Jews must leave the line." So the Jews in the line leave the store and head for home, empty-handed.

After some more of a wait the same official reappears and announces, "We are even lower on meat than we thought. All non-party members must leave the line." So all the non-card-carrying members standing in line begin heading for home, equally empty-handed.

After some more time the official appears to declare, "All Serbs and Croats must leave the line. We haven't got enough meat for you." Disappointed, they leave the line and wander off.

Well, you guessed it: a bit later the same official appears and informs the re-maining people, "Unfortunately we have run out of meat entirely. You may as well all go home," and disappears back into the store.

"Isn't that just the way it always is," mutters one old man as he departs. "Those damn Jews get all the breaks!"

* * *

Mr. Weissenblat, a middle-aged meek Jew, is on a plane for Israel, in a window seat. Just before take-off, this HUGE Arab wearing a beautiful gaudy multi-colored gown walks up and sits down beside him. A few minutes later, the plane takes off.

All is well. For a while. But then, Mr. Weissenblat realizes that he has to go to the bathroom. That wouldn't be a problem, but he looks over and notices that the Arab beside him is sound asleep, and Mr. Weissenblat, being a meek man is afraid to disturb him. So he figures he'll hold it in until the Arab wakes up.

But as luck would have it, the Arab just keeps snoring away, and Mr. Weiseenbalt is feeling increasingly more uncomfortable. After a while, he starts to feel nauseous as well, from holding it in combined with the plane ride.

He tries and tries to hold it in, but then "AAARRGGHH!!" He throws up all over the Arab and his beautiful garment. He thinks, "Oh, no! Now he's gonna kill me!" and sits there in apprehension waiting for the Arab to wake up.

Finally, the Arab wakes up, and finds all this vomit all over him. Thinking quickly, Mr. Weissenblat says to him, "Well, do you feel better now?"

* * *

The Catholic chauffeur was bragging to his friend how well the Jewish family who employed him treated him. "You wouldn't believe it," he said. "I get tips galore, and they always buy me lunch or dinner when I drive. My salary is great, with benefits. I get off all holidays, including the Jewish ones, like Rosh Hashanah."

"That sounds pretty good," said the friend. "But what is Rosh Hashanah?"

"Oh, that's when they blow the shofar," replied the chauffeur.

"Wow!" said the amazed friend. "Those really *are* benefits!"

* * *

A mohel retires after 40 years of service and decides he needs something to remind him of his long career, but what? It soon becomes clear to him what it must be.

So the next day, he goes to a leather factory and takes with him all the skin he has saved over the 40 years. He says to the foreman, "I vant you should make me a memento of my years as a mohel."

The foreman assures him that something can be done and that he should come back next week to pick it up.

When the mohel returns, the foreman presents him with a wallet.

The mohel is shocked and incensed. "I vork for 40 years and all you can make for me is a vallet?"

The foreman replies, "But it is a special kind of wallet. When you rub it, it becomes a suitcase!"

* * *

Goldie was sitting on a beach in Florida, attempting to strike up a conversation with the attractive gentleman reading on the blanket beside hers. "Hello," she said, "do you like movies?"

"Yes, I do," he responded, then returned to his book.

Goldie persisted. "Do you like gardening?"

The man again looked up from his book. "Yes, I do," he said politely, before returning to his reading.

Undaunted, Goldie asked. "Do you like pussycats?"

With that, the man dropped his book and pounced on Goldie, ravaging her as she'd never been ravaged before. As the cloud of sand began to settle, Goldie dragged herself to a sitting position and panted, "How did you know that was what I wanted?"

The man thought for a moment and replied, "How did you know my name was Katz?"

* * *

A rabbi and a priest buy a car together and it's being stored at the priest's house. One day the rabbi goes over to use the car and he sees the priest sprinkling water on it.

The rabbi asked, "What are you doing?"

The priest responded, "I'm blessing the car."

So the rabbi said, "Okay, since we're doing that..." Then he takes out a hacksaw and cuts two inches off the tail pipe.

* * *

A tax official has come to a rural synagogue for an inspection.

The rabbi is accompanying him. "So Rabbi, tell me, please, after you have distributed all your unleavened bread, what do you do with the crumbs?"

"Why, we gather them carefully and send them to the city and then they make bread of them again and send it to us."

"Ah. So what about candles? What do you do with the ends?"

"We send them to the city as well, and they make new candles from them and send them to us."

"And what about circumcision? What do you do with those leftover pieces?"

The rabbi wearily, replies, "We send them to the city as well."

"To the city? And what do they send to you?"

"Today, they have sent you."

* * *

A congregation honors a rabbi for twenty-five years of service by sending him to Oahu for a week, all expenses paid. When he enters his hotel room, there's a nude girl lying on the bed.

He picks up the phone, calls his temple, and says, "Where is your respect? As your rabbi, I am extremely angry with you."

Hearing this, the girl immediately gets up and starts to get dressed.

He says, "Where are you going? I'm not angry at you..."

* * *

A man is standing at the urinal in a public toilet when another man stands in the next urinal.

The man looks over at the new arrival, stares him up and down. "Hey, what the hell are you looking at?" says the second man.

The first man quickly answers, "No, no, it's not what you think. I couldn't help but notice that you've been circumcised."

"Yeah," says the second man, "I'm Jewish, I was circumcised at birth."

"I guessed," says the first, "I know the surgeon who did the procedure."

"Oh come on," says the second man, "it was thirty years ago!"

"It was Dr. Abraham Winklehock. No doubt about it," says the first man.

"You're right," says the second. "How did you know that??" he asked, amazed.

"Bastard never could cut straight," says the first man "You're pissing on my shoes!"

* * *

A young, religious Jewish couple had only recently set up housekeeping when an unfortunate incident occurred. Early one morning, the wife, drowsy from bed, went to the toilet for the morning's relief, and neglected to notice that the seat was up. She was very skinny, and when she sat down, she literally fell in! She was just the right size and shape so that she became jammed into the toilet past her waist with her legs sticking straight up in front of her.

She cried for her husband, who rushed in, and for the next hour tried desperately to extricate her. In this process they removed her night gown, but this only left her naked and still stuck, with a particular part of her anatomy prominently visible between her splayed legs.

Finally, the couple resolved to call a plumber, despite the embarrassing nature of their problem. When the plumber arrived, the young man let him in, but as they were walking to the bathroom, the young man realized that his wife was exposed in a very compromising and humiliating way.

Thinking fast, he ran ahead of the plumber and placed the first thing he could think of, his yarmulka, over his wife's exposed privates.

The plumber walked into the bathroom, took one long look, and commented, "Well, I think I can save your wife, buddy, but the rabbi's a goner."

* * *

"Last week, my wife and I made great amour. I rubbed her body all over with olive oil, we made passionate love, and she screamed for five full minutes at the end," the Italian boasted.

"Last week when my wife and I made love, I rubbed her body all over with butter. We then made passionate love and she screamed for fifteen minutes," the Frenchman man said.

The Jewish man looked at the other two and said, "Well, last week my wife and I also did the do. I rubbed her body all over with schmaltz (chicken fat). We made love, and she screamed for over six hours."

The other two were stunned.

The amazed Frenchman asked, "What could you have possibly done to make your wife scream for six hours?"

The Jewish man said: "I wiped my hands on the bedspread."

* * *

Q & A Round Up
Jews

Q Did you hear about the new brand of tires - Firestein?
A They not only stop on a dime, they pick it up.

Q Why do Jewish divorces cost so much?
A Because they're worth it.

Q Have you seen the newest Jewish-American Princess horror movie?
A It's called "Debbie Does Dishes."

Q Where does a Jewish husband hide money from his wife?
A Under the vacuum cleaner.

Q Why are Jewish men circumcised?
A Because Jewish women won't touch anything unless it is 20% off.

Q What does a Jewish woman do to keep her hands soft and her nails so long and beautiful?
A Nothing, nothing at all.

Q What's a Jewish woman's idea of natural childbirth?
A No make up whatsoever.

Q Why did the Jewish Mother want to be buried near the mall?
A To be sure her daughter would visit her twice a week.

Q What did the Jewish mother say when her daughter told her she was having an affair?
A Who's doing the catering?

Q What is the most common disease transmitted by Jewish Mothers?
A Guilt.

Q What is a genius?
A An average pupil with a Jewish Mother.

Mexicans

Mexicans are some festive f#@kers. They love bright colors, tequila, beans, and whatever that sh*t is, polka? They are also smiley people. I don't just mean the people you see on the streets. Every time I see Mexican gang bangers on TV or in front of the lottery ticket joint, they have a big smile on their faces. It's a smile that says, "I just did some seriously f#@ked up sh*t, ese."

Here in sunny Southern California (I stare out at an absolutely perfect day as I toil in shadows for you unappreciative animals. I damn you all to hell), we frequently interact with our Mexican neighbors. Always present is the maelstrom of family activity that circles around them like a circus on nitrous oxide. Trying to pass them in, say, a supermarket aisle is like a video game. It's as if they and their seventeen or eighteen children are being controlled remotely by a maniac who wishes to keep you and the almond butter from ever meeting.

Having Mexicans or people from points way south working near you for awhile will teach you one thing: they are all a-tonal whistlers. Some can whistle one lonely note and will pace that note through an entire commercial-free radio set of whatever that sh*t is, polka?

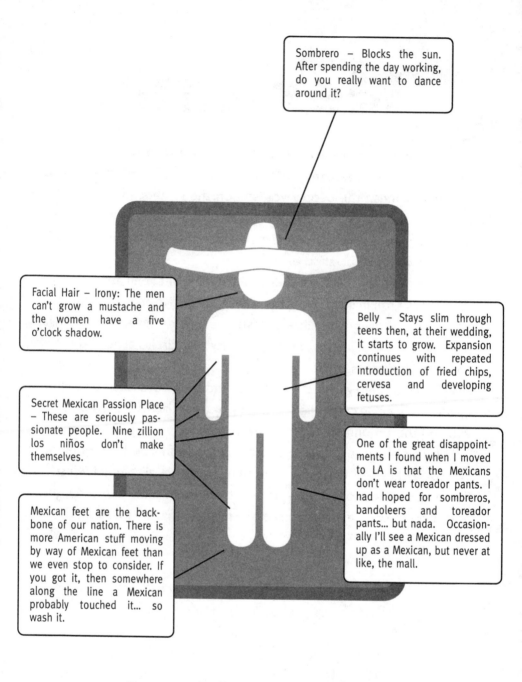

Common Indicators That You Are A

MEXICAN

Juan comes up to the Mexican border on his bicycle. He's got two large bags over his shoulders.

The border guard stops him and says, "What's in the bags?"

"Sand," answered Juan.

The guard says, "We'll just see about that, get off the bike!"

The guard takes the bags and rips them apart; he empties them out and finds nothing in them but sand.

He detains Juan overnight and has the sand analyzed, only to discover that there is nothing but pure sand in the bags.

The guard releases Juan, puts the sand into new bags, hefts them onto the man's shoulders, and lets him cross the border.

A week later, the same thing happens. The guard asks, "What have you got?"

"Sand," says Juan.

The guard does his thorough examination and discovers that the bags contain nothing but sand.

He gives the sand back to Juan, and Juan crosses the border on his bicycle.

This sequence of events is repeated every day for three years.

Finally, Juan doesn't show up one day and the guard meets him in a Cantina in Mexico.

"Hey, Buddy," says the guard, "I know you are smuggling something. It's driving me crazy. It's all I think about... I can't sleep. Just between you and me, what are you smuggling?"

Juan sips his beer and says, "Bicycles."

* * *

A Mexican bandit made a specialty of crossing the Rio Grand from time to time, and robbing banks in Texas. Finally, a reward was offered for his capture, and an enterprising Texas ranger decided to track him down.

After a lengthy search, he traced the bandit to his favorite cantina, snuck up behind him, put his trusty six-shooter to the bandit's head, and said, "You're under arrest. Tell me where you hid the loot or I'll blow your brains out." But the bandit didn't speak English, and the Ranger didn't speak Spanish.

Fortunately, a bilingual lawyer was in the saloon and translated the Ranger's message. The terrified bandit blurted out, in Spanish, that the loot was buried under the oak tree in back of the cantina.

"What did he say?" asked the Ranger.

The lawyer answered, "He said 'Get lost, Gringo. You wouldn't dare shoot me.'"

* * *

When young Jose, newly arrived in the United States, made his first trip to Yankee Stadium, there were no tickets left for sale. Touched by his disappointment, a friendly ticket salesman found him a perch near the American flag.

Later, Jose wrote home enthusiastically about his experience. "And the Americans, they are so friendly!" he concluded. "Before the game started, they all stood up and looked at me and asked, 'Jose, can you see?'"

* * *

The American investment banker was at the pier of a small coastal Mexican village when a small boat with just one fisherman docked. Inside the small boat were several large yellow fin tuna. The American complimented the Mexican on the quality of his fish and asked how long it took to catch them.

The Mexican replied, "Only a little while."

The American asked, "Why didn't you stay out longer and catch more fish?"

The Mexican said, "With this I have more than enough to support my family's needs."

The American then asked, "But what do you do with the rest of your time?"

The Mexican fisherman said, "I sleep late, fish a little, play with my children, take siesta with my wife, stroll into the village each evening where I sip wine and play guitar with my amigos, I have a full and busy life."

The American scoffed, "I am a Harvard MBA and could help you. You should spend more time fishing, and with the proceeds, buy a bigger boat. Then with the proceeds from the bigger boat you could buy several boats. Eventually you would have a fleet of fishing boats. Instead of selling your catch to a middleman you would sell directly to the processor; eventually opening your own cannery. You would control the product, processing and distribution. You would need to leave this small coastal fishing village and move to Mexico City, then Los Angeles and eventually New York where you will run your ever-expanding enterprise."

The Mexican fisherman asked, "But, how long will this all take?"

To which the American replied, "15 to 20 years."

"But what then?" asked the Mexican.

The American laughed and said that's the best part. "When the time is right you would announce an IPO and sell your company stock to the public and become very rich, you would make millions."

"Millions? Then what?"

The American said, "Then you would retire. Move to a small coastal fishing village where you would sleep late, fish a little, play with your kids, take siesta with your wife, stroll to the village in the evenings where you could sip wine and play your guitar with your amigos."

* * *

Two guys are bungee-jumping one day. The first guy says to the second. "You know, we could make a lot of money running our own bungee-jumping service in Mexico." The second guy thinks this is a great idea, so the two pool their money and buy everything they'll need, a tower, an elastic cord, insurance, etc.

They travel to Mexico and begin to set up on the square. As they are constructing the tower, a crowd begins to assemble. Slowly, more and more people gather to watch them at work. The first guy jumps. He bounces at the end of the cord, but when he comes back up, the second guy notices that he has a few cuts and scratches.

Unfortunately, the second guy isn't able catch him, he falls again, bounces and comes back up again. This time, he is bruised and bleeding. Again, the second guy misses him.

The first guy falls again and bounces back up. This time, he comes back pretty messed up, he's got a couple of broken bones and is almost unconscious. Luckily, the second guy finally catches him this time and says, "What happened? Was the cord too long?"

The first guy says, "No, the cord was fine, but what the heck is a piñata?"

* * *

A big Texan cowboy stopped at a local restaurant following a day of drinking and roaming around in Mexico. While sipping his tequila, he noticed a sizzling, scrumptious looking platter being served at the next table.

Not only did it look good, the smell was wonderful.

He asked the waiter, "What is that you just served?"

The waiter replied, "Ah senor, you have excellent taste! Those are bull's testicles from the bull fight this morning. A delicacy!"

The cowboy, though momentarily daunted, said, "What the heck, I'm on vacation down here! Bring me an order!"

The waiter replied, "I am so sorry senor. There is only one serving per day because there is only one bull fight each morning. If you come early tomorrow and place your order, we will be sure to save you this delicacy!"

The next morning, the cowboy returned, placed his order, and then that evening he was served the one and only special delicacy of the day.

After a few bites, and inspecting the contents of his platter, he called to the waiter and said, "These are delicious, but they are much, much smaller than the ones I saw you serve yesterday!"

The waiter shrugged his shoulders and replied, "Si, Senor. Sometimes the bull wins."

* * *

A U.S. Navy cruiser pulled into port in Mississippi for a week's liberty. The first evening, the Captain was more than a little surprised to receive the following letter from the wife of a wealthy plantation owner:

"Dear Captain, Thursday will be my daughter Melinda's, coming of age party. I would like you to send four well-mannered, handsome, unmarried officers. They should arrive at 8 p.m. prepared for an evening of polite southern conversation and dance with lovely young ladies. One last point: No, Mexicans. We don't like Mexicans."

Sure enough, at 8 p.m. on Thursday, the lady heard a rap at the door. She opened the door to find, in dress uniform, four exquisitely-mannered, smiling black officers. Her jaw hit the floor, but pulling herself together she stammered, "There must be some mistake!"

"On no, madam," said the first officer, "Captain Martinez doesn't make mistakes."

* * *

Three men are traveling in the Amazon, a German, an American, and a Mexican, and they get captured by some Amazons. The head of the tribe says to the German, "What do you want on your back for your whipping?"

The German responds, "I will take oil!" So they put oil on his back, and a large Amazon whips him ten times. When he is finished the German has these huge welts on his back, and he can hardly move.

The Amazons haul the German away, and say to the Mexican, "What do you want on your back?"

"I will take nothing!" says the Mexican, and he stands there straight and takes his ten lashings without a single flinch.

"What will you take on your back?" the Amazons ask the American.

He responds, "I'll take the Mexican."

* * *

An Englishman, Frenchman, Mexican, and Texan were flying across country on a small plane when the pilot comes on the loud speaker and says "We're having mechanical problems and the only way we can make it to the next airport is for three of you to open the door and jump, at least one of you can survive."

The four open the door and look out below.

The Englishman takes a deep breath and hollers, "God Save The Queen," and jumps.

The Frenchman gets really inspired and hollers, "Viva La France," and he also jumps.

This really pumps up the Texan so he hollers, "Remember the Alamo," and he grabs the Mexican and throws him out of the plane.

* * *

Q & A Round Up
Mexicans

Q Why doesn't Mexico have an Olympic Team?

A Because everybody who can run, jump, and swim are already in the U.S.

Q Why do black people go to Mexican garage sales?

A So they can get all their shit back.

Q: What do you get when you cross a Mexican and an Iranian?

A Oil of Ole.

Q Why does a Mexican re-fry their beans?

A Have you seen a Mexican do anything right the first time?

Q Why does a Mexican eat tamales for Christmas?

A So they have something to unwrap.

Q What are the first 3 words in the Mexican national anthem?

A "Attention K-Mart shoppers."

Q What are the first three words in every Mexican cookbook?

A "Steal a chicken."

Q Why did God give Mexicans noses?

A So they'll have something to pick in the winter.

Q Why don't Mexicans teach Driver's Education and Sex Education on the same day?

A Because they don't want to wear out the donkey.

Q What do you get when you cross a Mexican and an octopus?

A Got me, but it sure can pick lettuce.

Q What's the difference between a Jewish girl and a Mexican girl?

A The Mexican girl has real orgasms and fake jewelry!

Q When does a Mexican become Spanish??

A When he marries your daughter.

The French

Nobody. Repeat NOBODY in the world gets more sh*t than the French. This comes mainly from their perceived cowardice and lack of appreciation for us saving their asses in WWII. Some also resented them for their choice to not be part of the force in Iraq, but, well, we know how that turned out; over at the Capitol the fries are French again.

I was once visiting a small medieval village near Dijon and found myself drinking a bunch of white wine with a man of about eighty. He was just what you'd picture: old, French, drunk. Though my French seriously blows, enough of their language is sprinkled into our language (including the word "language") for me to pull together what he was saying. Since the village was off the beaten track and didn't cater to tourists, my wife and I were apparently the first Americans to stop in since the liberation. This old man took this rare opportunity to thank America from the bottom of his heart for the Marshall plan! We, as a nation, said, "You're welcome."

France has done and continues to do a ton of sucky things, but what country doesn't? (If you answered Sweden, you've clearly forgotten Abba) So, instead of coughing up some hack graphic of a beret-wearing, baguette-clutching Frenchy, I am going to share some French jokes about Americans. Issues of integrity aside, I think we're much funnier.

French Jokes About America
"The "Cheez-Whiz-eating Lewinsky addicts."

Q How do Republicans reduce unemployment?
A By prosecuting oral sex.

Q How many times did employers fire Saddam Hussein?
A Only once, the CIA paid for the rest of his work.

Q How many Americans does it take to buy a gallon of gas?
A 250,000 to seize it and one to pump it.

Q Why do American wars always come in twos?
A The first one creates terrorists and the second one does too.

Reporter's Question: "What is your opinion of American civilization?"
Frenchman: "I think it would be an excellent idea."

What do you call someone who speaks three languages? ... "Multilingual"
What do you call someone who speaks two languages? ... "Bilingual"
What do you call someone who speaks one language? ... "American"

If an American is interested in the European culture he is considered as an intellectual.
If a European is interested in the American culture he is considered retarded!

America is:
- a country where everyone has time to mow their three-acre lawn each week, but no one has time to cook their own food;
- a country where "evil-doer" and "do-gooder" are both negative characterizations;
- a country whose academic institutions are better known for their athletes than for their scholars;
- a country where it is possible to purchase sugar-frosted honey-coated deep-fat-fried cheese sticks;

Pierre, a brave French fighter pilot, takes his girlfriend, Marie, out for a pleasant little picnic by the River Seine. It's a beautiful day and love is in the air. Marie leans over to Pierre and says, "Pierre, kiss me!" Our hero grabs a bottle of Merlot and splashes it on Marie's lips.

"What are you doing, Pierre?" says the startled Marie.

"I am Pierre, the fighter pilot! When I have red meat, I like to have red wine!" She smiles and they start kissing. When things begin to heat up a little, Marie says, "Pierre, kiss me lower." Our hero tears her blouse open, grabs a bottle of Chardonnay and starts pouring it all over her breasts.

"Pierre! What are you doing?" asks the bewildered Marie.

"I am Pierre the fighter pilot! When I have white meat, I like to have white wine!" They resume their passionate interlude and things really steam up. Marie leans close to his ear and whispers, "Pierre, kiss me lower!" Our hero, grabs a bottle of Cognac and pours it in her lap. He then strikes a match and lights it on fire. Marie shrieks and dives into the river.

Standing waist deep, Marie throws her arms upwards and screams furiously, "Pierre, what in the hell do you think you're doing?"

Our hero stands up, defiantly, and says, "I am Pierre the fighter pilot! When I go down, I go down in flames!"

* * *

A husband and wife are on a nude beach in the south of France when suddenly a wasp buzzes into the wife's business end. Naturally enough, she panics. The husband is also quite shaken but manages to put a coat on her, pull up his shorts and carries her to the car. Then he makes a mad dash to the doctor. The doctor, after examining her, says that the wasp is too far in to remove with forceps. So he says to the husband that he will have to try and entice it out by putting honey on his penis and withdraw as soon as he feels the wasp.

The honey is smeared, but because of his wife's screaming and his frantic dash to the doctor, and the general panic, he just can't rise to the occasion. So the doctor says he'll perform the deed if the husband and wife don't object. Naturally both agree for fear the wasp will do any damage.

The doctor quickly undresses, smears the honey on and instantly gets an erection, at which time he begins to plug the wife. Only he doesn't stop and withdraw but continues with vigor. The husband shouts, "What the hell is happening?"

To which the doctor replies, "Change of zee plans. I'm going to drown the little bastard!"

* * *

A captain in the French Foreign Legion was transferred to a desert outpost. On his orientation tour he noticed a very old, seedy looking camel tied out back of the enlisted men's barracks. He asked the sergeant leading the tour, "What's the camel for?"

The sergeant replied, "Well sir, it's a long way from anywhere, and the men have natural sexual urges, so when they do, we have the camel."

The captain said, "Well, if it's good for morale, then I guess it's all right with me."

After he had been at the fort for about six months, the captain could not stand it anymore, so he told his sergeant, "Bring in the camel!"

The sarge shrugged his shoulders and led the camel into the captain's quarters. The captain got a footstool and proceeded to have vigorous sex with the camel.

As he stepped, satisfied, down from the stool and was buttoning his pants he asked the sergeant, "Is that how the enlisted men do it?"

The sergeant replied, "Well sir, they usually just use it to ride into town."

* * *

A long time ago, Britain and France were at war. During one battle, the French captured an English major. Taking the major to their headquarters, the French general began to question him. The French general asked, "Why do you English officers all wear red coats? Don't you know the red material makes you easier targets for us to shoot at?"

In his bland English way, the major informed the general that the reason English officers wear red coats is so that if they are shot, the blood won't show and the men they are leading won't panic. And that is why from that day to now all French Army officers wear brown pants.

* * *

Two young Frenchmen decided to make a bet as to which one of them could make love more times in one night. They agreed that sunrise would be the end of the contest and each went to their respective motel rooms.

The more boastful of the two went right to it and made love to his date, leaned over and marked a "I" on the wall. Feeling sprightly, he went again and once again at the completion of the act marked another "I" on the wall next to the first. Figuring he had the bet in the bag, he decided to relax a bit and in relaxing... fell asleep.

Awakened by the sun's rays coming in the window, he quickly grabbed his lady and did it one more time and marked another "I" on the wall. Just at that time, his friend enters and upon seeing the marks on the wall exclaims, "Damn! A hundred and eleven! You beat me by three."

* * *

There was once a sheep farmer who had a French farmhand working with him to help castrate his sheep. As the farmer castrated the sheep, the French farmhand took the parts and was about to throw them into the trash.

"No!" yelled the farmer. "Don't throw those away! My wife fries them up and we eat them, they're delicious! They're called sheep fries!"

The farm hand saved the parts and took them to the farmer's wife who cooked them up for supper. This went on for three days, and each evening they had sheep fries for supper.

On the fourth night the farmer came in to the house for supper. He asked his wife where the farm hand was and she replied, "It's the strangest thing! When he came in and asked what was for supper, I told him french fries and he ran like hell!"

* * *

In the middle of an international gynecology conference, an English and a French gynecologist are discussing various cases they have recently treated. The French gynecologist said, "Only last week, zer was a woman ooh came to see me, and 'er cleetoris - eet was like a melon."

The English gynecologist replied, "Don't be absurd. It couldn't have been that big. My goodness, man. She wouldn't have been able to walk if it was."

The French gynecologist said, "Aaah, you eenglish, zare you go again, always talkeeng about ze size. I was talkeeng about ze flavor."

* * *

There was this artist, who worked from a studio in his home in the South of France. He specialized in nudes, and had been working on what he thought would be a masterpiece for several months now. As usual, his model reported, and after exchanging the usual greetings and small talk, she began to undress for the day's work.

He told her not to bother as he felt pretty bad with a cold he had been fighting. He told her that he would pay her for the day, but that she could just go home; he just wanted some hot tea and then, off to bed.

The model said, "Oh, please, let me fix it for you. It's the least I can do." He agreed and told her to fix herself a cup too. They were sitting in the living room just exchanging small talk and enjoying their tea, when he heard the front door open and close, then some familiar footsteps.

"Oh my God!" he whispered loudly, "It's my wife, Quick! Take all your clothes off."

* * *

A thief in Paris planned to steal some paintings from the Louvre. After carefully planning, he got past security, stole the paintings and made it safely to his van. However, he was captured only two blocks away when his van ran out of gas.

When asked how he could mastermind such a crime and then make such an obvious error, he replied, "Monsieur, that's the reason I stole the paintings. I had no Monet to buy Degas to make the Van Gogh."

* * *

An Italian chicken and a French egg are lying in bed. The chicken is smoking a cigarette with a satisfied smile on its face. The egg is frowning and looking very frustrated.

The egg mutters, to no one in particular, "Well, I guess we answered ZAT question!"

* * *

A mother took her six-year-old daughter to the famed Ballet de France. This was the first time the little girl had ever seen a ballet and she watched wide-eyed as the ballerinas pranced around the stage on their toes.

When the ballet was over, the mother asked her daughter if she had any questions.

"Yes, Mommy," the little girl replied, "Wouldn't it be easier if they just hired taller dancers?"

* * *

Q & A Round Up
The French

Q How do you get a French waiter's attention?
A Start ordering in German.

Q What is the difference between a French woman and a basketball team?
A The basketball team showers after four periods.

Q Where's the best place to hide your money?
A Under the soap of a Frenchman

Q Why do the French cook with lots of garlic?
A To improve their breath.

Q How many Frenchmen does it take to screw in a light bulb?
A All of them: One to screw the bulb in, the rest to brag about how great the French are at screwing.

Q How many Frenchmen does it take to screw in a light bulb?
A It doesn't matter; if you're depending on the French to do the job, it's screwed anyway.

Q Why is there a dead fish on the altar at a French wedding?
A To keep the flies off the bride.

Q How do you break a Frenchman's finger?
A Hit him on the nose.

Q Why do Frenchmen wear berets?
A So they know which end to wipe.

Q Did you hear about England's new zoo?
A They put a fence around France.

Q How many jokes are there about the French?
A One, the rest are true.

Irish

What is it with the Irish and jokes? There aren't but a few dozen of them in a country the size of a Costco, but they seem to generate more jokes than anybody! "Jokes, Jokes, Jokes III" could easily be a collection of just Irish jokes.

But, go around asking for Mexican jokes and you get twelve... the same twelve over and over. How are the Mexicans not better fodder for jokes than the Irish? Who do I talk to about this?

What I think it must be is the Irish character as we understand it. They have the capacity to be at once heroically selfless, ready to help anyone passionately with little or no encouragement, yet at the same time looking as desperately in need as the lowliest cast beggar in India. They can appear to be decidedly well turned-out in even the most hastily laundered of outfits. They can be greeted by the Pope in an attempt to save the world, yet still smoke and drink and tour with their rock super-group. Of course this assumes that all Irish people are Bono, but I think that's fair.

Though the derby only appears on St. Patrick's Day and New Years Eve, the Irish have a tradition of wearing hats that began about three weeks after their tradition not to wash their hair.

Jackets too, have long adorned the Irish. It was the advent of the inner pocket that so impressed these warmly humorous, flask sharing alcoholics. It has been said, "An Irishman wit out a nip to offer has not the worth of a School marm's turd." Okay, it was said by me, but I stand by it.

Pants – When the Irish get drunk, these are the first things to go. Irish women or "lassies," wear dresses specifically because they can be hiked up to offer access to their unmentionables but they don't keep leaving them behind when they stagger home.

Feet – Once you have smelled the breath of an Irishman, you understand terror. Now, consider this; the smells grow increasingly worse as you head south. In the mid-to late 18th century, ships sailing for the new world would always try to have at least one Irish crewman aboard to keep the gulls from following the ship. Those sharing a cabin with an Irishman considered a fart to be an air freshener and a properly gassy Belgian could do quite well for himself flatulating in the rooms of the less well equipped.

Legs – These are the first line of Irish defense; if they can't kick you in the balls, they will run away. This is not to say that Ireland hasn't provided the world with their share of great boxers, "Gentleman" Jim Corbett, Jerry Cooney, but if 'running while drunk' were an Olympic event, you'd see an Irishman struggling to keep his balance on that top platform step every time.

Common Indicators That You Are A

IRISHMAN

Pat was found dead in his back yard, and as the weather was a bit on the warm side, the wake was held down to only two days, so his mortal remains wouldn't take a bad turn. At last his friends laid him in the box, nailed it shut and started down the hill into the churchyard. As it was a long, sloping path and the mourners were appropriately tipsy, one fellow lurched into the gatepost as they entered the graveyard. Suddenly a loud knocking came from in the box. Paddy was alive!

They opened the box up and he sat up, wide eyed, and they all said, "Sure, it's a miracle of God!" All rejoiced and they went back and had a few more drinks but later that day, the poor lad died. Really died. Stone cold dead.

They bundled him back into his box, and as they huffed and puffed down the hill the next morning, the priest said, "Careful now, boys; mind ye don't bump the gatepost again."

* * *

An Irish priest and a rabbi get into a car accident. They both get out of their cars and stumble over to the side of the road.

The rabbi says, "Oy vey! What a wreck!"

The priest asks him, "Are you all right, Rabbi?"

The rabbi responds, "Just a little shaken."

The priest pulls a flask of whiskey from his coat and says, "Here, drink some of this it will calm your nerves."

The rabbi takes the flask and drinks it down and says, "Well, what are we going to tell the police?"

"Well," the priest says, "I don't know what your aft' to be tellin' them. But I'll be tellin' them to give you a breathalyzer!"

* * *

McAteer arrived at JFK Airport and wandered about the terminal with tears streaming down his cheeks. An airline employee asked him if he was already homesick. "No," replied McAteer. "I've lost all me luggage!"

"How did that happen?"

"The cork fell out," said the Irishman.

* * *

One day an Englishman, a Scotsman, and an Irishman walked into a pub together. They each bought a pint of Guinness. Just as they were about to enjoy their creamy beverage, three flies landed in each of their pints, and were stuck in the thick head. The Englishman pushed his beer away in disgust. The Scotsman fished the fly out of his beer, and continued drinking it, as if nothing had happened. The Irishman, too, picked the fly out of his drink, held it out over the beer, and started yelling, "SPIT IT OUT!"

* * *

A woman followed her husband to the public house. "How can you come to this hole," she said, taking a sip of his pint of Guinness, "and drink that garbage?"

"Now!" he cried, "and you always said I was out enjoying meself."

* * *

Irishman trying to learn golf and having a terrible time of it. "I'd give just about anything to get this right!" he says aloud.

Straight on the devil appears and says, "Anything?"

"Well, short of selling my soul, yes."

"How about giving up sex for the rest of your life?"

"Done and done!" He finishes the game in rare good form and rumor of his deal spreads through the clubhouse.

One of the members, a reporter, sees a story here and asks him, "Sir, is it true you made a deal with the devil to become a great golfer?"

"True, enough."

"And you gave up sex as your part of the bargain?"

"True again!"

"And may I have your name, sir?"

"Father Mike O'Ryan."

* * *

Two drunks coming home, stumbled up the country road in the dark.

"Faith, Mike, we've stumbled into the graveyard and here's the stone of a man lived to the age of 103!"

"Glory be, Patrick and was it anybody we knew?"

"No, 'twas someone named, 'Miles from Dublin!'"

* * *

An American walks into an Irish pub and says, "I'll give anyone $100 if they can drink 10 Guinnesses in 10 minutes."

Most people just ignore the absurd bet and go back to their conversations. One guy even leaves the bar. A little while later that guy comes back and asks the American, "Is that bet still on?"

"Sure."

So the bartender lines 10 Guinnesses up on the bar the Irishman drinks them all in less than 10 minutes. As the American hands over the money he asks, "Where did you go when you just left?"

The Irishman answers, "I went next door to the other pub to see if I could do it."

* * *

After the Great Britain Beer Festival in London, all the brewery presidents decided to go out for a beer. The guy from Corona sits down and says, "Hey Senor, I would like the world's best beer, a Corona." The bartender dusts off a bottle from the shelf and gives it to him.

The guy from Budweiser says, "I'd like the best beer in the world, give me 'The King Of Beers.' a Budweiser." The bartender gives him one.

The guy from Coors says, "I'd like the only beer made with Rocky Mountain spring water, give me a Coors." He gets it.

The guy from Guinness sits down and says, "Give me a Coke." The bartender is a little taken aback, but gives him what he ordered.

The other brewery presidents look over at him and ask "Why aren't you drinking a Guinness?"

The Guinness president replies, "Well, I figured if you guys aren't drinking beer, neither would I."

* * *

A couple of Irish drinkin' buddies, who are airplane mechanics, are in the hangar at Logan; it's fogged in and they have nothing to do.

One of them says to the other, "Man, have you got anything to drink?"

The other one says, "Nah, but I hear you can drink jet fuel, and that it will kinda give you a buzz."

So they drink it, get smashed and have a great time; like only drinkin' buddies can do.

The following morning, one of them gets up and is surprised he feels good, in fact, he feels great, no hangover! The phone rings, it's his buddy.

The buddy says, "Hey, how do you feel?"

He said, "I feel great!"

And the buddy says, "I feel great too! You don't have a hangover?"

He says, "No, that jet fuel is great stuff, no hangover, we ought to do this more often."

"Yeah, we could, but there's just one thing..."

"What's that?"

"Did you fart yet?"

"No."

"Well, don't, 'cause I'm in Phoenix!"

* * *

Paddy and his two friends are talking at work. His first friend says, "I think my wife is having an affair with the electrician. The other day I came home and found wire cutters under our bed and they weren't mine."

His second friend says, "I think my wife is having an affair with the plumber the other day I found a wrench under the bed and it wasn't mine."

Paddy says, "I think my wife is having an affair with a horse."

Both his friends look at him with utter disbelief.

"No, I'm serious. The other day I came home and found a jockey under our bed."

* * *

An Irishman goes for a job on a building site. The foreman says, "Can you brew tea?"

The Irishman says, "Yes."

"Good. Can you drive a fork lift?"

The Irishman looks at him and says, "My God, how big is the teapot?"

* * *

O'Connell was staggering home with a pint of booze in his back pocket when he slipped and fell heavily. Struggling to his feet, he felt something wet running down his leg.

"Please, God," he implored, "let it be blood!"

* * *

The Irish girl knelt in the confessional and said, "Bless me, Father, for I have sinned."

"What is it, child?"

The girl said, "Father, I have committed the sin of vanity. Twice a day I gaze at myself in the mirror and tell myself how beautiful I am."

The priest turned, took a good look at the girl, and said, "My dear, I have good news. That isn't a sin, it's a mistake!"

* * *

Three Englishmen were in a bar and spotted an Irishman. So, one of the Englishmen walked over to the Irishman, tapped him on the shoulder, and said, "Hey, I hear your St. Patrick was a drunken loser."

"Oh really? Hmm, didn't know that."

Puzzled, the Englishman walked back to his buddies. "I told him St. Patrick was a loser, and he didn't care."

The second Englishman remarked, "You just don't know how to set him off... watch and learn." So, the second Englishman walked over to the Irishman, tapped him on the shoulder and said, "Hey, I hear your St. Patrick was lying, cheating, idiotic, low-life scum!"

"Oh really? Hmm, didn't know that."

Shocked beyond belief, the Englishman went back to his buddies. "You're right. He's unshakable!"

The third Englishman remarked, "Boys, I'll really tick him off... just watch." So the third Englishman walked over to the Irishman, tapped him on the shoulder and said, "I hear St. Patrick was an Englishman!"

"Yeah, that's what your buddies were trying to tell me."

* * *

An Irish girl went to London to work as a secretary and began sending home money and gifts to her parents.

After a few years, they asked her to come home for a visit as her father was getting frail and elderly. She pulled up to the family home in a Rolls Royce and stepped out wearing furs and diamonds.

As she walked into the house, her father said, "Hmmm, they seem to be paying secretaries awfully well in London."

The girl took his hands and said, "Dad, I've been meaning to tell you something for years, but I didn't want to put it in a letter. I can't hide it from you any longer. I've become a prostitute."

Her father gasped, put his hand on his heart and keeled over. The doctor was called, but the old man had clearly lost the will to live. He was put to bed and the priest was called.

As the priest began to administer Extreme Unction, with the mother and daughter weeping and wailing, the old man muttered weakly, "I'm a goner, killed by me own daughter! Killed by the shame of what you've become!"

"Please forgive me," his daughter sobbed, "I only wanted to have nice things! I wanted to be able to send you money and the only way I could do it was by becoming a prostitute."

Brushing the priest aside, the old man bolted upright in bed, smiling. "Did ye say prostitute? I thought ye said PROTESTANT!!"

* * *

Mrs. O'Donovan was walking down a street in Dublin and coming in the opposite direction was Father O'Reilly.

"Hello," the father said, "and how is Mrs. O'Donovan? Did I not marry you a couple of years ago?"

"That you did, Father," she replied.

"And are there any little ones yet?" he asked.

"No, Father, not as yet," she replied.

"Well, I'm off to Rome next week and I'll light a candle for you," said Father O'Reilly.

"Thank you, Father," she replied and continued on her way.

A few years later they met again. "Well now, Mrs. O'Donovan," the Father said, "how are you?" And tell me, have you any little ones yet?"

"Oh yes, Father," she replied. I've had three sets of twins and four singles, ten in all."

"Now isn't that wonderful," he replied. "And how is that lovely husband of yours?"

"He's well, Father. He's gone off to Rome for a wee spell," she said.

"And what would he be doing in Rome?" asked the Father.

"Blowing out that fucking candle!" she answered.

* * *

A man walks into an Irish pub one night. He goes up to the bar and asks for a beer.

"Certainly sir, that'll be one cent."

"ONE CENT!" exclaimed the guy.

The barman replied, "Yes."

So the guy glances over at the menu and he asks, "Could I have a nice juicy T-bone steak, with chips, peas and a fried egg?"

"Certainly sir," replies the bartender, "but all that comes to real money."

"How much money?" inquires the guy.

"Four cents," he replies.

"Four cents!" exclaims the guy. Where's the guy who owns this place?"

The barman replies, "Upstairs with my wife."

The guy says, "What's he doing with your wife?"

The bartender replies, "Same as I'm doing to his business."

* * *

Q & A Round Up
Irish

Q What are the best ten years of an Irishman's life?
A Third grade.

Q How do you sink an Irish submarine?
A Knock on the hatch.

Q Did you hear about the Irishman who was tap dancing?
A He broke his ankle when he fell into the sink.

Q How can you tell the Irish guy in the hospital ward?
A He's the one blowing the foam off of his bed pan.

Q How can you identify an Irish pirate?
A He's the one with patches over both eyes.

Q Have you heard about the Irish boomerang?
A It doesn't come back, it just sings songs about how much it wants to.

Q What is Irish diplomacy?
A It's the ability to tell a man to go to hell so that he will look forward to making the trip!

Q How do we know that Christ was Irish?
A Because he was 33 still lived at home, thought his mother was a virgin, and she thought he was the son of God.

Q Why did God invent whiskey?
A So the Irish would never rule the world.

Scottish

Have you seen the movie Braveheart? Well then we're even on Scottish knowledge. There are a couple of things everyone knows. They're cheap, they wear skirts and they like to grip the bag and blow the pipe.

Now, on to haggis. We've all heard a lot about it, but few of us really know what goes into making its horrific-ness legendary. So, instead of our usual human graphic, I give you the recipe for traditional Beef Haggis...

Beef Haggis

1 lb beef heart
1 lb boneless beef brisket
1 lb boneless lamb shoulder
1/4 c onions (dried) or 1 large, chopped
water or beef stock, as required
1 lb beef liver
3 cups pinhead oatmeal or rolled oats
1 cup beef suet
2 tbs. salt
1 tbs. black pepper
pinch cayenne pepper
cow's bladder or sheep's stomach

Chop coarsely heart, brisket, lamb and onion. Put in large saucepan, cover with water/stock. Bring to a boil and simmer 30 minutes. Add coarsely chopped liver and simmer a further 30 minutes. Pour off cooking liquid and reserve. Chop cooked meat finely and in a bowl mix in, one at a time, oatmeal, suet, salt, pepper and cayenne.

Pour in reserved liquid until firm and moist. Spoon mixture into bladder and secure ends with string. Place in top half of a steamer and steam over simmering water for 1 1/2 hours.

Eat. Wait five seconds. Vomit.

In Scotland, the most important time for a young lad is when he "comes of age" and is permitted to purchase and wear his first kilt.

A couple of weeks before his important birthday, a young lad went to a tailor shop and found the material he wanted for his first kilt. He took the material to the tailor and said, "I'd like ye to make me a kilt with this material here and, if ye don't mind, I'd like ye to make me a pair of matching underwear for it. I hear it gets a might drafty up dem tings!"

So, the tailor took the material and promised to call the young lad when the order was completed.

A few days later, the tailor called the lad back to the shop. "Here's ye kilt, and here's ye matching underwear, and here's five yards of the material left over. Ye might want to take it home and keep it in case ye want anything else made of it."

So, the lad rushed home with his order, threw the material in his room, and donned his kilt. In his excitement, he decided to run to his girlfriend's house to show off his new purchase. Unfortunately, in his excitement, he forgot to don his underwear. When his girlfriend answered the door, he pointed to his kilt and said, "Well, what'd ye think?"

"Ah, but dat's a fine looking kilt," she exclaimed.

"Aye, and if ye like it, ye'll really like what's underneath," he stated as he lifted his kilt to show her.

"Oh, but dat's a dandy," his girlfriend shouted admiringly.

Still not realizing that he didn't have his underwear on, he exclaimed quite proudly, "Aye, and if ye like it, I've got five more yards of it at home!"

***

An American, a Scot and a Canadian were in a terrible car accident. They were all headed to the same emergency room, but all three of them died before they arrived. Just as they were about to put the toe tag on the American, he stirred and opened his eyes.

Astonished, the doctors and nurses present asked him what happened.

"Well," said the American, "I remember the crash, and then there was a beautiful light, and then the Canadian and the Scot and I were standing at the gates of heaven. St. Peter approached us and said that we were all too young to die, and said that for a donation of $50, we could return to earth. So of course I pulled out my wallet and gave him the $50, and the next thing I knew I was back here."

"That's amazing!" said the one of the doctors, "But what happened to the other two?"

"Last I saw them," replied the American, "the Scot was haggling over the price and the Canadian was waiting for the government to pay his."

***

A Scottish private walked into the pharmacy near his base, pulled a beat-up, mutilated condom out of his pocket, and asked the pharmacist how much it would cost to repair the condom. The pharmacist replied that including replacing the band and spot welding the holes, it would cost 26 pence, but that for 29 pence, he could sell the private a new one.

The private said, "Aye, that is a weighty decision, I shall be back in two hours with an answer."

Two hours later, The Scotsman returns and said, "The regiment has voted to replace."

* * *

Mrs. Pete MacDonald came into the newsroom to pay for her husband's obituary. She was told by the kindly newsman that it was a dollar a word and he remembered Pete and wasn't it too bad about him passing away. She thanked him for his kind words and bemoaned the fact that she only had two dollars. But she wrote out the obituary, "Pete died."

The newsman said he thought old Pete deserved more and he'd give her three more words at no charge.

Mrs. Pete MacDonald thanked him and rewrote the obituary: "Pete died. Boat for sale."

* * *

There was an Scotsman, an Englishman and Kate Beckinsale sitting together in a carriage in a train going through Tasmania. Suddenly the train went through a tunnel and as it was an old style train, there were no lights in the carriages and it went completely dark. Then there was this kissing noise and the sound of a really loud slap.

When the train came out of the tunnel, Kate Beckinsale and the Scotsman were sitting as if nothing had happened and the Englishman had his hand against his face as if he had been slapped. The Englishman thought, "The Scottish fella must have kissed Kate Beckinsale and she missed him and slapped me instead."

Kate Beckinsale thought, "The English fella must have tried to kiss me and actually kissed the Scotsman and got slapped for it."

And the Scotsman thought, "This is great. The next time the train goes through a tunnel I'll make that kissing noise and slap that English bastard again."

* * *

Five Englishmen boarded a train just behind five Scots, who, as a group had only purchased one ticket. Just before the conductor came through, all the Scots piled into the toilet stall at the back of the car. As the conductor passed the stall, he knocked and called out "Tickets, please!" one of the Scots slid a ticket under the door. It was punched, pushed back under the door, and when it was safe all the Scots came out and took their seats.

The Englishmen were tremendously impressed by the Scots' ingenuity. On the trip back, the five Englishmen decided to try this themselves and purchased only one ticket. They noticed that, oddly, the Scots had not purchased any tickets this time.

Anyway, again, just before the conductor came through, the Scots piled into one of the toilet stalls, the Englishmen into the other. Then one of the Scots leaned out, knocked on the Englishmen's stall and called, "Ticket, Please!" When the ticket slid out under the door, he picked it up and quickly closed the door.

* * *

A Scotsman is strolling down the street in Moscow and kicks a bottle laying in the street. Suddenly out of the bottle comes a genie.

The Scotsman is stunned and the genie says, "Hello Master, I will grant you one wish, anything that you want."

The Scotsman begins thinking, "Well I really like drinking scotch." Finally the Scotsman says, "I wish to drink scotch whenever I want, so make me piss scotch."

The genie grants him his wish. When the Scotsman gets home he gets a glass out of the cupboard and pisses into it. He looks at the glass and it's golden brown. Looks like scotch. Then he smells the liquid. Smells like scotch. So he takes a taste and it is the best scotch that he has ever tasted.

The Scotsman yells to his wife, "Agnes, Agnes, come quickly."

She comes running down the hall and the Scotsman takes another glass out of the cupboard and pisses into it. He tells her to drink, that it's scotch. Agnes is reluctant but goes ahead and takes a sip. It is the best scotch that she has ever tasted. The two drink and party all night.

The next night the Scotsman comes home from work and tells his wife to get two glasses out of the cupboard. He proceeds to piss in the two glasses. The result is the same, the scotch is excellent and the couple drink until the sun comes up.

Finally, Friday night comes and the Scotsman tells his wife to grab one glass from the cupboard and we will drink scotch.

She gets the glass but asks him "Angus, why do we only need one glass?"

Angus raises the glass and says, "Because tonight my love, you drink from the bottle."

* * *

Callum decided to call his father-in-law the "Exorcist" because every time he came to visit he made the spirits disappear.

* * *

A Scotsman and a Englishman are strolling along the beach when they find a lamp. They clean it up and out pops a genie. "I'll give you each one wish for freeing me" says the genie.

The Englishman thinks then wishes. "I believe in an England for the English, I'm sick and tired of all these Scots coming into my country. I wish for a huge wall around England to keep the English in and the Scots out," POOF and it's done.

The Scotsman thinks. "Genie?" he says, "Tell me about this wall."

"Well," says the genie, "it's 500 feet high, a third of a mile thick, nothing can get in and nothing can get out,"

"Okay," says the Scotsman "Fill it with water."

* * *

A Scottish newspaper ad : "Lost - a £5 note. Sentimental value."

* * *

It was about a month ago when a Scotsman felt that he needed to confess, so he went to his priest.

"Forgive me Father, for I have sinned. During World War II, I hid a Jewish man in my attic."

"Well," answered the priest, "That's not a sin."

"But I made him pay me 20 quid for each week he stayed."

"I admit that wasn't good, but you did it for a good cause."

"Oh thank you Father; that eases my mind. Father, I have one more question."

"What is it son?"

"Do I now have to tell him the war is over?"

* * *

A Scotsman took a girl for a ride in a taxi. She was so beautiful he could hardly keep his eye on the meter.

* * *

A Scotsman left on a long trip across the country, taking a train the entire length of the line. At each station along the way, he insisted that he had to get off of the train to buy a new ticket. He chose to not buy a ticket to his final destination, but just one to take him to the next stop on the line.

After watching this go on for several hours, another passenger asked, "Why are you buying all of these individual tickets, man? Why not just save yourself time and money and just get one ticket for the rest of your trip? You'd save 25 percent."

The Scotsman scowled at the very idea, and darkly replied, "My doctor told me that I am not long for this world. I don't plan to waste any of my money on train tickets I may not use while I am here!"

* * *

In the beginning, God is telling all his angels about his plans for Scotland.

"It will be beautiful," He said. "There will be deep forests full of deer, rivers and lochs full of salmon, and magnificent coastline. The people will be handsome, intelligent and hardworking. They will even invent whiskey."

"Aren't you being a bit generous with these Scots?" asks one of the angels.

"Not really," says God. "I haven't told you yet who they'll have for neighbors."

* * *

A Scottish guy walks into a bar. The bartender says to the guy: "Mate, you've got a steering wheel down your pants."

The guy replies "Yeah I know. Its driving me nuts!"

* * *

Angus came by to see his friend Donald to find he was stripping the wallpaper from the walls. Rather obviously, he remarked "You're decorating, I see."

To which Donald replied, "Naw. I'm moving."

* * *

One day MacNaughton bought a bottle of fine scotch whiskey and while walking home he fell. Getting up he felt something wet on his pants.

He looked up at the sky and said, "Oh Lord! Please I beg you. Let it be blood!"

* * *

A Scotsmen and a Jewish man were having a magnificent meal at one of the finest restaurants in New York. At the end of the evening the waiter came over to present the check and a Scottish voice said, "That's all right laddie just gae the check to me."

The headlines in the local newspaper next day proclaimed "Jewish ventriloquist found beaten to death."

* * *

Seems that a clan chief's daughter was offered as a bride to the son of a neighboring chief in exchange for two cows and four sheep. The big swap was to happen on the shore of the stream that separated the two clans. Father and daughter showed up at the appointed time only to discover that the groom and his livestock were on the other side of the stream.

The father grunted, "The fool doesn't know which side his bride is bartered on."

* * *

A young Scottish lad and lass were sitting on a low stone wall, holding hands, gazing out over the loch. For several minutes they sat silently.

Then finally the girl looked at the boy and said, "A penny for your thoughts, Angus."

"Well, uh, I was thinkin'... perhaps it's aboot time for a wee kiss."

The girl blushed, then leaned over and kissed him lightly on the cheek.

Then he blushed. The two turned once again to gaze out over the loch.

Minutes passed and the girl spoke again. "Another penny for your thoughts, Angus."

"Well, uh, I was thinkin' perhaps it's noo time aboot time for a wee cuddle."

The girl blushed, then leaned over and cuddled him for a few seconds.

Then he blushed. Then the two turned once again to gaze out over the loch.

After a while, she again said, "Another penny for your thoughts, Angus."

"Well, uh, I was thinkin' perhaps it's aboot time you let me put my hand on your leg."

The girl blushed, then took his hand and put it on her knee. Then he blushed. The two turned once again to gaze out over the lock before the girl spoke again.

"Another penny for your thoughts, Angus."

The young man glanced down with a furled brow. "Well, noo," he said, "my thoughts are a wee bit more serious this time."

"Really?" said the lass in a whisper, filled with anticipation.

"Aye," said the lad, nodding.

The girl looked away in shyness, began to blush, and bit her lip in anticipation of the ultimate request.

Then he said, "Dae ye nae think it's aboot time ye paid me the first three pennies?"

* * *

An irate golfer, on his way to a round of 150 said, "You must be the worst caddie in the world!"

The Scottish caddie dryly said, "That would be too much of a coincidence, sir."

* * *

A student at an English university by name of Donald MacDonald from the Isle of Skye was living in the hall of residence in his first year there. After he had been there for a month, his mother came to visit, no doubt carrying reinforcements of oatmeal.

"And how do you find the English students, Donald?" she asked.

"Mother," he replied, "they're such terrible noisy people! The one on that side keeps banging his head against the wall, and won't stop. The one on the other side screams and screams and screams away into the night!"

"Oh, Donald! How ever do you manage to put up with these awful noisy English neighbors?"

"Mother, I do nothing, I just ignore them! I just keep to myself and practice my bagpipes!"

* * *

Sandy said, "Please whisper those three little words that will make me walk on air."

The girl said, "Go hang yourself!"

* * *

A fierce Highlander is drinking in a Glasgow pub. He consumes about ten pints, but just as he starts on his eleventh, he feels the call of nature.

Dubious about the character of the Glaswegian, he gets a post-it note and scribbles on it "This pint belongs to the Inverness Heavyweight Boxing Champion" and sticks it to the glass.

On his return he sees another note stuck over his, which reads "This pint is now inside the Glasgow Half Mile Sprint Champion!"

* * *

A bunch of Highland women are making their way back to their village when they are aghast to see just outside it a cart that has fallen on top of a kilted man, right across his stomach, so that only his legs are visible.

"I'll go get help," says Morag, "the rest of you try and lift that cart off him."

The three remaining women try but the damned thing is just too heavy.

"Here," says the first one, "I hope that isn't my man!" she lifts his kilt and peers, "No, that's definitely not my man."

The second woman lifts his kilt, and with no little relief says, "And I'm certain, thank the Lord, that he isnae my man either."

The third woman lifts the man's kilt and looks. With profound certainty she says,

"Hey lassies, he's not even from oor village!"

* * *

Q & A Round Up
Special Bagpipe Edition!

Q   What's one thing you never hear people say?

A   Oh, that's the bagpipe player's Porsche.

Q   How do you get two bagpipes to play in perfect unison?

A   Shoot one.

Q   Why do bagpipers leave their cases on their dashboards?

A   So they can park in handicapped zones.

Q   How can you tell a bagpiper with perfect pitch?

A   He can throw a set into the middle of a pond and not hit any of the ducks.

Q   How is playing a bagpipe like throwing a javelin blindfolded?

A   You don't have to be very good to get people's attention.

Q   What do you call a bagpiper with half a brain?

A   Gifted.

Q   How many bagpipers does it take to screw in a light bulb?

A   Five, one to do it, and four to criticize his fingering style.

Q   If you were lost in the woods, who would you trust for directions, an in-tune bagpipe player, an out of tune bagpipe player, or Santa Claus?

A   The out of tune bagpipe player. The other two indicate you have been hallucinating.

Q   How do you make a chain saw sound like a bagpipe?

A   Add vibrato.

Q   What's the definition of a gentleman?

A   Someone who knows how to play the bagpipe and doesn't.

Q   What's the difference between a dead bagpiper in the road and a dead country singer in the road?

A   The country singer may have been on the way to a recording session.

Q What's the range of a bagpipe?

A Twenty yards if you have a good arm.

Q Why are bagpipers fingers like lightning?

A They rarely strike the same spot twice.

Q How can you tell if a bagpipe is out of tune?

A Someone is blowing into it.

Q Why is a bagpipe like a Scud missile?

A Both are offensive and inaccurate.

Q How do you know if a bagpipe band is at your front door?

A No one knows when to come in.

Q Why do bagpipers always walk when they play?

A Moving targets are harder to hit.

Q Why do they call it a "kilt"?

A Because a lot of people got kilt when they called it a skirt.

Q What's the definition of "optimism?"

A A bagpiper with a beeper.

Q What's the difference between a bagpiper and a frog?

A The frog might be getting a gig.

Bonus non-bagpipe riddle:

Q What's the difference between a Scotsman and a Rolling Stone?

A A Rolling Stone says, "hey you, get off of my cloud!"
     While a Scotsman says, "Hey McLeod, get off of my ewe!"

Animals

Animals are what the Jewish folks call, "shnorers." It's kind of a moocher that hovers around wanting sh*t. All animals really do sleep and shnore.

Cats have this great trick where they try to lead you to wherever they want you. They get out ahead of you by a couple of steps and when you're about to go one way and they want you to go the other, they do a kind of, "How about this way?!" skip step. And, according to cats, the time span between the opening of the food can and getting it to their spot on the floor should come in at around NOW! Want to have some fun? If you're a cat owner, put some car wax on your bare ankles and take your sweet time dishing out the food. The cat will rub back and forth, polishing your ankles to a high sheen. Then, get your best gal out on the dance floor, roll up those pant legs and enjoy some serious attention.

Every monkey hand and elephant trunk at the zoo will stretch your way if you're carrying a little sumpin, sumpin, but dogs take the cake (and anything else they can wrap their dank kissers around). Of course there is the live vacuum benefit to having a dog around at dinner time, but when there's no food to shnore, dogs do my least favorite animal shnoring technique; the love shnore. This is where they push their moist nose up under your dry, relaxed hand and make you pet them.

I feel so violated.

Head – Insane in the membrane. Combination of instinct and conditioning create perfect storm of cuddles and flesh removal. All animals are messed-up in the head – yes, even yours.

Neck – It-chy!!! There is not an animal on Earth that doesn't have an itchy neck. There is a limit on how much they can eat, sleep or hunt, but they will let you scratch their necks until they can't bear the ecstasy another second (see "head" above).

Nose – Moist mobile phone. Has scent waiting and three-way sniffing. Animals don't follow smells; they trace calls.

Animals uniformly love getting scratched or whacked on the ass. Right on the coccyx - the animal G-spot. You could swing a boat oar at an elephant's ass until the cows came home and demand spankings of their own. Some get strung out on it and have to mate for "favors."

Animals piss on everything, and then other animals inhale it. It's how they communicate. It's like damp, disgusting gang graffiti. Mr. Poopiebuttons got to represent.

Legs – Most animals have them. Used largely for running away from shit sneaking up on shit, and burying shit. An animal will shit, run away from its shit, sneak back up on its own shit be totally surprised and bury the shit.

You've got your webbed, hoofed, cloven, paws, claws, talons, fins, hands, the elephant has some big garbage can-looking things; animals have weird feet. And if you look at most of the designs, they have got to hurt like hell after a long day of whatever their species does all day. But nobody can help them. Forget Dr. Doolittle, they need Dr. Scholl's!

Common Indicators That You Are An

ANIMAL

A lady on vacation took a stroll through the woods.

Suddenly a little white duck, all covered with poop, crossed her path.

"Oh, my," exclaimed the lady. "Come on, I'll clean you!"

She took a Kleenex from her purse and cleaned the little critter.

She walked a little farther and another duck, with poop all over it, crossed her way. Again she took a Kleenex and cleaned the little bird.

Then she encountered a third duck, with the same problem.

And for the third time, cleaned the bird

She walked on still farther and she heard a voice from the bushes calling, "Pssssst...Hey, lady!"

"Yes?" she responded.

"Do you have any tissue?" asked the voice from the bushes.

"No, not anymore," she answered.

"Damn! Have ya' seen any ducks?"

* * *

Deep within a forest a little turtle began to climb a tree.

After hours of effort he reached the top, jumped into the air waving his front legs and crashed to the ground.

After recovering, he slowly climbed the tree again, jumped, and fell to the ground. The turtle tried again and again while a couple of birds sitting on a branch watched his sad efforts.

Finally, the female bird turned to her mate.

"Dear," she chirped, "I think it's time to tell him he's adopted."

* * *

A man walked by a table in a hotel and noticed three men and a dog playing cards. The dog was exhibiting an extraordinary performance.

"That is a very smart dog," the man commented.

"He's not so smart," said one of the irked players. "Every time he gets a good hand he wags his tail."

* * *

A man follows a woman out of a movie theater. She has a dog on a leash.

He stops her and says, "I'm sorry to bother you, but I couldn't help noticing that your dog really seemed to be enjoying the movie. He cried at the right spots, he moved nervously in his seat at the boring parts, but most of all, he laughed like crazy at the funny parts. Don't you find it strange?"

"Yes," she replied, "I found it very strange. He hated the book!"

* * *

A visiting professor at the University of Montana is giving a seminar on the supernatural.

To get a feel for his audience, he asks, "How many people here believe in ghosts?"

About 90 students raise their hands.

"Well that's a good start," says the professor. "Out of those of you who believe in ghosts, do any of you think you've ever seen a ghost?"

About 40 students raise their hands.

"That's really good," continues the professor. "I'm really glad you take this seriously. Has anyone here ever talked to a ghost?"

15 students raise their hands.

"That's a great response," remarks the impressed professor. "Has anyone here ever touched a ghost?"

Three students raise their hands.

"That's fantastic. But let me ask you one question further. Have any of you ever made love to a ghost?" asks the professor.

One student in the back raises his hand.

The professor is astonished.

He takes off glasses, takes a step back, and says, "Son, all the years I've been giving this lecture, no one has ever claimed to have slept with a ghost. You've got to come up here and tell us about your experience."

The redneck student replies with a nod and begins to make his way up to the podium.

The professor asks, "Well, tell us what it's like to have sex with a ghost."

The student replies, "'Ghost?!?' Dang, I thought you said 'goats.'"

* * *

A doctor had just finished a marathon sex session with one of his patients. He was resting afterwards and was feeling a bit guilty because he thought it wasn't really ethical to screw one of his patients.

However, a little voice in his head said "Lots of other doctors have sex with their patients so its not like you're the first..."

This made the doctor feel a little bit better until still another voice in his head said, "...but they probably weren't veterinarians."

* * *

A poor man was poaching lobster at a beach. A game warden, his first day on the job saw him and said, "I'm going to have to arrest you. Poaching is illegal."

"I'm not poaching lobsters," the man said. "These are my pets. I'm exercising them. I throw them into the sea, then whistle, and they come back."

"Show me," the warden said in disbelief.

The man threw the lobsters into the water and started to walk away.

"Wait!" the warden shouted. "Don't you have to whistle to call your lobsters back?"

The man looked at the warden, paused, and said, "What lobsters?"

* * *

A man is walking his dog in a park when he meets another man, also walking his dog. They say hello and start to talk about their dogs. One has a chihuahua and the other a doberman.

They decide to rest for coffee and they walk into a local cafe.

Upon seeing a 'No Animals Allowed' sign, the man with the doberman says, "Don't worry, put on these dark glasses. We'll pretend these are our guide dogs."

So the men do this and go into the cafe.

When the waiter comes over, he says to the man with the doberman, "I'm sorry sir, but we do not allow animals in here. You'll have to take that dog outside."

"But this is my guide dog," says the man.

"A doberman! A doberman isn't a guide dog," says the waiter.

"Actually, a doberman is particularly suited to being a guide dog nowadays. They provide lots of security and they are very well mannered."

"Oh, alright then," says the waiter, and then he notices the other dog. "Excuse me sir, but you can't have that dog in here," he says to the other man.

"Oh yes I can, this is my guide dog," says the man.

"But that dog is a chihuahua! A chihuahua isn't a guide dog!" says the waiter.

The man exclaims "What, they gave me a fucking chihuahua?"

* * *

A man left his cat with his brother while he went on vacation for a week. When he came back, the man called his brother to see when he could pick the cat up.

The brother hesitated, then said, "I'm so sorry, but while you were away, the cat died."

The man was very upset and yelled, "You know, you could have broken the news to me better than that. When I called today, you could have said he was on the roof and wouldn't come down. Then when I called the next day, you could have said that he had fallen off and the vet was working on patching him up. Then when I called the third day, you could have said he had passed away."

The brother thought about it and apologized.

"So how's Mom?" asked the man.

"She's on the roof and won't come down."

* * *

An old snake goes to see his doctor. He says, "Doctor, I need something for my eyes. I can't see well these days." The doctor fixes him up with a pair of glasses and tells him to return in two weeks.

The snake comes back in two weeks, and tells the doctor he's very depressed.

The doctor says, "What's the problem? Didn't the glasses help you?"

"The glasses are fine doc. I just discovered I've been living with a water hose the past two years!"

* * *

A vampire bat came flapping in from the night, covered in fresh blood, and parked himself on the roof of the cave to get some sleep.

Pretty soon all the other bats smelled the blood and began hassling him about where he got it. He told them to go away and let him get some sleep. However, the bats persisted until finally he gave in.

"Okay, follow me," he said, and flew out of the cave with hundreds of bats behind him. Down through a valley they went, across a river and into a forest full of trees. Finally he slowed down and all the other bats excitedly milled around him.

"Now, do you see that tree over there?" he asked.

"Yes, yes, yes!" the bats all screamed in a hungry frenzy.

"Good," said the first bat tiredly, "Because I didn't!"

* * *

A man brought a very limp dog into the veterinary clinic. As he lay the dog on the table, the doctor pulled out his stethoscope, placing the receptor on the dog's chest. After a moment or two, the vet shook his head sadly and said, "I'm sorry, but your dog has passed away."

"What?" screamed the man. "How can you tell? You haven't done any testing on him or anything. I want another opinion!"

With that, the vet turned and left the room. In a few moments, he returned with a labrador retriever. The retriever went right to work, checking the poor dead dog out thoroughly with his nose. After a considerable amount of sniffing, the retriever sadly shook his head and said, "Bark" (meaning, dead as a doornail).

The veterinarian then took the labrador out and returned in a few moments with a cat, who also carefully sniffed out the poor dog on the table. As had his predecessors, the cat sadly shook his head and said, "Meow" (meaning, he's history). He then jumped off the table and ran out of the room.

The veterinarian handed the man a bill for $600.

The dog's owner went berserk. "$600! Just to tell me my dog is dead?"

The vet shook his head sadly and explained. "If you had taken my word for it, the charge would only have been $50, but you wanted the lab work and the cat scan."

* * *

A young boy, about eight years old, was at the store picking out a large box of laundry detergent. The grocer walked over and, trying to be friendly, asked the boy if he had a lot of laundry to do.

"Oh, no laundry," the boy said. "I'm going to wash my dog."

"But you shouldn't use this to wash your dog. It's very powerful and if you wash your dog in this, he'll get sick. In fact, it might even kill him."

But the boy was not stopped by this and carried the detergent to the counter and paid for it, even as the grocer still tried to talk him out of washing his dog.

About a week later the boy was back in the store doing some shopping. The grocer asked the boy how his dog was doing.

"Oh, he died," the boy said.

The grocer said, "I tried to tell you not to use that detergent on your dog."

"Well," the boy replied, "I don't think it was the detergent that killed him."

"Oh I'm sorry. How did he die?"

"I think it was the spin cycle."

* * *

A man was driving along a freeway when he noticed a chicken running along side the road, beside his car.

He was amazed to see that the chicken was keeping up with him. Glancing down at his speedometer, he noticed that he was doing 50 miles per hour.

He accelerated to 60 and the chicken stayed right next to him. He sped up to 75 and the chicken kept up.

The man then noticed that the chicken had three legs. Growing even more curious, he followed the chicken down a road and into a farm. He got out of his car and saw that all the chickens around him had three legs.

He asked the farmer, "What's up with these three legged chickens?"

The farmer said, "Well, whenever we have chicken for dinner, everyone in the family fights over the legs, but there are only two. I have bred a three legged bird. It's going to make me a millionaire."

"How do they taste?" the man asked.

The farmer said, "Don't know yet, I haven't been able to catch one."

* * *

A city guy was taking a vacation at a farm out in the country.

The farmer he was staying with said, "It's a beautiful morning. Why not take the dogs and do a bit of shooting?"

"Great! Thanks."

At lunch the farmer inquired, "How was the shooting?"

"Terrific. Got any more dogs?"

* * *

A dog walks into a butcher shop, spends a number of minutes looking at the meat on display, and eventually indicates with a nod of his head and a bark that he would like some lamb chops.

The butcher, thinking the dog would know no better, picks up the lowest quality chops in the shop.

The dog barks furiously and continues to bark until the butcher selects the finest chops from the display counter.

The butcher weighs the meat and asks the dog for $5.90. Again, the dog barks furiously until the butcher reduces the bill to the correct price of $3.60.

The dog hands over a five dollar note and the butcher gives him 40 cents in change. Once again, the dog barks continuously until the butcher tenders the correct change. The dog then picks up his package and leaves the shop.

Now, the butcher is extremely impressed and decides that he would like to own a dog so clever. He shuts up shop and follows the dog to see where it goes.

After ten minutes or so, the dog climbs the steps to a house. When it gets to the top, it shakes its head as though in frustration, gently places the package of meat on the floor and, standing on its hind legs, rings the doorbell.

A man opens the door and starts to yell obscenities at the dog.

As he does so, the horrified butcher leaps up the steps and begs the man to stop. "It's such an intelligent dog," he says, "surely it doesn't deserve this kind of treatment."

He then went on to explain how the dog had procured the best lamb chops in the shop, insisted on paying the advertised price and quibbled over incorrect change!

The man looked at the butcher and said, "Intelligent he may be, but this is the third time this week he's forgotten his keys."

* * *

One day, a young camel decided to ask his father some questions about growing up. "Daddy, why is it that we have humps on our backs?"

"Well son, we have humps on our backs which contain fat to sustain us through many days when we are out in the desert."

"Oh thanks, dad," said the youngster. He then asked, "Daddy, why is it that we have long eye lashes over our eyes?"

"Well son," said the father, "in the desert, there are many sandstorms which whip up a lot of sand that can get into our eyes. The long eye lashes protect our eyes from being blinded."

"Oh thanks, dad," said the youngster. "Dad, why is it that we have great big padded feet?"

"Well son, in the desert, the sand is very soft and we need big feet to be able to walk on the sand without our feet sinking into the soft sand."

"Well thanks, dad, but what are we doing in the London Zoo?"

* * *

A couple was going out for the evening to celebrate the wife's birthday. While they were getting ready, the husband put the cat out.

The taxi arrived, and as the couple walked out of their home, the cat shot back into the house.

Not wanting their cat to have free run of the house while they were out, the husband went back upstairs to chase the cat out.

The wife, not wanting it known that the house would be empty, explained to the taxi driver, "He's just going upstairs to say goodbye to my mother."

A few minutes later, the husband got into the car, and said, "Sorry I took so long" he says, "stupid old thing was hiding under the bed and I had to poke her with an umbrella to get her to come out!"

* * *

On reaching his plane seat, a man is surprised to see a parrot strapped in next to him. He asks the stewardess for a coffee where upon the parrot squawks, "And get me a whiskey you stupid cow."

The stewardess, flustered, brings back a whiskey for the parrot and forgets all about the coffee. When this omission is pointed out to her, the parrot drains its' glass and squawks, "And get me another whiskey you airhead."

Quite upset, the poor girl comes back shaking with another whiskey, but still no coffee.

Unaccustomed to such slackness, the man tries the parrot's approach, "I've asked you twice for a coffee. Go and get it now you stupid idiot."

Next moment, both he and the parrot have been wrenched up and thrown out of the emergency exit by two burly stewards.

As they plunge downwards, the parrot turns to the man and says, "You've sure got an attitude for someone who can't fly."

* * *

Recently, the Psychic Hotline launched hotlines for frogs. Here is the story of one frog and his conversation with a psychic.

A frog telephones the Psychic Hotline and is told, "You are going to meet a beautiful young girl who will want to know everything about you."

The frog says, "This is great! Will I meet her at a party, or what?"

"No," says the psychic. "Next semester in her biology class."

* * *

There was once a man from the city who was visiting a small farm, and during this visit he saw a farmer feeding pigs in a most extraordinary manner. The farmer would lift a pig up to a nearby apple tree, and the pig would eat the apples off the tree directly. The farmer would move the pig from one apple to another until the pig was satisfied, then he would start again with another pig.

The city man watched this activity for some time with great astonishment. Finally, he could not resist saying to the farmer, "This is the most inefficient method of feeding pigs that I can imagine. Just think of the time that would be saved if you simply shook the apples off the tree and let the pigs eat them from the ground!"

The farmer looked puzzled and replied, "What's time to a pig?"

* * *

A lion woke up one morning feeling really rowdy and mean. He went out and cornered a small monkey and roared, "Who is mightiest of all jungle animals?"

The trembling monkey says, "You are, mighty lion!

Later, the lion confronts a ox and fiercely bellows, "Who is the mightiest of all jungle animals?"

The terrified ox stammers, "Oh, great lion, you are the mightiest animal in the jungle!"

On a roll now, the lion swaggers up to an elephant and roars, "Who is mightiest of all jungle animals?"

Fast as lightning, the elephant snatches up the lion with his trunk, slams him against a tree half a dozen times leaving the lion feeling like it'd been run over by a safari wagon. The elephant then stomps on the lion till it looks like a corn tortilla and ambles away.

The lion lets out a moan of pain, lifts his head weakly and hollers after the elephant, "Just because you don't know the answer, you don't have to get so upset about it!"

* * *

A three legged dog walks into a saloon in the old west. He slides up to the bar and says, "I'm looking for the man who shot my paw."

* * *

An elderly woman buys two parrots with the understanding that one is male and the other female, but she's unable to identify their sexes. She calls the pet store and asks how she's to tell which is which. The man at the store advises her to watch them carefully and, in time, all would become clear.

She spends weeks staring at the cage and eventually catches them doing what comes naturally. Not wanting to get them mixed up again, she makes a small cardboard ring and places it around the male parrot's neck.

A few days later, the local parish priest pays the woman a visit.

The male parrot takes one look at the priest's collar, lets out a whistle and says, "I see she caught you at it, too!"

* * *

A fundamentalist Christian couple felt it important to own an equally fundamentally Christian pet, so they went shopping.

At Jesus Saves Breeders, a kennel specializing in what they were looking for, they found a dog they took a liking to. When they asked the dog to fetch the Bible, he did it in a flash. When they instructed him to look up Psalm 23, he complied equally fast, using his paws with dexterity. Thoroughly impressed, they purchased the animal and took him home, all the while praising the Lord for bringing this dog to them.

That night they had friends over. They were so proud of their new fundamentalist dog and his major skills, they called the dog and showed off a little.

The friends were impressed and asked whether the dog could also do any of the 'usual' dog tricks. This stopped the couple cold, as they hadn't thought about 'normal' tricks.

"Well," they said, "let's try and see."

Once more they called the dog, and they clearly pronounced the command, "Heel!"

Quick as a wink, the dog jumped up, put his paw on the man's forehead, closed his eyes in concentration, and bowed his head.

* * *

Little Red Riding Hood is skipping down the road when she sees the Big Bad Wolf crouched down behind a log.

Stopping, she says, "My, Mr. Wolf, what big eyes you have."

The startled wolf jumps up and runs away.

Further down the road, Little Red Riding Hood sees the wolf again. This time he's crouched behind a tree stump.

"My, what big ears you have Mr. Wolf," says Little Red Riding Hood.

Again the wolf quickly jumps up and runs away.

A couple of miles further, Little Red Riding Hood sees the wolf again. This time he's crouched down behind a road sign.

"My, what big teeth you have, Mr. Wolf," says Little Red Riding Hood.

With that, the Big Bad Wolf jumps up and screams, "Will you get lost!!! I'm trying to take a dump!!!"

* * *

As Mickey and Minnie were before the judge in divorce court, the judge looked at Mickey and said, "Listen here, Mr. Mouse, I cannot grant you a divorce from Minnie."

"But why not, Your Honor?" a stunned Mickey asked.

"I have reviewed all the information you submitted to the court and I can find no evidence to support the allegation that she's crazy," explained the judge.

"Your Honor," Mickey exclaimed, "I didn't say she was crazy. I said she was fucking Goofy."

* * *

A group of prisoners were attending their rehabilitation meeting. Their assignment was to each stand up in turn, state their name and admit to the other inmates what crime they had committed.

The first prisoner stood up and said, "My name is Stuart, and I'm in for armed robbery."

Everyone gave him approving looks and pats on the back for admitting his wrongdoing.

The next prisoner stood up and said, "My name is Dennis, and I'm in for murder."

Again, there was a round of approving looks and pats on the back. This continued around the circle until it was the last inmate's turn.

He stood up and said, "My name is Louie, and I'm not saying what I'm in for."

"Come on now, Louie," the group leader said, "in order for you to make any progress, you must disclose what your crime was. Now, tell us what you're in for."

"Okay, okay," Louie said, "I'm in for screwing dogs."

A disgusted look came over the other prisoners as they yelled, "That is disgusting! How low can you go!?"

"Chihuahuas."

* * *

The Colorado State Department of Fish and Wildlife is advising hikers, hunters, fishermen, and golfers to take extra precautions and be on the alert for bears while in the Dillon, Breckenridge, and Keystone area.

They advise people to wear noise-producing devices such as little bells on their clothing to alert but not startle the bears unexpectedly. They also advise you to carry pepper spray in case of an encounter with a bear.

It is also a good idea to watch for signs of bear activity. People should be able to recognize the difference between black bear and grizzly bear droppings.

Black bear droppings are smaller and contain berries and possibly squirrel fur.

Grizzly bear droppings have little bells in them and smell like pepper spray.

* * *

Q & A Round Up
Animals

Q Why did the chicken cross the road?
A To show the armadillo that it was possible.

Q Why do birds fly South?
A Because it's too far to walk.

Q Is it good manners to eat fried chicken with your fingers?
A No, you should eat your fingers separately.

Q Why do seagulls live near the sea?
A Because if they lived near the bay, they would be called bagels.

Q What has four legs and an arm?
A A happy pit bull.

Q What is the difference between a Rottweiler and a social worker?
A It is easier to get your kids back from a Rottweiler!

Q Did you hear about the new breed in pet shops?
A They crossed a pit bull with a collie; it bites your leg off and goes for help.

Q What do you get when you cross an elephant with a kangaroo?
A Holes all over Australia.

Q Why do gorillas have big nostrils?
A Because they have big fingers.

Q What do fish say when they hit a concrete wall?
A Dam!

Rednecks

I live near a lot of rednecks in a little part of the world we call "America." It is amazing to me how pervasive the redneck lifestyle really is. They're very much like the French in many ways (oh, the rednecks are gonna like that). Think about it. They both eat what they want, smoke like chimneys, drink like fish, take lunch breaks that last sometimes months and they don't always smell… perfect. Yet, somehow the French stay thin.

I have spent some time outside the big Jew/fag cities of this nation, a good deal of it moving among our redneck brothers and sisters. To ingratiate myself I would allow a pseudo accidental "y'all" slip into my conversation and then catch it with, "Well, now you've got me saying it!" Well sir, they would just love it. That is one thing about the redneck community; y'all are welcome to join up! And I'm guessing the dues aren't cost-prohibitive.

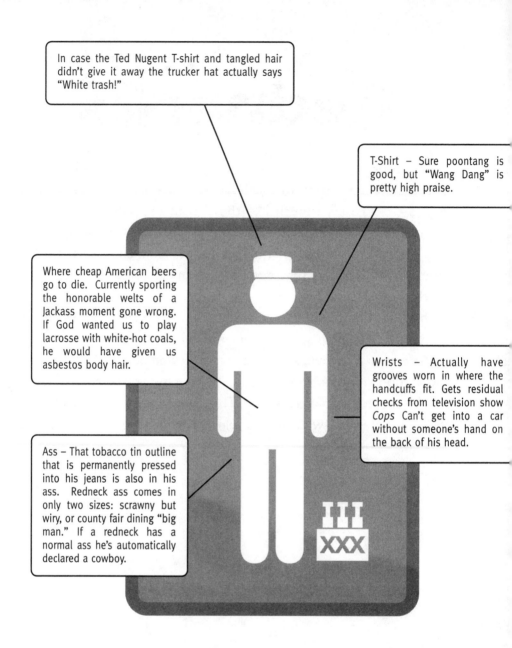

Common Indicators That You Are A

REDNECK

A redneck took his daughter to the gynecologist they were in the room waiting for the doctor. The doctor walked in and asked the father, "What are we here for today?"

The father said, "To get my daughter on birth control."

The doctor then asked the father, "so is your daughter sexually active?" The father said, "no, she just lays there like her mother."

* * *

Two Italian guys are driving through Texas when they get pulled over by a state trooper. The trooper walks up and taps on the window with his nightstick.

The driver rolls down the window, and the trooper smacks him in the head with the stick.

The driver says, "Why did you do that?"

The trooper says, "You're in Texas, son. When I pull you over, you'll have your license ready."

Driver says, "I'm sorry, officer, I'm not from around here."

The trooper runs a check on the guy's license, and he's clean. He gives the guy his license back and walks around to the passenger side and taps on the window. The passenger rolls his window down, and the trooper smacks him with the nightstick.

The passenger says, "What'd you do that for?"

The cop says, "Just making your wishes come true."

The passenger says, "Huh?"

The cop says, "I know that two miles down the road you're gonna say, 'I wish that guy would've tried that crap with me.'"

* * *

A hillbilly boy and his new bride were on their honeymoon. The husband jumps into bed to wait for his wife to get herself ready.

The wife comes out of the bathroom in a sexy negligee and says "Honey, I have something to tell you. I'm a virgin."

The idiot grabs his clothes and rushes out of the house yelling at the top of his lungs. He heads straight to his father's house.

When he gets there his father says, "Boy, what are you doing here? You're supposed to be on your honeymoon."

The son says, "Dad, my new wife told me a big secret of hers. She's a virgin."

The father says, "Damn, son. You did the right thing by leaving. If she wasn't good enough for her family, she sure as hell isn't good enough for ours."

* * *

Cleon goes to the doctor to arrange a sperm count. The doctor gives him a sealed plastic cup and says, "Use this and bring me a sample tomorrow." Next day Cleon goes back to the doctor and gives him an empty cup.

"So why is this empty?" asks the doctor.

Cleon explains, "Well, doctor, first I tried it with my right hand, but nothing. Then I tried it with my left hand, but still nothing. Then I asked my wife Katy for help. She tried it with her right hand, then with her left, but nothing. Katy even tried with her mouth and with her teeth in, then with her teeth out, but still no luck. We then called in our next door neighbor and she tried it with both hands, and with her mouth too, but with no results, I'm sad to say."

The doctor was shocked. "You mean you asked your neighbor to try?!"

Cleon replied, "Yup, but no matter what we tried we couldn't open that damn cup!"

* * *

A salesman is lost in a rural area and stops at a farm to get directions. As he is talking to the farmer he notices a pig with a wooden leg. "How did the pig get a wooden leg?" he asks the farmer.

"Well," says the farmer, "that is a very special pig. One night not too long ago we had a fire start in the barn. Well, sir, that pig set up a great squealing that woke everyone, and by the time we got there he had herded all the other animals out of the barn and saved every one of them."

"And that was when he hurt his leg?" asked the salesman.

"Oh no," says the farmer. "He was fine after that. Though a while later I was in the woods out back and a bear attacked me. Well, sir, that pig was near by and he came running and set on that bear and chased him off. Saved me for sure."

"So... the bear injured his leg then." says the salesman.

"Oh no. He came away without a scratch from that. Though a few days later my tractor turned over in a ditch and I was knocked unconscious. Well, that pig dove into the ditch and pulled me out before I drowned."

"So he hurt his leg then?" asks the salesman.

"Oh no," says the farmer.

"So how did he get the wooden leg?" the salesman asks.

"Well," the farmer tells him, "A pig like that, you don't want to eat all at once."

* * *

A farmer ordered a high-tech milking machine. Since the equipment arrived when his wife was out of town, he decided to test it on himself first. So, he inserted his penis into the equipment, turned the switch on and everything else was automatic!

Soon, he realized that the equipment provided him with as much pleasure as his wife did. When the fun was over, though, he quickly realized that he couldn't remove the instrument from his penis, and his discomfort was quickly building.

He read the manual but didn't find any useful information. He tried every button on the instrument, but still without success.

Finally, the farmer decided to call the supplier's Customer Service Hot Line. "Hello, I just bought a milking machine from your company. It works fantastically, but how do I remove it from the cow's udder? I -- I mean, the cow seems to be in a lot of pain."

"Don't worry," replied the customer service rep, "the machine was programmed to release automatically once it has collected two gallons."

* * *

A redneck walks into a hardware store and asks for a chain saw. The next day he brings it back and says, "This chain saw is defective. It would only cut down one tree and it took *all damn day!*" The salesman takes the chain saw, starts it up to see what's wrong, and the redneck says, "What's that noise?"

* * *

Bobby-Joe was riding in Jed's truck. Jed pulled over, got out and pointed down yonder and said, "That's where I first had sex."

Bobby-Joe asked, "How was it?"

Jed said, "It was great 'til I looked up and saw her mom was watching."

Bobby-Joe yelled, "Oh shit! What did she say?"

Jed replied, "Baaa!"

* * *

A woman went to the Welfare Office to get aid. The office worker asked her how many children she had.

"I have ten," she answered.

"What are their names?" he asked.

"LeRoy, LeRoy, LeRoy, LeRoy, LeRoy, LeRoy, LeRoy, LeRoy, LeRoy and LeRoy," she replied.

"All of them are named LeRoy?" he asked. "What if you want them to come in from playing outside?"

"That's easy," she said. "I just call 'LeRoy' and they all come running in."

"And, if you want them to come to the table for dinner?" he asked.

"Then I just say, 'LeRoy, come eat your dinner,'" answered the woman.

"But, what do you do if you just want *one* of them to do something?"

"Oh, that's easy too," she said. "I just use their last name!"

* * *

A good old boy works at a new job on Thursday and Friday. On Monday he calls in and says, "I can't come in today. I'm sick." He worked the rest of the week, but the following Monday he calls in and says, "I can't come in today. I'm sick."

The boss asks the foreman about him, and the foreman says, "He's great. He does the work of two men. We need him."

So the boss calls the guy into his office, and says, "You seem to have a problem getting to work on Mondays. You're a good worker and I'd hate to fire you. What's the problem? Anything we can help you with? Drugs? Alcohol?"

The guy says, "No, I don't drink or do drugs. But my brother-in-law drinks every weekend, and then beats on my sister. So every Monday morning, I go over to make sure she's all right. She puts her head on my shoulder and cries, one thing leads to another, and the next thing you know, I'm screwing her."

The boss says, " You screw your sister?"

The guy says, "Hey, I told you I was sick."

* * *

There were these two rednecks out hunting when they came upon an old, abandoned mine shaft. Curious about its depth they threw in a pebble and waited for the sound of it striking the bottom, but they heard nothing.

They went and got a bigger rock, threw it in and waited. Still nothing. They searched the area for something larger and came upon a railroad tie. With great difficulty the two men carried it to the opening and threw it in. While waiting for it to hit bottom, a goat suddenly darted between them and leapt into the hole!

The guys were still standing there with astonished looks upon their faces when a man walked up to them. He asked them if they had seen a goat anywhere in the area and they said that one had just jumped into the mine shaft in front of them!

The man replied, "Oh no, that couldn't be my goat, mine was tied to a railroad tie."

* * *

Three dead bodies turn up at the mortuary, all with very big smiles on their faces. The coroner calls the police to tell them what has happened.

The coroner tells the inspector, "First body: A Frenchman, 72, died of heart failure while with his mistress. Hence the enormous smile."

"Second body: "Irishman, 25, won a thousand dollars on the lottery, spent it all on whiskey. Died of alcohol poisoning, hence the smile."

The inspector asked, "What of the third body?"

"Ah," says the coroner, "This is the most unusual one. Danny Earl, the redneck from West Virginia, 30, struck by lightning."

"Why is he smiling then?" inquires the inspector.

"Thought he was having his picture taken."

* * *

A farm boy accidentally overturned his wagon load of corn. The fa.
lived nearby heard the noise and yelled over to the boy, "Hey Willis, forg.
troubles. Come in and visit with us. I'll help you get the wagon up later."

"That's mighty nice of you," Willis answered, "but I don't think Pa would lik
me to."

"Aw come on boy," the farmer insisted.

"Well okay," the boy finally agreed, and added, "but Pa won't like it."

After a hearty dinner, Willis thanked his host. "I feel a lot better now, but I
know Pa is going to be real upset."

"Don't be foolish!" the neighbor said with a smile. "By the way, where is he?"

"Under the wagon."

* * *

Two women, one from the north and one from the south, are seated next
to one another on a plane. "Where you flyin' to?" says the southern woman. The
northern woman turns up her nose.

"Don't you know you should *never* end a sentence with a preposition?" The
southern woman thinks about this for a second.

"Where you flyin' to, bitch?"

* * *

The girl asked her redneck boyfriend, "Darling, if we get engaged will you give
me a ring?"

"Sure," he replied "What's your phone number?"

* * *

After living in the remote wilderness of Kentucky all his life, an old hillbilly decided it was time to visit the big city. In one of the stores, he picked up a mirror and
looked into it. Not knowing what it was, he remarked, "How about that! Here's a
picture of my daddy."

He bought the 'picture,' but on the way home he remembered his wife, Lizzy,
didn't like his father. So he hung it in the barn, and every morning before leaving for
the fields, he would go there and look at it. Lizzy began to get suspicious of these
many trips to the barn.

One day after her husband left, she searched the barn and found the mirror. As
she looked into the glass, she fumed, "So that's the ugly bitch he's runnin' around
with."

* * *

se three farmers that wanted to win the state fair contest for
og. They decide that they should stick a cork in the pigs ass
onth before the fair. The only problem was that none of them
to stick the cork in. So they bought a monkey and trained him
es.

... or two of this, they stick the monkey in the pen with the pig and a
cork, and after a minute, the monkey did what he was supposed to do. The farmers
fed the pig for a month and sure enough, they won first prize. Once they got home,
they realized they still had to take the cork out. So they trained this same monkey
to take corks out of bottles.

They stuck the monkey in the pen with the pig, and the farmers woke up three
days later in the hospital with a reporter sitting next to them.

The reporter asked the first farmer, "What is the last thing you remember?"

"Shit flying everywhere," the farmer replied.

The reporter asked the second farmer the same question and got the same response. When she got to the third farmer and asked him what he could remember,
he started crying. The reporter asked, "What's the matter?"

The farmer replied, "The last thing I remember is the look on the poor monkey's face as he tried to stick the cork back in."

* * *

Two men from the country were sitting at a bar when a young lady nearby began to choke on a hamburger. As she gasped and gagged, one turned to the other
and said, "That gal is havin' a bad time. I'm a gonna go over there and help."

The man ran over to the young lady, held both sides of her head in his big hands
and asked, "Kin ya swaller?" Gasping, she motioned that she couldn't swallow.

Then, the man asked, "Kin ya breathe?" Still gasping, she motioned that she
couldn't breathe. With that, the man yanked up her skirt and licked her butt. The
young woman was so shocked and humiliated that she coughed up the piece of hamburger and began breathing on her own. The man sat back down with his friend and
said, "Ya know, it's sure amazin' how that hind-lick maneuver always works!"

* * *

A redneck wanted to learn how to skydive. He got an instructor and started
lessons. The instructor told the redneck to jump out of the plane and pull his rip
cord. The instructor then explained that he himself would jump out right behind him
so that they would go down together. The redneck understood and was ready.

The time came to have the redneck jump from the airplane. The instructor
reminded the redneck that he would be right behind him. The redneck proceeded
to jump from the plane and after being in the air for a few seconds pulled the rip
cord. The instructor followed by jumping from the plane. The instructor pulled his

rip cord but the parachute did not open. The instructor, frantically trying to get his parachute open, darted past the redneck.

The redneck, seeing this, yelled as he undid the straps to his parachute, "So you wanna race, eh?"

* * *

A newlywed farmer and his wife were visited by her mother, who immediately demanded an inspection of the place. While they were walking through the barn, the farmer's mule suddenly reared up and kicked the mother-in-law in the head, killing her instantly.

At the funeral a few days later, the farmer stood near the casket and greeted folks as they walked by. The pastor noticed that whenever a woman would whisper something to the farmer, he would nod his head "yes" and say something. Whenever a man walked by and whispered to the farmer, he would shake his head "no" and mumble a reply. Curious, the pastor later asked the farmer what that was all about.

The farmer replied, "The women would say, 'What a terrible tragedy,' and I would nod my head and say, 'Yes, it was.' The men would ask, 'You wanna sell that mule?' and I would shake my head and say, 'Can't. It's all booked up for a year.'"

* * *

A little country boy was sitting on the curb with a quart of turpentine and just shaking it all up; just watching all the bubbles.

A priest came along and asked the little boy what he was doing. The little boy replied, "Well, I'm a just shakin' the most powerful liquid in the world, it's called turpentine."

The priest said, "No, son, the most powerful liquid in the world is Holy Water." If you take some of this Holy Water and rub it on a pregnant woman's belly, she'll pass a healthy baby boy."

The little boy replied, "Shoot, that ain't nothin'. You take some of this here turpentine and rub it on a dog's ass, he'll pass a motorcycle."

* * *

Somewhere in the deep South, Bubba called an attorney and asked, "Is it true they're suing the cigarette companies for causing people to get cancer?"

"Yes, Bubba, that is true."

"And people are suing the fast food restaurants for making them fat and clogging their arteries with all them burgers and fries... is that true, mister lawyer?"

"Sure is Bubba, but why do you ask?"

"Cause I was thinkin'.... Maybe I can sue Budweiser for all them ugly women I've been wakin' up with!"

* * *

A man walked up to a farm house and knocked on the door. When a woman opened the door, the man asks if she knew how to have sex. Not amused, she slammed the door. Again, though, the man knocked, and asked the same question. Not amused, the woman screamed at him and told him to leave.

Later that evening, the woman told her husband of the incident. He said he'd stay home the following day just in case the man returned.

Sure enough, the next day the same man returned. The husband hid with his gun while his wife answered the door. When she was asked again if she knew how to have sex, she replied, "Sure, I do! Why do you ask?"

"Good," said the man at the door, "give some to your husband the next time you see him, and tell him to keep away from my wife!"

* * *

The old couple had lived together in the backwoods for over fifty years. To celebrate their fiftieth anniversary, he took her to the big city and they checked into a plush hotel.

She said to the bellman, "We refuse to settle for such a small room. No windows, no bed, and no air conditioning."

"But, madam!" replied the bellman.

"Don't 'But madam' me," she continued. "You can't treat us like we're a couple of fools just because we don't travel much, and we've never been to the big city, and never spent the night at a hotel. I'm going to complain to the manager."

"Madam," the bellman said, "this is the elevator."

* * *

This guy walks into a bar down in Alabama and orders a mudslide. The bartender looks at the man and says, "You're not from round here are ya?"

"No," replied the man, "I'm from Pennsylvania."

The bartender looks at him and says, "Well what do you do in Pennsylvania?"

"I'm a taxidermist," said the man.

The bartender, looking very bewildered, now asked, "What in the world is a tax-e-derm-ist?"

The man looked at the bartender and said, "Well, I mount dead animals."

The bartender stands back and hollers to the whole bar which is staring at him "It's okay, boys! He's one of us!"

* * *

A small redneck Wild Animal Park had acquired a very rare species of gorilla. Within a few weeks, the female gorilla became very 'in the mood' and difficult to handle.

Upon examination, the park veterinarian determined the problem. The gorilla was in heat. To make matters worse, there were no male gorillas of the species available.

While reflecting on their problem, the park administrators noticed Ed, a part-time redneck intern, responsible for cleaning the animals' cages. Ed, like most rednecks, had little sense, but possessed ample ability to satisfy a female of *any* species.

So, the park administrators thought they might have a solution. Ed was approached with a proposition. Would he be willing to have sex with the gorilla for $500? Ed showed some interest, but said he would have to think the matter over carefully.

The following day, Ed announced that he would accept their offer, but only under three conditions.

"First," he said, "I don't want to have to kiss her. Secondly, you must never tell anyone about this."

The park administration quickly agreed to these conditions, so they asked what was his third condition.

"Well," said Ed, "You gotta give me another week to come up with the $500."

* * *

Two Texas A&M Aggies were out hunting in central Texas when they encountered a scantily clad young lass lounging against a tree.

"What y'all boys doing?" she inquired.

They, being manly men responded, "Well ma'am, we're huntin' wild game."

"Well I'm wild, and I'm game!" she replied.

So they shot her.

* * *

The National Transportation Safety Board recently divulged they had covertly funded a project with the U.S. auto makers for the past five years, whereby the auto makers were installing black box voice recorders in pick-up trucks.

This was done in an effort to determine, when accidents occurred, the circumstances in the last 15 seconds before the crash. They were surprised to find in 49 of the 50 states the last words of drivers in 61.2 percent of crashes were, "Oh, shit!"

Only the state of Montana was different, where 89.3 percent of the final words were: "Hold my beer and watch this!"

* * *

Emily Sue passed away and Bubba called 911.

The 911 operator told Bubba that she would send someone out right away. "Where do you live?" asked the operator.

Bubba replied, "At the end of Eucalyptus Drive."

The operator asked, "Can you spell that for me?"

There was a long pause and finally Bubba said, "How 'bout if I drag her over to Oak Street, and you pick her up there?"

* * *

Cletus finally found the nerve to tell his fiancée that he had to break off their engagement so he could marry another woman.

"Can she cook like I can?" the distraught woman asked between sobs.

"Not on her best day," he replied.

"Can she buy you expensive gifts like I do?"

"No, she's broke."

"Well, then, is it sex?"

"Nobody does it like you, babe."

"Then what can she do that I can't?"

"Sue me for child support."

* * *

It was a nice sunny day and three redneck men were walking down a country road, when they saw a bush with a pig's ass popping out.

The first man says, "I wish that was Jessica Simpson's ass."

The second man says, "I wish that was Pamela Anderson's ass."

Then the third man says, "I wish it was dark."

* * *

This woman is driving into a small town and slams on the brakes as a coyote runs across the road in front of her. Just as she regains her wits and gets ready to proceed, a cowboy runs right in front of her and catches the coyote by the hind legs and starts screwing it.

"Oh my God!" she exclaims and drives into town to find the local law. She sees the local sheriff's car parked in front of the town bar.

"It figures," she says as she storms inside.

The first thing she notices is an old, old man with a long white beard sitting in the corner jacking-off. She runs up to the sheriff who's sitting at the bar with his drink.

"What kind of sick town are you running here? I drive into town and almost run over some cowboy sodomizing an animal... and then... I come in here... and see this old man in the corner jacking-off right in public!"

"Well, ma'am," the sheriff slowly replies, "you don't expect him to catch a coyote at his age, do ya?"

* * *

A redneck stopped at his favorite watering hole after a hard day's work to relax. He noticed a man next to him ordered a shot and a beer. The man drank the shot, chased it with the beer and then looked into his shirt pocket.

This continued several times before the man's curiosity got the best of him. He leaned over to the guy and said, "Excuse me, I couldn't help but notice your little ritual, why in the world do you look into your shirt pocket every time you drink your shot and beer?"

The man replied, "There's a picture of my girlfriend in there, and when she starts looking good, I'm heading home!"

* * *

After years of listening to her plead, the redneck finally decided to let his wife come hunting with him. He led her into the woods and left her in a blind with instructions on what to do when a deer came within range.

He had no sooner arrived at his own blind when he heard a shot coming from his wife's direction. The first shot was quickly followed by several more. He immediately ran back to see what had happened; only to find a man standing in front of his wife with his hands up shouting, "Okay lady, it's your deer! Just let me take the saddle off!"

* * *

Three aspiring student psychiatrists from various colleges were attending their first class on emotional extremes. "Just to establish some parameters," said the professor to the student from the University of Houston, "What is the opposite of joy?"

"Sorrow," replied the student.

"And the opposite of depression?" the professor asked of the young lady from Rice.

"Elation," said she.

"And you sir," he said to the young man from Texas, "how about the opposite of woe?"

The Aggie replied, "Sir, I believe that would be giddy-up."

* * *

On a shopping trip to the city, a backwoods farmer bought a 24-piece jigsaw puzzle. He worked on it every night for two weeks. Finally, the puzzle was finished.

"Look what I've done, Jess," he said proudly to a visiting neighbor.

"That's surely somethin', Willard. How long did it take you?"

"Only two weeks."

"Never done a puzzle myself," Jess said. "Is two weeks fast?"

"Darn tootin'," Willard said. "Look at the box. It says, 'From two to four years.'"

* * *

Bubba decided to visit Colorado to do something he could never do back home… snow skiing.

Unfortunately for Bubba, before he was even able to make it up the hill, he was knocked unconscious by the chairlift.

As soon as he could, he called his insurance company from the hospital only to be told that they were refusing to cover his injury.

"What do you mean?!" Bubba screamed. "Why wouldn't you cover an injury like this?"

"You got hit in the head with a chairlift," the insurance representative explained. "That makes you a moron, and we consider that to be a pre-existing condition."

* * *

Maw is outside hanging up the laundry, when she sees Paw come out onto the porch.

"Paw," she yells, "git over thar and fix that thar outhouse!"

Paw walks over to the outhouse, looks it over and says, "Maw, thar ain't nuthin' wrong with this here outhouse!"

"Stick yer head down that thar hole, Paw," Maw says.

Paw puts his head down in the hole and says, "Maw, I still says thar ain't nuthin' wrong with this here outhouse!"

Paw goes to lift his head and screams, "Owwwww! Maw, my beard's stuck!"

"Aggravatin', ain't it?" says Maw.

* * *

An Irishman, with quite a pronounced limp, sits down at a bar and orders a whiskey. As he looks down at the end of the bar, he sees someone who resembles Jesus, so he asks the bartender, "Is that Jesus down there?" The bartender confirms that it is, so the Irishman tells him to give Jesus a whiskey, too.

Next, a hunchbacked Italian enters the bar and orders a glass of wine. When he sees Jesus sitting down at the end of the bar, he asks the bartender to give a glass of wine to the son of God, too.

Finally, a redneck swaggers in, dragging his knuckles on the floor, and hollers, "Barkeep, set me up a cold one. Hey, is that God's boy down there?" The bartender nods and the redneck tells him to give Jesus a cold one, too.

As Jesus gets up to leave, he walks over to the Irishman, touches him, and says, "For your kindness, you are healed!" Feeling the strength return to his legs, the Irishman gets up and dances a jig out the door.

Jesus then touches the Italian, and says, "For all your kindness, you too are healed!" Feeling his back straighten, the Italian raises his hands above his head and does a flip out the door.

As Jesus is walking towards the redneck, the redneck jumps up and screams, "Don't touch me! I'm drawing disability!"

* * *

A young man graduated from the University of Alabama with a degree in journalism. His first assignment for the newspaper that hired him was to write a human interest story. Being from Alabama, he went back to the country to do his research.

He went to an old farmer's house way back in the hills, introduced himself to the farmer, and proceeded to explain to him why he was there. The young man asked, "Has anything ever happened around here that made you happy?"

The farmer thought for a minute and said, "Yep! One time one of my neighbor's sheep got lost. We formed a posse and found it. We all screwed it, then took it home."

"I can't print that!" the young man exclaimed. "Can you think of anything else that happened that made you or a lot of other people happy?"

After another moment, the farmer said, "Yep! One time my neighbor's wife, a real good lookin' gal, got lost. We formed a big posse that time and found her. After we all screwed her, we took her back home."

Again, the young man said, "I can't print that either." He decided to try a new line of questioning. "Has anything ever happened around here that made you sad?"

The old farmer dropped his head as if he were ashamed. After a few seconds, he looked up timidly and said, "I got lost once..."

* * *

Glen bought his wife a beautiful diamond ring for her birthday.

After hearing about this extravagant gift, a friend of his said, "I thought she wanted one of those sporty four-wheel-drive vehicles."

"She did," Glen replied, "but where the heck was I going to find a fake Jeep?"

* * *

A hillbilly is on his wedding night and, since he's never been with a woman before, he phones his dad for some tips on what he's supposed to do.

"What do I do first?" he asks.

"Take off all her clothes and put her in bed," his dad says.

Five minutes later, he calls his dad back and says, "She's naked and in bed, now what do I do?"

"Now take your clothes off and get in bed," replies his dad.

Five minutes later, he calls back again and says, "I'm naked and in bed with her. What do I do next?"

"Must I spell it all out for you, son?" his father says, losing his patience. "Just put the hardest thing on your body where she pees!"

Again, he calls his father five minutes later and says, "Okay, I have my head in the toilet bowl, now what?"

* * *

Deep in the back woods of Kentucky, a redneck's wife went into labor in the middle of the night and the doctor was called to help with the delivery.

Since there was no electricity, the doctor handed the father-to-be a lantern and said, "Hold this lantern high so I can see what I'm doing." A short time later, a baby girl was delivered.

"Hold on now, don't be so quick to put that lantern down," the doctor said, "I think there's yet another one to come."

Sure enough, within minutes, he had delivered another baby girl.

"Land sakes, son," exclaimed the doctor, "don't be in such a hurry to put that lantern down. It looks like there's still another one in there!"

The redneck scratched his head in bewilderment and asked, "Doc, does ya think it's the light that's attractin' em?"

* * *

A man was driving down a quiet country lane when a rooster suddenly strayed out into the road.

Whack! With a cloud of feathers, the rooster disappeared under his car.

Shaken, the man pulled over at the farmhouse, rang the bell and an old farmer appeared.

Nervously, the man said, "I'm sorry, but I think I killed your rooster. Please allow me to replace him."

"Suit yerself," the farmer replied, "the hens are 'round back."

* * *

Bubba and Earl got promoted from Privates to Sergeants. Shortly after, they were out walking when Bubba said, "Hey, Earl, there's the NCO Club. Let's go in and have us a drink."

"But we's privates," protested Earl.

Pointing out their stripes, Bubba replied, "No we ain't Earl, we's Sergeants now!"

They went in and ordered their drinks.

A few minutes later, a hooker walked up to Bubba and said, "You're real cute. I'd love to take you somewhere and make you feel real good, but I've got a bad case of gonorrhea."

Bubba pulled Earl closer and whispered, "Quick, go look in the dictionary and see what that gon-o-rea means. If it's good, give me the okay sign."

Earl came back and gave Bubba the okay sign.

A couple of weeks later, Bubba was in the infirmary with a case of gonorrhea. "Earl," he said, "why did you gimme the okay fer?"

"Bubba, in the dictionary it says gonorrhea only affects the privates. But, we's Sergeants now!"

* * *

While visiting a relative in Chicago, a University of Alabama student went to a party where he met a very attractive co-ed. Attempting to strike up a conversation with her, he asked, "Where does you go to school?"

The co-ed, not at all impressed with his grammar or southern drawl, thought she would at least be polite and answer.

"Yale," she said.

Taking a deep breath, the UA student shouted, "I SAYS, WHERE DOES YOU GO TO SCHOOL?"

* * *

Bubba and Billy Bob were talking one evening. "Billy Bob," Bubba said, "I reckon I'm ready for vacation. This time I'm gonna do things different. These past few years I've taken your suggestions. You said go to Hawaii, I did and Mary got pregnant. Then you said go to Bermuda, I did and again Mary got pregnant. Last year you said go to Barbados, I did and yet again Mary gets pregnant."

"What you gonna do different this time Bubba?" asked Billy Bob.

"This time, Mary's coming with me," replied Bubba.

* * *

Hoping to get a little practice in before final exams, a proctology student is in the morgue. He goes over to a table where a body is lying face down. He removes the sheet covering the body and, much to his surprise, he finds a cork in the corpse's rectum.

Thinking this is pretty unusual, he pulls the cork out and is surprised when music begins playing:

"On the road again… just can't wait to get on the road again…"

Amazed, he places the cork back in the backside and the music stops. Totally freaked out, he calls the medical examiner over to the corpse.

"Take a look at this. This is really something," the student tells the examiner as he pulls the cork out again. "On the road again… just can't wait to get on the road again…"

"So what?" replies the medical examiner, obviously unimpressed with the student's discovery.

"What do you mean, so what? Isn't that the most amazing thing you've ever seen?" the student asks.

"You must be kidding," the examiner replies. "Any asshole can sing country music."

* * *

A mangy redneck youth walks into the kitchen where his mom is fixing that night's dinner.

"Mom, I got a splinter in my finger. Can I have a glass of cider?" asks the slack-jawed youth.

"Are you sure you don't want me to pull it out?"

"No thanks, just the cider."

"Well sure," responds the youth's mother and gives her boy the cider and watches him trot contentedly off.

About fifteen minutes later the boy returns to the kitchen and again asks his mother for a glass of cider. His mother, not wanting to question his reasoning, gives him another glass and again watches him leave happy.

Ten minutes later the boy returns once again asks for a glass of cider. The mother complies with her son's wishes again, but her curiosity has been piqued to the point where she can't resist knowing why any longer. So she wanders into the family room and sees her son sitting in front of the TV with his finger in the glass.

"Why on earth do you have your finger in that glass?" asks the boy's mother.

"Well Mom, I heard Sis on the phone say that whenever she had a prick in her hand, she couldn't wait to get it in cider."

* * *

Chester and Earl are going hunting. Chester says to Earl, "I'll send my dog out to see if there are any ducks out in the pond. If there aren't any ducks out there, I'm not going hunting."

So he sends the dog out to the pond. The dog comes back and barks twice.

Chester says, "Well I'm not going to go out. He only saw two ducks out there."

Earl says, "You're going to take the dog's barks for the truth?" Earl doesn't believe it, so he goes to look for himself. When he gets back he says, "I don't believe it where did you get that dog? There really are only two ducks out there!"

Chester says, "Well, I got him from the breeder up the road. If you want, you can get one from him, too."

So Earl goes to the breeder and says he wants a dog like the one his friend Chester has.

The breeder obliges and Earl brings the dog home, tells it to go out and look for ducks. Minutes later the dog returns with a stick in it's mouth and starts humping Earl's leg.

Outraged, Earl takes the dog back to the breeder and says, "This dog is a fraud. I want my money back!"

The breeder asks Earl what the dog did. So Earl tells him that when he sent the dog out to look for ducks, it came back with a stick in it's mouth and started humping his leg.

The breeder says, "Earl, all he was trying to tell you was that there are more fucking ducks out there than you can shake a stick at."

* * *

An Indian enters a trading post and asks the clerk for some toilet paper. The good old boy behind the counter asks him which one he would like, Charmin, White Cloud or no name.

"White Cloud sounds like good Indian toilet paper," the Indian says. "How much for that one?"

"$1.25 for a roll," replies the clerk.

"That seems quite expensive," the Indian responds. "How much are the other two?"

"Charmin is $2.00 a roll and no name is 75 cents a roll," the clerk says.

Since he doesn't have very much money, the Indian opts for the no name paper. Within a few hours he returns to the trading post.

"I have a name for the no name toilet paper," he announces to the clerk. "We shall call it John Wayne."

Confused, the clerk asks, "Why?"

"Because it's rough and it's tough and it don't take no shit off an Indian!"

* * *

Q & A Round Up
Rednecks

Q How do you circumcise a redneck?
A Kick his sister in the chin.

Q Why do folks in Kentucky go to the movie theater in groups of 18 or more?
A 'Cuz 17 and under not admitted.

Q What do they call "Hee Haw" in Arkansas?
A A documentary.

Q What do they call it in Kentucky?
A Life Styles of the Rich & Famous.

Q How do you know when you're staying in a redneck hotel?
A When you call the front desk and say "I've gotta leak in my sink" and the person at the front desk says "go ahead."

Q How can you tell if a Texas redneck is married?
A There is dried chewing tobacco on both sides of his pickup truck.

Q Did you hear that they have raised the minimum drinking age in Tennessee to 32?
A It seems they want to keep alcohol out of the high schools!

Q How many rednecks does it take to eat a 'possum?
A Two. One to eat, and one to watch out for traffic.

Q Why did God create armadillos?
A So that Texas rednecks can have 'possum on the half shell.

Q Where was the toothbrush invented?
A Oklahoma. If it was invented anywhere else it would have been called teethbrush.

Q Did you hear about the $3,000,000 Tennessee State Lottery?
A The winner gets $3 a year for a million years.

Q Did you hear that the governor's mansion in Little Rock, Arkansas burned down?

A Yep. Perty' near took out the whole trailer park.

Q What's the best thing to ever come out of Arkansas?

A I-40

Q What do a divorce in Alabama, a tornado in Kansas, and a hurricane in Florida have in common?

A Somebody's fixin' to lose them a trailer.

Q What do you get when you have 32 rednecks in the same room?

A A full set of teeth.

Q What's the most popular pick-up line in Arkansas?

A Nice tooth!

Q Did you hear about the redneck who passed away and left his entire estate in trust for his beloved widow?

A She can't touch it till she's fourteen!

Q What's the difference between a good ol' boy and a redneck?

A The good ol' boy raises livestock. The redneck gets emotionally involved.

Q What happens if you don't pay your garbage bill in West Virginia?

A They stop delivery

Q Why do the Arkansas cheerleaders wear bibs?

A To keep the tobacco juice off their uniforms.

Q What's the last thing you hear before a redneck dies?

A "Hey y'all! Watch this!"

Q What's the difference between a Northern and a Southern Fairytale?

A A Northern Fairytale begins with "Once Upon A Time" A Southern Fairytale begins with "Y'all ain't gonna believe this shit."

Polish

No other nationality is as closely associated with a stereotype as the Polish. This is because they are actually stupid. The Italians were once the Puerto Ricans in terms of ethnic pigeon-holing, but they elevated themselves to revenge-driven thugs. The Polish, not so much.

A little while back, there was an article published in the Haverford College alumni magazine describing a Polish neighborhood called Greenpoint in New York. The community was rightfully upset as the author wrote that Greenpoint was "infested" with Polish people and that the business district was, "even uglier than the morons who work there."

The real question here is not whether the author of the offending article was correct or not, look into your heart for that answer, but how he had the balls to write it! Talk that sh*t about the Jews, they'll sue you. Every other nationality will just kill you – except the Italians who will still kill you, but they'll do something horrifically "special" first.

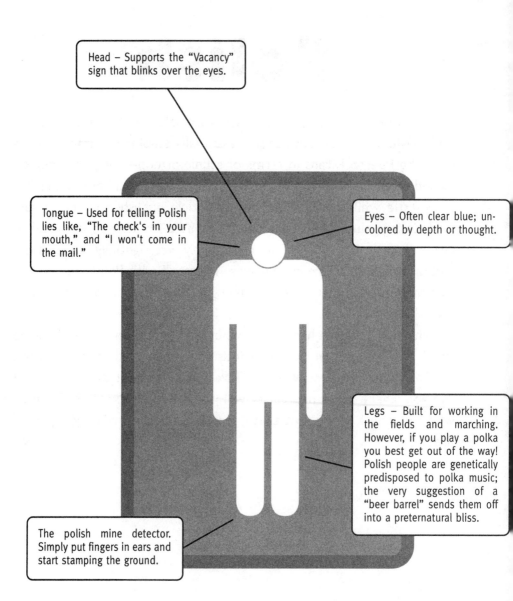

Common Indicators That You Are A

POLACK

A Polish man is skydiving, enjoying his free-fall, when he realizes that he has reached the altitude where he must open his parachute. So he pulls on the ripcord, but nothing happens.

"No problem," he says to himself, "I still have my emergency chute."

So he pulls the ripcord on his emergency parachute, and once again, nothing happens.

Now the man begins to panic. "What am I going to do?" he thinks, "I'm a goner!" Just then he sees a another Polish guy flying up from the earth toward him.

He can't figure out where this Polish guy is coming from, or what he's doing, but he thinks to himself, "Maybe he can help me. If he can't, then I'm done for."

When the Polish guy gets close enough to him, the skydiver cups his hands and shouts down, "Hey, do you know anything about parachutes?"

The Polish guy replies, "No! Do you know anything about gas stoves?"

* * *

Long ago lived a Polish seaman named Captain Bravo. He was a manly man who showed no fear in facing his enemies. One day, while sailing the seven seas, a look-out spotted a pirate ship and the crew became frantic. Captain Bravo bellowed, "Bring me my Red Shirt." The First Mate quickly retrieved the captain's red shirt and whilst wearing the bright red frock he led his men into battle and defeated the pirates.

Later on that day, the look-out spotted not one, but two pirate ships. The captain again called for his red shirt and once again, though the fighting was fierce, he was victorious over the two ships.

That evening, all the men sat around on the deck recounting the day's triumphs and one of the them asked the captain, "Sir, why do you call for your red shirt before battle?"

The captain replied, "If I am wounded in the attack, the shirt will not show my blood and thus, you men will continue to fight, unafraid."

All of the men sat in silence and marveled at the courage of such a manly man as Captain Bravo. As dawn came the next morning, the look-out spotted not one, not two, but TEN pirate ships approaching from the far horizon. The crew stared at the captain and waited for his usual reply.

Captain Bravo calmly shouted, "Get me my brown pants."

* * *

Knock, Knock?
Who's there?
Polish burglar.

* * *

Stanley and Buddy are walking down the street, and they see a sign on a store which reads, "Suits $5.00 each, shirts $2.00 each, trousers $2.50 per pair."

Stanley says to his pal, "Buddy, Look here! We could buy a whole bunch of these, take 'em back to Poland, sell them to our friends and make a fortune."

"Now when we go in there you be quiet, okay? Just let me do the talkin' 'cause if they hear your Polish accent, they might think we're ignorant, and not wanna sell that stuff to us. Now, I'll talk like I'm from America so they don't know."

They go in and Stanley says, "I'll take 50 of them suits at $5.00 each, 100 of them there shirts at $2.00 each, and 50 pairs of them there trousers at $2.50 each. I'll back up my pickup and..."

The owner of the shop interrupts, "You're both from Poland, aren't you?"

"Well... yeah," says a surprised Stanley, "How come you know that?!"

The owner replied, "Cause this here's a dry-cleaners."

* * *

A passenger in a Woznuski's taxi tapped the driver on the shoulder to ask him something. The driver screamed, lost control of the cab, nearly hit a bus, drove up over the curb, and stopped just inches from a large plate glass window.

For a few moments everything was silent in the cab, then the driver said, "Please, don't ever do that again. You scared the daylights out of me."

The passenger, who was also frightened, apologized and said he didn't realize that a tap on the shoulder could frighten him so much.

The driver replied, "I'm sorry, it's really not your fault at all, today is my first day driving a cab; I have been driving a hearse for the last 25 years."

* * *

A Polish, English, and French guy are running away from the German soldiers when they come up to a forest and they decide to hide by each climbing a tree.

When the Germans arrive, they go to the first tree where the English guy is, and shout, "We know you're up there! Come down."

The English guy, thinking fast, says, "Tweet, tweet, tweet."

The Germans, thinking that it's a bird, move on to the next tree where the French guy is and once again shout, "We know you're up there! Come down."

The French guy, thinking fast, says, "Hoot, Hoot, Hoot."

The Germans, thinking that it's an owl, move on to the next tree where the Polish guy is and once again shout, "We know you're up there! Come down."

The Polish guy thinks for a while and then says, "Moo, moo, moo."

* * *

Stanley walked into a doctor's office and the receptionist asked him what he had.

Stanley said, "Shingles."

So she took down his name, address, medical insurance number and told him to have a seat. Fifteen minutes later a nurse's aid came out and asked him what he had.

Stanley said, "Shingles."

So she took down his height, weight, a complete medical history and told him to wait in the examining room. A half-hour later a nurse came in and asked him what he had.

Stanley said, "Shingles."

So she gave him a blood test, a blood pressure test, an electrocardiogram, told him to take off all his clothes and wait for the doctor. An hour later the doctor came in and asked him what he had.

Stanley said, "Shingles."

The doctor said, "Where?"

Stanley said, "Outside on the truck. Where do you want them?"

* * *

There were these three guys, a Polish guy, an Italian guy, and a Jewish guy. They all worked together at a factory. Everyday they noticed that their boss leaves work a little early. So one day they meet together and say that today when the boss leaves, they'll all leave early too.

The boss leaves and so did they. The Jewish guy goes home and goes to rest so he can get an early start the next morning. The Italian guy goes home and cooks dinner.

The Polish guy goes home and walks to his bedroom. He opens the door slowly and sees his wife in bed with his boss, so he shuts the door and leaves.

The next day the Italian and Jewish guys are talking about going home early again. They ask the Polish guy if he wants to leave early again and he says, "No."

They ask him why not and he says, "Because yesterday I almost got caught!"

* * *

A two-seater plane crashed into a cemetery early this afternoon in central Poland. Polish search and rescue workers have recovered 300 bodies so far and expect that number to climb as digging continues into the evening.

* * *

Two Polish guys were in a bar watching the television when the news came on. It showed a guy on a bridge that was about to jump, obviously suicidal.

"I'll bet you $10 he'll jump," said the first guy.

"Bet you $10 he won't," replied the second.

Then, the guy on the television closed his eyes and threw himself off the bridge. The second guy hands the first his money.

"I can't take your money," said the first guy. "I cheated you. The same story was on the five o'clock news."

"No, no. Take it," said the second guy. "I saw the five o'clock news too. I just didn't think the guy was dumb enough to jump again!"

* * *

A prominent Polish scientist conducted a very important experiment. He trained a flea to jump upon giving her a verbal command 'Jump!'

In the first stage of experiment he removed flea's leg, told her to jump, and the flea jumped. So he wrote in his scientific notebook: "Upon removing one leg all flea organs function properly."

So, he removed the second leg, asked the flea to jump, she obeyed, so he wrote again: "Upon removing the second leg all flea organs function properly."

Thereafter he removed all the legs but one, the flea jumped when ordered, so he wrote again: "Upon removing the next leg all flea organs function properly."

Then he removed the last leg. Told flea to jump, and nothing happened. He did not want to take a chance, so he repeated the experiment several times, and the legless flea never jumped. So he wrote the conclusion: "Upon removing the last leg the flea loses sense of hearing."

* * *

A Polish guy, an American and a Frenchman were all going to be executed. The executioner told them that they would each get to choose the method by which they would die.

Their choices were: lethal injection, electric chair or by hanging.

The American was afraid of needles and didn't want to be hanged. The American chose the electric chair.

He sat in the chair and they pulled the switch and nothing happened. The executioner said that if this happens a second time that he could go free.

They tried a second time and again nothing happened so they set him free.

The guy from France was also afraid of needles and didn't want to be hanged so he too chose the electric chair.

Once again, the chair didn't work and he was free.

Next it was the Polish guy's turn to pick how he was to be executed.

He said, "I'm afraid of needles, and the electric chair won't work... so you're going to have to hang me."

* * *

A Polish man was suffering from constipation, so his doctor prescribed suppositories. A week later the Pole complained to the doctor that they didn't produce the desired results.

"Have you been taking them regularly?" the doctor asked.

"What do you think I've been doing," the Pole said, "shoving them up my ass?"

* * *

These two Poles are building a house. One of them is putting on the siding. He picks up a nail, hammers it in. Picks up another nail, throws it away. Picks up a nail, hammers it in. Picks up another, throws it away.

This goes on for a while, and finally his friend comes over and asks him why he is throwing half of the nails away.

He replies, "Those ones were pointed on the wrong end."

The buddy gets exasperated and says, "You idiot, those are for the other side of the house!"

* * *

A Pole came home one day from work, hung up his coat, took off his hat and walked into his bedroom shouting, "Honey I'm home!"

What should he see but his best friend in bed with his wife. Infuriated, he rushed to the cupboard, pulled out his gun and put it to his head. His wife started laughing.

"Don't laugh!" he screams. "You're next!"

* * *

Two Poles immigrated to America. On their first day off the boat in New York City, they spied a hot dog vendor in the street. "Did you know they eat dogs in America?" one asked the other.

"I did not know that."

"Well, If we're going to live here, we might as well learn to eat like Americans."

So they each bought a hot dog wrapped up in wax paper and sat down to eat them on a nearby park bench. One Pole looked inside his wax paper, then over at the other Pole and asked, "What part did you get?"

* * *

Two Polish truck drivers are barreling along when they come up to an overpass. A sign says, "Clearance: 11" 2'." So they get out, measure their truck, and realize that it's 11"6'.

So the first man looks at his friend and says, "I don't see any police around... let's go for it!"

* * *

Following the assault of a young woman, the police rounded up the usual suspects for a lineup; suddenly, the Polish suspect stepped forward and screamed "That's her!"

* * *

Three POW's, an American, a German, and a Pole, are scheduled to be executed by firing squad. They bring out the American and stand him in front of the firing squad.

He points and shouts, "Tornado!" They all look and the American runs away. Next, they place the German in front of the firing squad.

He yells, "Earthquake!" They all hit the dust and the German escapes.

Next up is the Pole. He looks around and shouts, "Fire!"

* * *

Three men were all applying for the same detective job. One was Polish, one was Jewish, and one was Italian. Rather than ask the standard questions during the interview, the chief decided to ask each applicant just one question and base his decision upon that answer.

When the Jewish man arrived for his interview, the chief asked, "Who killed Jesus Christ?"

The Jewish man answered without hesitation "The Romans killed him." The chief thanked him and he left.

When the Italian man arrived for his interview, the chief asked the same question.

He replied "Jesus was killed by the Jews." Again, the chief thanked the man who then left.

When the Polish man arrived for his interview, he was asked the exact same question.

He thought for a long time, before saying, "Could I have some time to think about it?"

The chief said, "Okay, but get back to me tomorrow."

When the Polish man arrived home, his wife asked "How did the interview go?"

He replied, "Great, I got the job, and I'm already investigating a murder!"

* * *

Some men in a pickup truck drove into a lumberyard. The Polish driver walked into the office and said, "We need some four-by-twos."

The clerk said, "You mean two-by-fours, don't you?"

The man said, "I'll go check," and went back to the truck. He returned in a minute and said, "Yeah, I meant two-by-fours."

"Alright. How long do you need them?"

The driver paused for a minute and said, "I'd better go check."

After awhile, the customer returned to the office and said, "A long time. We're gonna build a house."

* * *

Several days before Halloween, Tom, Dick and Stan were sitting in a bar enjoying a few quiet drinks, when they decided to get in on the Halloween raffle. Since the raffle was for charity, they bought five $1 tickets each. When the raffle was drawn a few days later, they each won a prize.

Tom won the first prize, a year's supply of gourmet spaghetti sauce. Dick was the winner of the second prize, a six month supply of extra-long gourmet spaghetti. And Stan won the sixth prize, a toilet brush.

The next time they met at the bar, Stan asked the others how they were enjoying their prizes.

"Great," said Tom. "I love spaghetti."

"Me too," replied Dick. "And how's the toilet brush, Stan?"

"Not so good," Stan groaned, "I'll probably go back to paper."

* * *

A purse snatcher named Walczak was on trial and the defendant was stating what had taken place.

"Yes, that's him," she said. "I would remember his face anywhere!"

At that point, the defendant yelled out, "You didn't even see my face, lady. I was wearing a mask!"

* * *

A fifth grade class was putting on a school play about the Knights of the Round-table. One little Polish boy was not terribly good at remembering lines, so the teacher asked him to be responsible for saying just one line in the play. He was to go up to a young girl dressed as a fair maiden and say, "Oh, fair young damsel, I've come to snatch a kiss and fill your soul with hope."

The boy practiced the line for hours on end to make sure he would say it perfectly. But, the night the play was done for the school children and all the parents, the boy was true to form. When the play got to his line, it came out, "Oh, damn young fairsel, I've come to kiss your snatch and fill your hole with soap!"

* * *

There once was a Polish prince who, through no fault of his own, was cast under a spell by an evil Polish witch. The curse was that the Polish prince could speak only one word each year. He could, however, save up the words so that if he did not speak for a whole year, then the following year he was permitted to speak two words. This was well before the time of letter writing or sign language.

One day he met a Polish princess who had luscious ruby lips, long golden hair and sapphire eyes, and he immediately fell in love. With the greatest of difficulty, he decided to refrain from speaking for two whole years so that he would be able to look at her and say, "My darling." However, at the end of the two years he wished to tell her he loved her. Because of this, he waited an additional three years without speaking, bringing the total number of silent years to five.

At the end of the five years he realized that he had to ask her to marry him, so he waited another four years without speaking.

Finally, as the ninth year of silence ended, his joy knew no bounds. Leading the lovely princess to the most secluded and romantic place in the beautiful royal garden, he placed a hundred red roses on her lap, knelt before her, took her delicate hand in his and huskily said, "My darling, I love you! Will you marry me?"

Tucking a strand of golden hair behind her dainty ear, the princess opened her sapphire eyes in wonder, parted her luscious ruby lips and said, "Pardon?"

* * *

Q & A Round Up
Polish

Q If Tarzan and Jane were Polish what does that make Cheetah?
A Smarter than the pair of them.

Q Did you hear about the Polish family that froze to death outside a theater?
A They were waiting to see the movie "Closed for the Winter."

Q Did you hear about the Polish Admiral who wanted to be buried at sea when he died?
A Five sailors died digging his grave.

Q Did you hear about the gay Pole?
A He slept with women.

Q Did you hear about the Polish loan shark?
A He lends out all his money, then skips town.

Q Who wears a dirty burlap sack and rides a pig?
A Lawrence of Poland.

Q Heard about the Polish hockey team?
A They all drowned during spring training.

Q What is long and hard, and a Polish bride gets one on her wedding night?
A A new last name.

Q How do you get a one-armed Pole out of a tree?
A Wave.

Q How do you ruin a Polish party?
A Flush the punch bowl.

Q How do you get a Pole out of the bath tub?
A Throw in a bar of soap.

Q What happened to the Polish National Library?
A Someone stole the book.

Q Why are there no ice cubes in Poland?
A They forgot the recipe.

Q What do you do if a Pole throws a hand-grenade at you?
A Take the pin out and throw it back.

Q How did the Polish mother teach her son which way to put his underwear on?
A Yellow in the front, brown in the back!

Q Why do Polish names end in "ski" ?
A Because they can't spell toboggan.

Q What's delaying the Polish space program?
A Development of a working match.

Q How do you know Poland is going "green?"
A When you see toilet paper hanging on the clotheslines.

Q Did you know that Poland just bought 10,000 septic tanks?
A As soon as they learn how to drive 'em, they are going to invade Russia.

Q Did you hear about the big Polish tragedy?
A There was a power outage in Poland's busiest shopping mall. People were stuck on the escalators for four hours.

Q How do you sink a Polish battleship?
A Put it in water.

Q Why wasn't Christ born in Poland?
A Because they couldn't find three wise-men and a virgin.

Q How did the Germans conquer Poland so fast?
A They marched in backwards and the Polish thought they were leaving.

Q Why do Polish police cars have stripes on the side?
A So the cops can find the handles.

Q Did you hear about the new automatic Polish parachutes?
A They open on impact.

Q Do you know why the new football stadium they built in Warsaw could not be used?
A No matter where you sat you were behind a Pole.

Q What's the motto of the Polish Solidarity Union?
A Every man for himself.

Q How do you keep a Pole in suspense?
A

Q How do Poles form a car pool?
A They meet at work.

Q Why did the Polish couple decide to have only four children?
A They'd read in the newspaper that one out of every five babies born in the world today is Chinese.

Q What did the Polish mother say when her daughter announced that she was pregnant?
A "Are you sure it's yours?"

Q Why did the Pole sell his water skis?
A He couldn't find a lake with a hill in it.

Q You go to a cockfight. How do you know if a Pole is there?
A He's the one with a duck.

Q How do you know if an Italian is there?
A He bet on the duck.

Q How do you know if the Mafia is there?
A The duck wins.

Q Why did the Pole put ice in his condom?
A To keep the swelling down.

Q How does a Polish Firing Squad stand?
A In a circle

Italians

I was born in the Bronx and raised on Long Island, New York. The first Italian word I learned was, "Camaro." Many of my friends had names like Paulie, Frankie and Pete. Though I was not Italian myself, I found myself with a growing appreciation for all things Italian.

For those of you who only associate the Italians with adultery, murder and loan sharking, you should know there is far more to them. Nobody issues a beating like an Italian and, man, can they cook.

The term "agida" means indigestion and is very frequently used by the Italians. This is because for them a meal is an assault on their stomachs. First the foods, rich with fats, acids and parts of a pig that are more suited to being read by witches, attacks. They are chased by emotional bile stemming from long running feuds, mutual distrust and well-earned guilt. Meats are often slow cooked to butter-tender perfection to eliminate the need for too-convenient knives on the table.

Shoulder Holster – .44 Magnum is the handgun for stopping power; arguably the most powerful handgun in the world. Extra bonus, new "Magnum Flavor Sleeves™" wrap easily around the end of the barrel so that if intended victim / intimidation recipient is made to suck on it, the flavor helps send your personal message of fear. Available in garlic-basil for Italians, vodka for Russians and "Dank™" for ganstas.

Violine Case, Sub Machine Gun – Since 14th February, 1929, the day of the St. Valentine's Day massacre, the sub machine gun has been a sentimental favorite for mass murder enthusiasts. On that day six men were told to stand against a wall by hoods dressed as cops and promptly Swiss-cheeseoffied. Though the practice is still in use, the influence of Southern sociopaths has branded it with the clever moniker, "Line Dancing."

Behind Back, In Belt – The Colt 1911. Widely respected for its reliability and lethality though requiring serious practice for its single action operation, this is what you want "backing you up." Extra care required when leaning back as the gun faces straight down your crack. You need an accidental discharge like you need a second asshole.

Ankle Holster – The Smith & Wesson 442, .38 cal Revolver is cute. It's petite and weighs only 15 ounces. Keeping one of these in your ankle works great for when you've been shot a few times and the prick that did you is sauntering up sadistically so that he can see the fear in your eyes as he puts out your lights. But you, using the last of your strength wait until he levels his gun and says, "Fuck you" before you pull your 442, and reply, "No cocksucker; fuck you!" And blow his brains out. Oh sure, you still die painfully; full of regret and all alone, but man, if someone alive had seen that, it would have been cool.

Testicles – Even if you've got lead balls in the chamber, you'll need even bigger lead balls in your sack or you'll never pull the trigger.

Common Indicators That You Are An

ITALIAN

The Polish were upset because of their bad reputation. A group of them got together and approached a conference of Americans, Germans, and Japanese and asked for help on this matter.

An American replied, "You must do something so the world will respect you. The Japanese are known for their technology and the Germans are known for their resourcefulness. We Americans have had respect since we helped win the World War against the other two. See, you need to do something world-famous."

A German added, "Yes, he's right. Why don't you find a place in this world in need of a bridge that no one has dared build, build it, come back to us, and we will help publicize it."

With that, the Polish set off to build their bridge. They designed it and worked six months and finally completed it. They then went back to report it to the group. The bridge was a beautiful bridge but it had one flaw: it was erected in the middle of the Sahara Desert.

An American said, "No, no. See, that is why you have your reputation. There is no need for a bridge in the middle of the desert. Now go and dismantle it, and find a more strategic spot to erect it."

The Polish returned to the conference in two weeks. One of the Japanese said, "Two weeks! It only took you two weeks to dismantle that bridge and build a new one??? That is amazing!!"

To which a Polish man replied, "Well, not exactly. When we returned to the bridge we couldn't dismantle it because there were all these Italians fishing off it."

* * *

One day ima gonna Malta to bigga hotel. Ina morning I go down to eat breakfast. I tella waitress I wanna two pissis toast. She brings me only one piss. I tella her I want two piss. She say go to the toilet. I say you no understand, I wanna piss onna my plate. She say you better no piss onna plate, you sonna ma bitch. I don't even know the lady and she call me sonna ma bitch.

Later I go to eat at the bigga restaurant. The waitress brings me a spoon and knife but no fock. I tella her I wanna fock. She tell me everyone wanna fock. I tell her you no understand. I wanna fock on the table. She say you better not fock on the table, you sonna ma bitch.

So I go back to my room inna hotel and there is no shits onna my bed. Call the manager and tella him I wanna shit. He tell me to go to toilet. I say you no understand. I wanna shit on my bed. He say you better not shit onna bed, you sonna ma bitch.

I go to the checkout and the man at the desk say: "Peace on you". I say piss on you too, you sonna ma bitch, I gonna back to Italy.

* * *

There was once a hillbilly who was extremely sad with life because people always made fun of him. He decided to do something about it. He sat back and thought about it.

Suddenly he thought, "I have never seen anyone making fun of Italians. So, if I start talking and behaving like them, no one will be able to make out that I am a hillbilly and make fun of me."

He went into isolation for three months and after a lot of practice, he walked confidently into a shop and said, "Ima very hungry. Gimme some pepperoni and zucchini."

Immediately, the man behind the counter asked, "Are you a hillbilly?"

The hillbilly was taken aback and he repeated his request.

The man behind the counter asked, "Are you a hillbilly or not?"

The hillbilly was finally very ashamed and amazed at the shop owner's discerning ability, and so he admitted to the fact after which he asked; "But how did you know?"

The shopkeeper replied, "This is a hardware store!"

* * *

An Italian man walking along a California beach was deep in prayer. All of a sudden he said out loud, "Lord, grant me one wish."

Suddenly the sky clouded above his head and in a booming voice the Lord said, "Because you have had the faith to ask, I will grant you one wish." The man said, "Build a bridge to Hawaii, so I can drive over anytime I want to."

The Lord said, "Your request is very materialistic. Think of the logistics of that kind of undertaking. The supports required to reach the bottom of the Pacific! The concrete and steel it would take! I can do it, but it is hard for me to justify your desire for worldly things. Take a little more time and think of another wish, a wish you think would honor and glorify me."

The Italian man thought about it for a long time. Finally he said, "Lord, I have been married and divorced four times. All of my wives said that I am uncaring and insensitive. I wish that I could understand women. I want to know how they feel inside, what they are thinking when they give me the silent treatment, why they cry, what they mean when they say 'nothing' and how I can make a woman truly happy."

After a few minutes God said, "You want two lanes or four on that bridge?"

* * *

There once were two baby animals, one is a duck and the other a skunk. As they were walking along with their parents, a car came speeding down the road. The baby skunk and duck watched in horror as their parents were run over by the car. Now the two babies were orphans. They had to stay together and help each other. Soon enough they were curious and wanted to know what kind of animals they were. They asked each other to describe their looks and tell what they were.

The skunk went first and said, "Well, you have fluffy feathers, an orange bill, and you're white so you must be a duck!"

The duck was now happy because he knew what type of animal he was. It was the duck's turn to describe the skunk and tell him what he was. The duck said, "Well you're not really black, and you're not really white, and you stink so you must be Italian."

* * *

These four guys were walking down the street, a Saudi, a Russian, a North Korean, and a New York Italian.

A reporter comes running up and says, "Excuse me, what is your opinion about the meat shortage?"

The Saudi says, "What's a shortage?"

The Russian says, "What's meat?"

The North Korean says, "What's an opinion?"

The New York Italian says, "Excuse me? What's excuse me?"

* * *

Three men, a Frenchman, and Irishman and an Italian walk into a bar and the barman says, "If you can sit in my basement for a day I'll give you free beer forever."

So the Frenchman says, "Easy, I can do that."

But he walks out after five minutes and says, "It's impossible, you got a swarm of flies in there."

So the Irishman tries his luck, but can't take more than 10 minutes. Finally the Italian goes in and comes out a day later. The others ask him how he did it.

He said, "Easy, I took a dump in one corner and sat in the other corner!"

* * *

A Frenchman and an Italian were seated next to an Australian on a long flight.

After a few cocktails, the men began discussing their home lives. "Last night I made love to my wife four times," the Frenchman bragged, "and this morning she made me delicious crepes and she told me how much she adored me."

"Ah, last night I made love to my wife six times," the Australian responded, "and this morning she made me a wonderful omelet and told me she could never love another man."

When the Italian remained silent, the Frenchman smugly asked, "And how many times did you make love to your wife last night?"

"Once," he replied.

"Only once?" the Australian arrogantly snorted. "And what did she say to you this morning?"

"Don't stop."

* * *

An Italian man walks into the market followed by his ten-year-old son. The kid is spinning a 25 cent piece in the air and catching it between his teeth. As they walk through the market someone bumps into the boy at just the wrong moment and the coin goes straight into his mouth and lodges in his throat. He immediately starts choking and going blue in the face and the dad starts panicking, shouting and screaming for help.

A middle-aged, fairly unremarkable Italian man in a gray suit is sitting at a coffee bar in the market reading his newspaper and sipping a cup of coffee. At the sound of the commotion he looks up, puts his coffee cup down on the saucer, neatly folds his newspaper and places it on the counter. He gets up from his seat and makes his unhurried way across the market.

Reaching the boy (who is still standing, but just barely) the Italian man carefully takes hold of the kid's testicles and squeezes gently but firmly. After a few seconds the boy convulses violently and coughs up the 25 cent piece, which the man catches in his free hand. Releasing the boy, the man hands the coin to the father and walks back to his seat in the coffee bar without saying a word.

As soon as he is sure that his son has suffered no lasting ill effects, the father rushes over to the man and starts effusively thanking him. The man looks embarrassed and brushes off the father's thanks. As the man is about to leave, the father asks one last question: "I've never seen anybody do anything like that before, it was fantastic . What are you, a surgeon or something like that?"

"Oh good heavens, no," the man replies, "I work for the IRS."

* * *

This little Italian boy and this little Jewish boy lived about a block apart in the neighborhood and basically they grew up together. The Jewish boy was the son of a jeweler and the Italian boy was the son of a hit-man. Oddly enough, they had the same birthday. Well, for their 12th birthday, the little Jewish boy gets a Rolex watch and the little Italian boy gets a .22 Baretta.

The next day they are out on the street corner comparing their presents and neither is happy so they switch gifts with each other. The little Italian boy goes home to show his father and his father is NOT pleased!

"What're you, nuts? Lemme tell you something, you idiot!! Some day you're gonna meet a nice girl, you're gonna wanna settle down and get married. You'll have a few kids, all that stuff. THEN one day, you're gonna come home and find your wife in bed with another man. What the heck ya gonna do??? Look at your watch and say, 'Hey, how long you gonna be?'"

* * *

An Italian immigrant accused of theft was appearing before the judge. "Your Honor," his lawyer said, "I feel it is very unfair for my client to be accused of theft.

He arrived in this city only a few days ago and barely knows his way around. What's more, he is only able to speak a few words of English."

The Judge looked sternly at the defendant and asked, "How much English do you speak?"

The defendant looked up and replied, "Give-a me your wallet!"

* * *

A man was getting a haircut prior to a trip to Rome. He mentioned the trip to the barber who responded, "Rome? Why would anyone want to go there? It's crowded, dirty and full of Italians. You're crazy to go to Rome. So, how are you getting there?"

"We're taking United," was the reply. "We got a great rate!"

"United?" exclaimed the barber. "That's a terrible airline. Their planes are old, their flight attendants are rude, and they're always late. So, where are you staying in Rome?"

"We'll be at the downtown International Marriott."

"That dump! That's the worst hotel in the city. The rooms are small, the service is surly and they're overpriced. So, whatcha doing when you get there?"

"We're going to go to see the Vatican and we hope to see the Pope."

"That's rich," laughed the barber. "You and a million other people trying to see him. He'll look the size of an ant. Boy, good luck on this lousy trip of yours. You're going to need it."

A month later, the man again came in for his regular haircut. The barber asked him about his trip to Rome.

"It was wonderful," explained the man, "not only were we on time in one of United's brand new planes, but it was overbooked and they bumped us up to first class. The food and wine were wonderful, and I had a beautiful 28-year-old stewardess who waited on me hand and foot. And the hotel was great! They'd just finished a $25 million remodeling job and now it's the finest hotel in the city. They, too, were overbooked, so they apologized and gave us the presidential suite at no extra charge!"

"Well," muttered the barber, "I know you didn't get to see the Pope."

"Actually, we were quite lucky, for as we toured the Vatican, a Swiss Guard tapped me on the shoulder and explained that the Pope likes to personally meet some of the visitors, and if I'd be so kind as to step into his private room and wait, the Pope would personally greet me. Sure enough, five minutes later the Pope walked through the door and shook my hand! I knelt down and he spoke to me."

"Really?" asked the Barber. "What'd he say?"

"He said, 'Where'd you get the lousy haircut?'"

* * *

A Frenchman, an Englishman, and a New York Italian get captured by cannibals.

The chief comes to them and says, "The bad news is that now that we've caught you, we're going to kill you. We will put you in a pot and cook you, then we'll eat you, and then we'll use your skins to build a canoe. The good news is that you get to choose how you die."

The Frenchman says, "I take ze sword." The chief gives him a sword, the Frenchman cries "Vive la France!" and runs himself through.

The Englishman says, "A pistol for me, please." The chief hands him a gun, the Englishman points it at his head saying, "God save the Queen!" and blows his brains out.

The New Yorker says, "Gimme a fork." The chief is puzzled, but shrugs and gives him a fork. The New Yorker takes the fork and starts jabbing himself all over; the stomach, sides, chest, everywhere. There's blood gushing all over the place, it's horrible.

The chief is appalled and asks, "God almighty, what are you doing?"

The New Yorker sneers and says, "So much for your canoe, you stupid fuck!"

* * *

Q & A Round Up
Italians

Q Why did the Italian staple his nuts together?
A "If you can't lick 'em, join 'em"

Q Why is Italy shaped like a boot?
A Do you think they could fit all that shit in a tennis shoe?

Q Why is Italian bread so long?
A So they can dip it into the sewer.

Q How does an Italian get into an honest business?
A Usually through the skylight.

Q What do you get when you cross an Italian and a Pollack?
A A guy who makes you an offer you can't understand.

Q How do you kill an Italian?
A Smash the toilet seat on the back of his head when he is getting a drink.

Q If Tarzan and Jane were Italian, what would Cheetah be?
A The least hairy of the three.

Q What did the barber say to the Italian kid?
A Do you want your hair cut or should I just change the oil?

Q Why do Italian men have mustaches?
A So they can look like their mothers.

Q Why do Italians hate Johavah's Witnesses?
A Because Italians hate all witnesses.

Q Why does the new Italian Navy use glass bottomed boats?
A So they can see the old Italian Navy.

Q Why don't Italians have freckles?
A They all slide off.

Asians

Just labeling a chapter "Asians" is rude in itself. There are so many Asian cultures that the blanket term simply doesn't cover them. But there aren't enough, say, Laotian jokes, to justify a chapter, so here we are.

The ancient Chinese had jokes. They are different than the kind we're used to in that they have no measure of, say, funny? I have dredged one up for you and I think you'll agree that some dynasties just can't tell a joke.

During the Sui Dynasty (581-618), there lived a clever man who spoke with a slight stutter. Whenever the Minister Yang Su felt bored and listless, he would invite this man over to have a chat. One evening toward the close of the year when they sat facing each other, Yang asked him more in jest than in earnest: " Supposing you find yourself in a pit ten feet deep and ten feet in circumference, how would you get out?"

The man lowered his head, meditating for some time, and asked; "Is there a l-l ladder?"

"No," replied Yang. " I wouldn't have asked you if there were a ladder."

Again the man lowered his head meditating. Some time later, he inquired, "In br-br-broad daylight? Or at n-n-night?"

"No need to ask whether it's in broad daylight or at night," replied Yang." The question is how would you get out."

"I'm not blind," reported the man. "If it isn't after night-fall, how the hell could I fall into it?"

At that Yang burst out laughing and followed up with another question: " Supposing you were a general sent to a small city besieged by an enemy tens of thousands strong. The garrison there numbered less than one thousand, and the provisions would suffice only for a few days. What would you do?"

The man hung down his head, pondering over the problem for a long time. Then he asked; "Any re-reinforcements for-forthcoming?"

"No," replied Yang, "that's why I asked you."

After muttering to himself for a good while, the man raised his head and said, "If the situation is as you said, I'm afraid we're just about done for."

At that Yang burst into laughter again and then put to the man the last question:

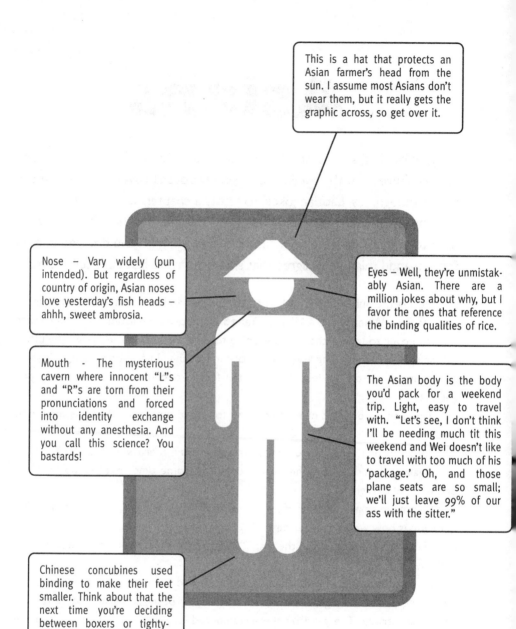

Common Indicators That You Are An

ASIAN

"I know you're a very capable man and there's scarcely anything you can't do. It so happened that someone in my family got bitten today by a snake. Will you see to the snake bite?"

"Well," said the man in response, "go to the south wall and get hold of some s-snow which fell on the fifth day of the fifth moon. Ap-apply it to the bite, and he'll get well in no time."

"But," protested Yang, "it never snows in the fifth moon."

" No," the man agreed. "In the twelfth moon, where can you find a snake that bites?"

Much amused by his remarks, Yang Su let the man go.

At the conclusion of the joke, the teller would do the honorable thing and take his own life.

Two whales spot a Japanese whaler.

First whale: "Those are the bastards who killed my folks. Let's drown them!"

Second whale: "If they killed your folks let's do it!"

First: "We'll dive down then surface and blow the ship over with our blow-holes."

This they did but the sailors were still alive swimming for it.

First: Darn it! "We'll have to swim up to them with our mouths open and swallow them all down!"

Second: "No way! I don't mind the blow-job but I'm not swallowing the seamen!"

* * *

A businessman was in Japan to make a presentation to the Toyota Motors people. Needless to say, this was an especially important deal and it was imperative that he make the best possible impression. On the morning of the presentation he awoke to find himself uncontrollably passing gas in large volumes. Additionally, the flatulence had the unpleasant characteristic of sounding like "*honda*." The man was beside himself. Every few minutes "*honda... honda...*" What would the Toyota people think?

Unable to stop this aberrant behavior, and in desperate need to terminate these odious and rather embarrassing emissions, he sought a physician's aid. After a full examination, the doctor told him that there was nothing inherently wrong with him and that he would just have to wait it out. Being unwilling to accept this state of affairs he visited a second and then a third doctor all of whom told him the same thing. Finally one medic suggested that he visit a dentist. Well, although he could not see how a dentist was going to be of any help, he visited one anyway.

Lo and behold, the dentist said, "Ah, there's the problem."

"What is it?" the man asked.

"Why you have an abscess," said the dentist.

"An abscess. How could that be causing my problem?" asked the man.

"That's easy," replied the dentist. "Everyone knows, abscess makes the fart go Honda."

* * *

An Asian guy walks into the New York City Currency Exchange with 2,000 yen and walks out with $72. The next week he walks in with 2,000 yen and gets $66. He asks the lady why he gets less money this week than last week.

The lady says, "Fluctuations."

The Asian guy storms out, and just before slamming the door, turns around and says: "Fluc you Amelicans, too!"

* * *

Two guys were arguing about the correct orientation of Japanese women's sex organs. One said that Japanese women have their private part going from side to side, while the other said it goes vertical, just like everybody else. The argument went on for hours until they decided to settle it once and for all by going to another friend who has a Japanese wife. Surely, he should know!

After being told of the subject of the argument, the friend quickly said, "Vertical, just like everybody else and I'll prove it!" He called his wife and she appeared from the second floor bedroom. "Honey, take off your panties and slide down the banister." Like a good obedient wife, she obliged and mounted the banister. On the way down there was a long screeeeeech, and she landed on the floor. "See? Didn't I tell you guys that it's vertical, just like everybody else?"

The two scratched their heads in wonder. "What does that prove?" one asks.

"If it were horizontal, the sound would have been *thpptpptpptpptppt*."

* * *

Moshe was eating in a Chinese restaurant and was chatting to his Chinese waiter. Moshe commented upon what a wise people the Chinese were.

"Yes," replied the waiter, "we're wise because our culture is 4,000 years old. But Jewish people are also very wise, are they not?"

Moshe replied, "Yes, we are. Our culture is 5,000 years old."

The waiter was surprised to hear this. "That can't be true," he replied, "where did your people eat for a thousand years?"

* * *

The beautiful secretary of the president of the Chase Manhattan Bank goes on a sight-seeing tour with a very rich Taiwanese client. Out of the blue, the client asks her to marry him. Naturally, the secretary is quite taken aback. However, she remembers what her boss told her: "Don't reject the guy outright."

So, she tries to think of a way to dissuade the businessman from wanting to marry her. After a few minutes, the woman says to the man, "I will only marry you under three conditions. First, I want my engagement ring to be a 75-carat diamond ring, with a matching 200-carat diamond tiara."

The Taiwanese man pauses for awhile. Then, he nods his head and says, "No problem! I buy. I buy."

Realizing that her first condition was too easy, the woman says to the man, "I want you to build me a 100-room mansion in New York. And as a vacation home, I want a chateau built in the middle of the best wine country in France."

The man pauses for awhile. He whips out his cellular phone, calls some brokers in New York, then he calls some brokers in France. He looks at the woman, nods his head and says, "Okay, okay. I build, I build."

Realizing that she has one last condition, the secretary knows that she'd better make this a good one. She takes her time to think and finally, she gets an idea. A sure-to-work condition. She squints her eyes, looks at the man and says, rather coldly, "Since I like sex, I want the man I marry to have a 12-inch penis."

The man seems a bit disturbed. He cups his face with his hands and rests his elbows on the table. All the while, he's uttering something in Chinese. Finally, after what seemed like forever, the man shakes his head, and looking really sad, says to the woman, "Okay, okay. I cut. I cut."

* * *

After the war, Americans and Japanese worked together guarding a bridge. The American asked his sergeant if he could go talk to the Japanese soldier at night when it's lonely out there. So in the middle of the night the American soldier went out on the bridge and so did the Japanese soldier, meeting half way.

To start conversation, the American asked what part of the military was he in. The Japanese soldier didn't answer.

So the American asked, "The Air Force?" while waving his index fingers way over head. The Japanese soldier still didn't answer.

The American asked, "The Marines?" while moving his hands in a swimming motion. The Japanese soldier still didn't answer.

The American asked, "Are you in the Calvary?" while motioning like riding a horse and smacking its behind. The Japanese soldier still had no reply.

Finally, the American asked, "Are you in the artillery?" while bringing his hands up to his eyes like goggles.

The Japanese soldier took off running. He ran into his sergeants office hollering, "Sergeant, Sergeant we have to get out of here!" His sergeant asked why, and the Japanese soldier replied, "That American back there said when the sun goes down he's gonna swim across the river and fuck me in my ass until my eyes pop out!"

* * *

Big Shuggie is on holiday and is stuck at the airport, and proceeds to get very drunk. After about his tenth big swig at his bottle a little Japanese man accidentally bumps into him, causing the bottle to smash to the floor.

Big Shuggie is furious, he grabs the wee fellah demanding compensation and drags him out of the building. Next thing he returns with bruises all over his face.

Behind him is the Japanese man who is smiling.

"It is just a small Japanese thing," he explained to the crowd of waiting passengers, who were astonished, "We call it aikido."

But despite having been overwhelmed and tossed to the pavement, Big Shuggie's anger builds up and once more he challenges the Japanese man to 'go ootside.'

They do and within a couple of minutes Shuggie is limping back into the building, with the smiling Japanese man behind him.

"It is just a small Japanese thing," he explains once more to the impressed crowd, "We call it karate."

As the effects of his mauling at the hands of the wee man wears off, Big Shuggie once more bellows at the Japanese guy that he wants to take him outside and 'batter him wan'.

Sighing and shrugging his shoulders, the Japanese man accompanies Shuggie outside.

A couple of minutes later the hushed crowd hear a thud, and Shuggie comes striding back into the airport building, beaming like a champion,

"It wiz just a small Japanese thing, " he explains to them, "The bumper aff a Toyota!"

* * *

An Italian, and Irishman and a Chinese fellow are hired at a construction site. The foreman points out a huge pile of sand and says to the Italian guy. "You're in charge of sweeping" To the Irishman, he says, "You're in charge of shoveling." And to the Chinese guy, "And you're in charge of supplies.

"Now, I have to leave for a little while. I expect you guys to make a dent in that pile." So the foreman goes away for a couple hours, and when he returns, the pile of sand is untouched. He says to the Italian, "Why didn't you sweep any of it?"

The Italian replies, "I didn't have a broom. You said the Chinese guy was in charge of supplies, but he disappeared and I couldn't find him."

So then the foreman turns to the Irishman and asks why he didn't shovel. The Irishman replies, "I couldn't get myself a shovel. You left the Chinese guy in charge of supplies, but I couldn't find him."

The foreman is really pissed off now, and storms off toward the pile of sand looking for the Chinese guy. Just then, the Chinese guy springs out from behind the pile of sand and yells, "SUPPLIES!"

* * *

A woman is just about to give birth in the hospital when she says to the doctor, "Doc, do me a favor. Tell me what color the baby is as it's being born."

The doctor is understandably a little puzzled at this. "Why don't you know what color the child is going to be?"

"Well," says the woman, "The problem is that I'm a porno actress and the child was conceived during the making of a film. I have no idea who the father is."

"Okay," says the doctor, "I'll do it for you but it is most unusual." The baby begins to be born and the doctor says, "Here comes the head, it seems to have yellow skin and the eyes are slanted. Was one of the actors Chinese?"

"Yes, doctor he was," says the woman.

"Wait," says the doctor, "The chest and arms are out and they seem to be very dark. Was one of the actors black?"

"Yes, doctor he was."

"Wait, now the legs are out and they're brown. Was one of the actors Mexican?"

"Yes, doctor he was." So the doctor pulls the baby free and gives it the traditional slap on the back. The baby lets out a healthy "Waaaahh" and starts crying.

"Oh, thank God for that!" says the woman. "For a moment there, I expected it to bark!"

* * *

A rich man often went to Bangkok for the night life and before long, he contracted a sexual disease. So one day, he went to the doctor for a checkup.

The doctor examined his private parts and said, "This is a very severe case. We have no other way but to cut it away. Otherwise, it will spread and become worse."

The businessman was shocked. The last thing he wanted was to have it cut and end his night life. He went to other doctors but all gave the same diagnosis.

Desperate he thought, "Why don't I consult traditional Chinese medicine. They might have some surprises."

So, the Chinese doctor gave him an examination and the doctor said, "We don't have to cut. I'll give you herbs to rub."

The rich man was so happy. "Wow no operation! You are better than Western medicine. I'm amazed, So what is the exact secret?"

The Chinese doctor said, "Just wait for three days. It will drop off by itself."

* * *

Three Chinese gentlemen approach St. Peter's gates requesting entrance to heaven. St. Peter informs the three that as they are not Christian, they can not come in. But after much pleading by the three Chinese men, St. Peter agrees to let them in on one condition: each one must explain a Christian holiday.

The first man says, "Christmas. Christmas is when young children dress up in scary costumes, say trick or treat, eat candy. Christmas."

St. Peter says, "No."

The second man says, "Lent. Lent is when everyone gather 'round big fire, cook hot dog, make fireworks. Lent."

St. Peter says, "No."

The third man says, "Easter. Put man on cross. Man dies on cross. Put man in tomb. Wait three days. After three days, roll the rock from tomb. Man come out of tomb. If man see shadow..."

* * *

A Chinese man enters a bar to find an Orthodox Jewish bartender. He says, "Hey Jew, give me a brew."

The bartender responds, "That's terrible! How would you like it if I said something like that to you? In fact, let's just switch places. You get behind the bar and I'll come in as a customer."

The Chinese man agrees and gets behind the bar. The Jewish man goes outside.

Upon reentering, he says, "Hey Chink, give me a drink."

To which the Chinese man answers, "Sorry, we don't serve Jews here."

* * *

The teacher asks Little Johnny to put the word INFATUATION in a sentence.

Johnny replies, "A Japanese tourist walks into Long John Silver's fish and chip shop, and asks the guy behind the counter 'How do you cook your chips?' so he tells him, 'In fat, you Asian.'"

* * *

A man suspected his wife of seeing another man. So, he hired a famous Chinese detective, Mr. Sui Tansow Pok, to watch and report any activities that might develop. A few days later, he received this report:

Most honorable sir:

You leave house.

He come house.

I watch.

He and she leave house.

I follow.

He and she get on train.

I follow.

He and she go in hotel.

I climb tree, look in window.

He kiss she.

She kiss he.

He strip she.

She strip he.

He play with she.

She play with he.

I play with me.

fall out of tree, not see.

...NO FEE

* * *

A pianist was hired to play background music for a movie. When it was completed he asked when and where he could see the picture. The producer sheepishly confessed that it was actually a porno film and it was due out in a month.

A month later, the musician went to a porno theater to see it. With his collar up and dark glasses on, he took a seat in the back row, next to an Asian couple who also seemed to be in disguise.

The movie was even raunchier than he had feared, featuring group sex, S&M and even a dog.

After a while, the embarrassed pianist turned to the couple and said, "I'm only here to listen to the music."

"Yeah?" replied the man. "We're only here to see our dog."

* * *

Back in the time of the Samurai there was a powerful emperor who needed a new head Samurai, so he sent out a declaration throughout the country that he was searching for one.

A year passed and only three people showed up, a Japanese Samurai, a Chinese Samurai and a Jewish Samurai.

The emperor asked the Japanese Samurai to come in and demonstrate why he should be head Samurai. The Japanese Samurai opened a match box and out pops a little fly. *Whoosh* goes his sword and the fly drops dead on the ground in two pieces.

The emperor exclaimed, "That is very impressive!"

The emperor then asked the Chinese Samurai to come in and demonstrate his skill. The Chinese Samurai also opened a match box and out pops a fly. *Whoosh, whoosh* goes his sword. The fly drops dead on the ground in four pieces.

The emperor exclaimed, "That is really very impressive!"

The emperor then had the Jewish Samurai demonstrate why he should be the head Samurai.

The Jewish Samurai also opened a match box and out pops a fly. His flashing sword goes *whooooosshhh, whooossshhh, whoooosssshhh, whoooooossshhh, whooooosssshhh*. A gust of wind fills the room, but the fly is still alive and buzzing around.

The emperor, obviously disappointed, asks, "After all of that, why is the fly not dead?"

The Jewish Samurai smiled, "Circumcision is not intended to kill."

* * *

After the baby was born, the panicked Japanese father went to see the obstetrician. "Doctor," he said, "I don't mind telling you, but I'm a little upset because my daughter has red hair. She can't possibly be mine."

"Nonsense," the doctor said. "Even though you and your wife both have black hair, one of your ancestors may have contributed red hair to the gene pool."

"It isn't possible," the man insisted. "We're pure Asian."

"Well," said the doctor, "let me ask you this. How often do you have sex?"

The man seemed ashamed. "I've been working very hard for the past year. We only made love once or twice a month."

"There you have it!" the doctor said confidently. "It's just rust."

* * *

A waitress walks up to a table where three Japanese men were seated. When she gets to the table, the waitress notices that the three men are furiously masturbating.

The waitress demandingly asks, "What the hell are you three perverts doing?"

One man replies, "We all very hungry!"

The waitress responded, "But why are you jerking off?"

And, the Japanese men answered, "Because menu say, 'First come, first served!'"

* * *

Q & A Round Up
Asians

Q How do you blind a Chinese person?
A Put a windshield in front of him.

Q How do you know when Chinese are moving into your neighborhood?
A When the Mexicans start getting car insurance.

Q What do you call a Jewish Chinese homosexual?
A A Heblew.

Q What happens to an Asian man who runs into a wall and has a full erection?
A He breaks his nose.

Q What's yellow and goes "cheep, cheep?"
A A Chinese prostitute.

Q There's an Asian, a Hispanic, and a Black riding in a car. Who's driving?
A The cop.

Q How do you know if you're Asian?
A When you've got a bucket in your bathroom.

Q What do you call a Filipino walking a poodle?
A A Gourmet.

Q Why is there no Disneyland in China?
A No one's tall enough to go on the good rides.

Q What do you get when you cross a Puerto Rican and a Chinaman?
A A car thief who can't drive.

Also From
National Lampoon Press

**National Lampoon
Jokes, Jokes, Jokes
Collegiate Edition**
*Steve Ochs
Mason Brown*
978-0977871-827
Price: $11.95 US

**National Lampoon
The Saddam Dump
Saddam Hussein's Trial Blog**
*Scott Rubin
MoDMaN*
978-0977871-858
Price: $14.95 US

**National Lampoon
Favorite Cartoons
Of The 21st Century**
*National Lampoon
Staff And
Contributors*
978-0977871-810
Price: $14.95 US

**National Lampoon
Not Fit For Print**
*National Lampoon
Staff And Contributors*
978-0977871-834
Price: $17.95 US

**National Lampoon
Help!**
Scott Rubin
978-0978832-322
Price: $14.95 US

**National LampoonVan Wilder
Guide to Graduating College
In Eight Years or More**
*MoDMaN
And National
Lampoon Contributors*
978-0978832-339
Price: $12.95 US

**National Lampoon
Magazine Rack**
*Ed. by
J. Naughton
MoDMaN,
P. Cummin*
978-0977871-803
Price: $17.95 US

**The 29th
Anniversary of
National Lampoon's
Animal House**
Chris Miller
978-0978832-346
Price: $12.95 US

**Balls!
An In-Your-Face
Look at Sports**
Steve Hofstetter
978-0978832353
Price: $12.95 US

Pimp It Yourself
*Dirty Mike &
Jeremy Roder*
978-09788383-7-7
Price: $14.95 US